AF513786

Time-Lapse Photography

Art and Techniques

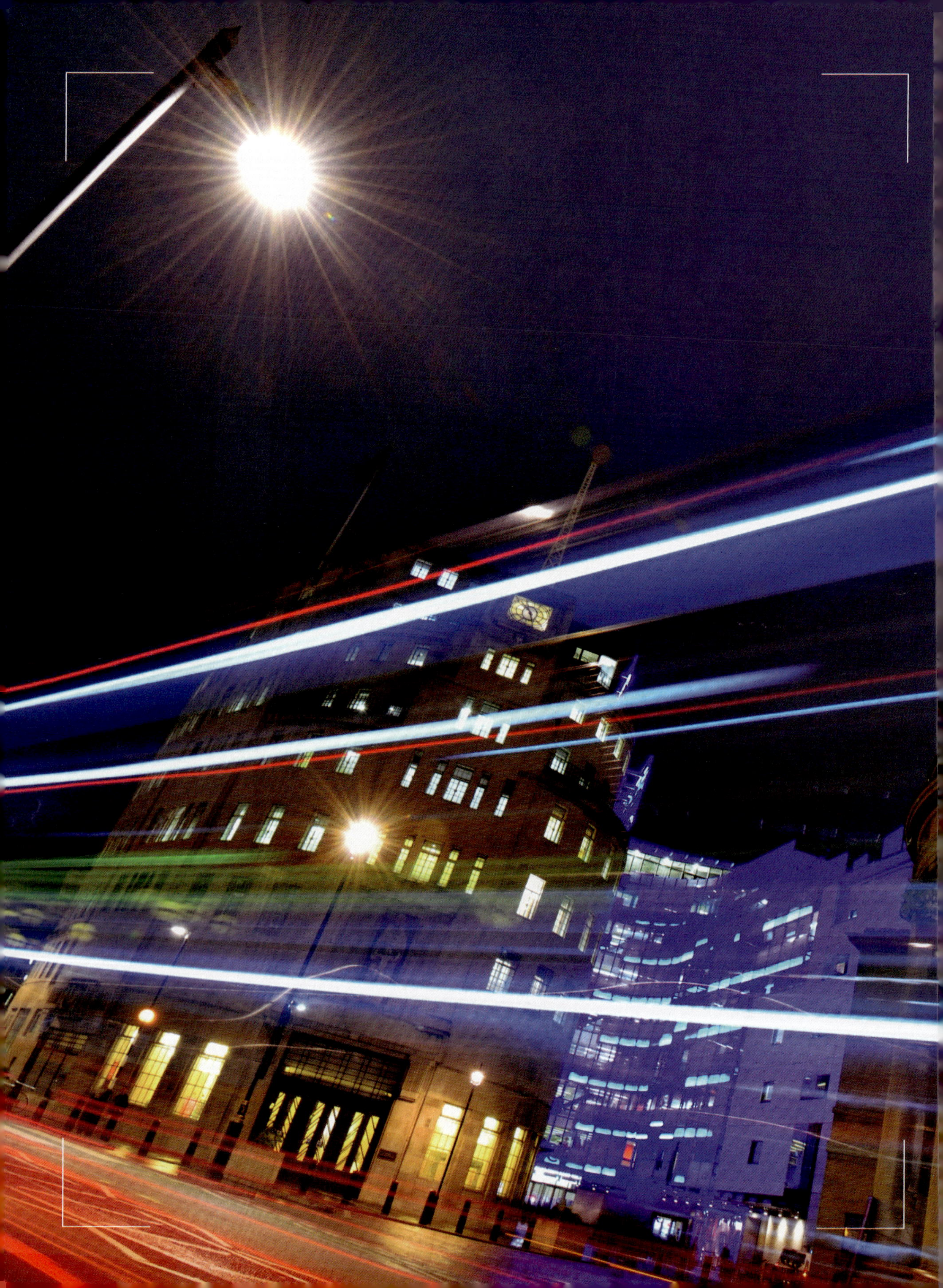

Time-Lapse Photography
Art and Techniques

Mark Higgins

CROWOOD

First published in 2016 by
The Crowood Press Ltd
Ramsbury, Marlborough
Wiltshire SN8 2HR

www.crowood.com

© Mark Higgins 2016

All rights reserved. No part of this publication may be reproduced or transmitted in any form or by any means, electronic or mechanical, including photocopy, recording, or any information storage and retrieval system, without permission in writing from the publishers.

British Library Cataloguing-in-Publication Data
A catalogue record for this book is available from the British Library.

ISBN 978 1 78500 209 0

Graphic design and layout by Peggy & Co. Design Inc.
Printed and bound in India by Parksons Graphics

CONTENTS

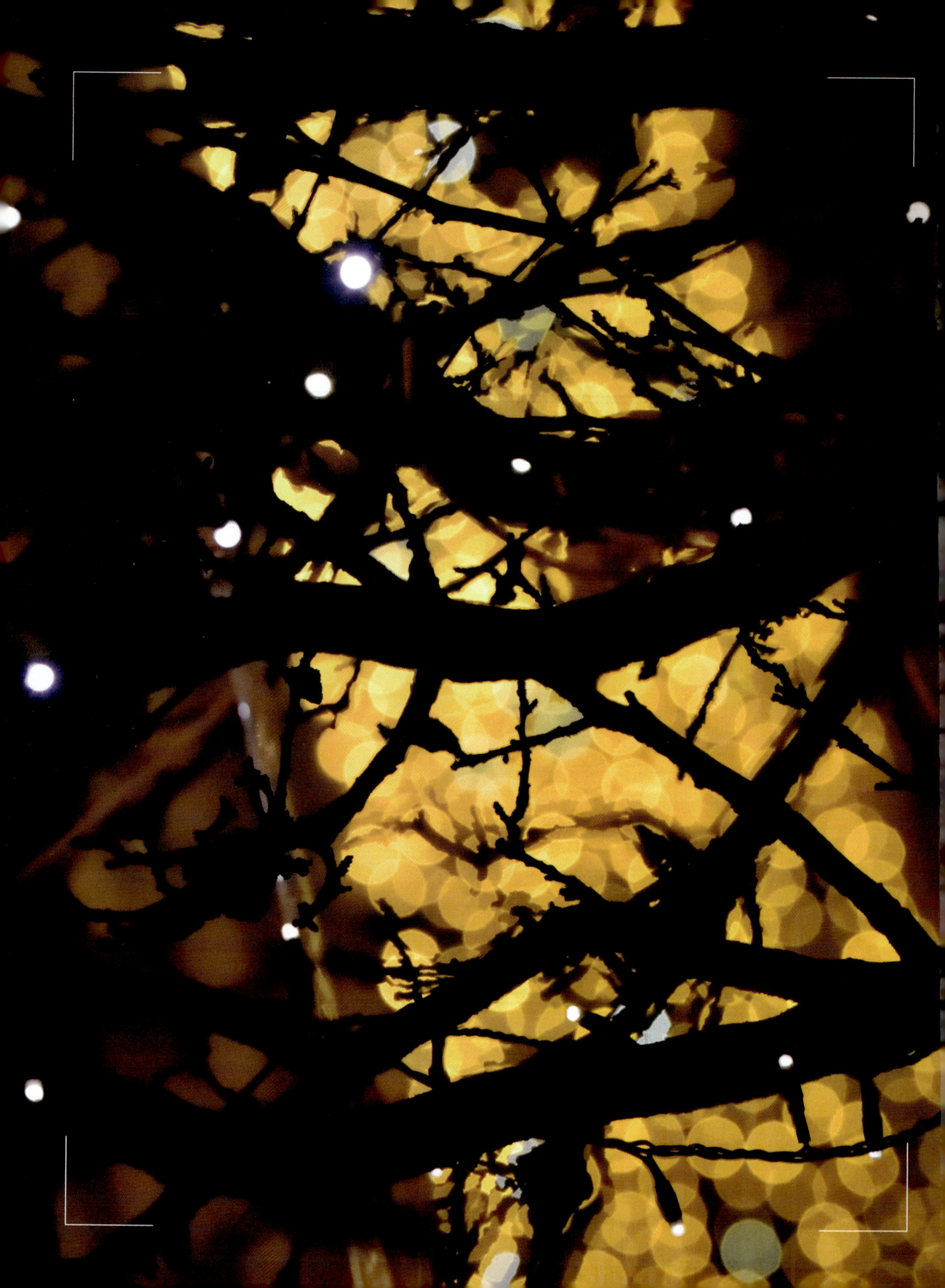

Introduction

Welcome to the exciting and inspiring world of time-lapse photography. We will explore techniques that will be invaluable to both the beginner who has only just picked up a camera and the professional who is looking to expand their creativity and skills. Many different approaches will be addressed, which will enable the learner to react to any shooting situation with confidence. Time-lapse photography in many ways is a bridge between shooting stills and video. Because of this crossover, the reader will be given an opportunity to explore all areas of photography and video that relate to time-lapse.

Time-lapse is a sector of photography that is constantly changing with the development of new technology and ideas; this should be embraced and explored in order to advance and evolve your learning. There is a wealth of information and technology available, and we can utilize it to our advantage.

HOW TO USE THIS BOOK

This book should be used as an informative and enjoyable resource for anyone interested in learning about time-lapse, as well as stills photography and video-making. The reader might choose to work through this book from cover to cover, or to use it as an occasional reference. Everyone learns in different ways and at different paces, so absorb the information in the way that works for you. Learning about photography is as much about practical experience as it is about theory.

◀ This image is an example of what can be achieved when ideas, colours and composition are explored. Whilst experimenting we can make our own path and create visually interesting imagery that excites and inspires us. Camera settings: 1/250s, *f*/9, ISO 400.

Sometimes too much time can be spent simply talking about photography, rather than actually going out and creating imagery. This is why throughout this book there will be practicals for you to engage with to reinforce the content covered. Building your knowledge in a practical manner is key to driving your work forward, and the aim of this book is to help the reader develop a portfolio of exciting work and to gain confidence and experience.

The learning process

Learning in itself is an interesting challenge, and we all learn in different ways, but generally if you take a positive and enquiring approach this will help your progress. When working on your time-lapse videos, never let small setbacks get in the way of your passion for imaging. You may find there are days when nothing is working at all. It happens to everyone; don't let this get you down. If you have created a time-lapse that you don't like, then use it as a learning experience; don't delete it but learn why you don't like it.

Getting started

At the beginning you might have a blank canvas, this is probably the most daunting part of the process, but it is also one of the most exciting. It may be worth starting in an area that you are comfortable with, such as landscape or street photography, for example. This will take some of the pressure or uncertainty away from the beginning of the exercise. All it takes is one or two successful results and you will start to gain valuable confidence. After this first step you will realize the rich scope of potential that you have with time-lapse photography.

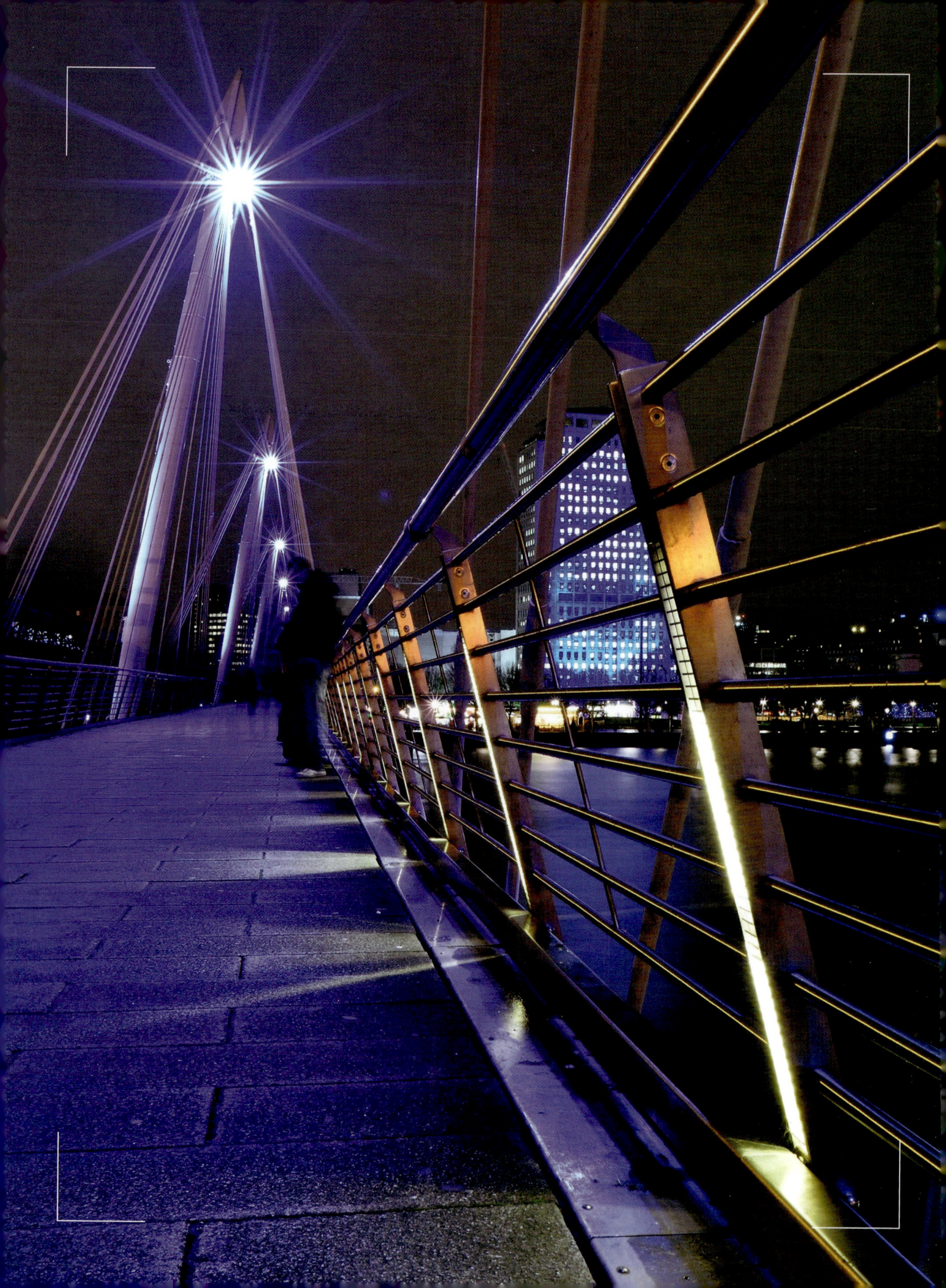

Chapter 1

What is time-lapse photography?

This chapter will establish the fundamentals of what time-lapse photography is by deconstructing its meaning and placing it within stills photography and video, as well as looking at the subject as a stand-alone area. We will consider it as a powerful communication tool and look at different ways in which it can be used. The ideas explored will help you define the genre and therefore help you create stunning content. Key questions will also be asked about how to go about producing your content.

WHAT DOES 'TIME-LAPSE' MEAN?

The Latin word *lapsus* means 'for time to pass by, or elapse', so time-lapse essentially means 'time passing'. Generally time-lapse photography shows time moving more quickly than in real life. The speed at which you choose to portray time passing will depend on how you want to communicate your content. There is no reason why you should not portray time moving both forwards and backwards, but it is more common for time-lapse photography to depict the former.

A healthy interest in science fiction can be useful (this might sound strange but keep reading) – time-lapse photography is essentially about time travel because we are able to see time passing in a way that we normally would not. The beauty of it is that we don't need a time machine to do the travelling: all we need is a camera and some imagination. When capturing a time-lapse, we take lots of still photographs, put them together in a video format and the result appears to fast forward time. Music is often used to accompany the final video and a well-chosen audio track can successfully enhance the viewing experience. Time-lapse clips are frequently used in the context of a larger video, such as a television series or movie and everything in between. Time-lapse is becoming much more popular and accessible because technology allows more photographers to be able to produce it. Large, expensive cameras have been used to create time-lapse videos for a very long time, but now we have smartphones, tablets and smaller advanced cameras, which can also be used. Although time-lapse has become easier from a technical standpoint, the creative side remains something that requires time and effort before you can achieve your aspirations.

Deconstructing time-lapse

To understand the concept of what time-lapse is, it's relevant to look at how a regular video is constructed because the two are very closely related. A video that is watched in the cinema, on television or online is made up of many still photographs that are played back consecutively, usually at 24 frames per second or faster. The actual capture when filming regular video is also at least 24 frames per second, which

◀ Working with strong colours and shapes is a fantastic way to achieve eye-catching imagery. Here the lines of the bridge have been used as a compositional tool. A star burst (top left) has been created by the using a particular aperture setting. The people on the bridge have been blurred by the use of a slow shutter speed. All of these elements come together to create evocative stills or time-lapse videos. Camera settings: 30s, ƒ/16, ISO 100.

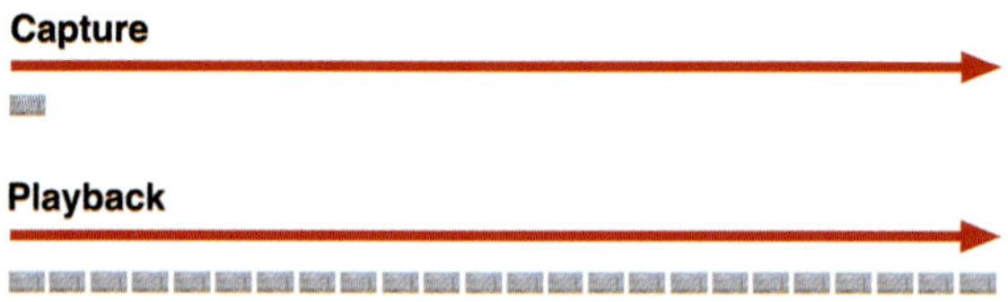

▲ This diagram represents the passing of a single second in time. In this example the time-lapse has been captured at one frame a second. The delivery is at least 24 frames per second. The final result will therefore be 24 times faster than how it looks in reality.

PAUSE A VIDEO AND LOOK AT INDIVIDUAL FRAMES

Watch a piece of video footage – this could be part of your favourite film or a television advert, it doesn't matter. Play the footage, pause it and look at the individual frames. Look at how the frame is composed in terms of colour and shape. Notice what happens when you pause when an object is moving. Sometimes the object will blur, which creates natural movement in the video. Find a time-lapse video online or on television and do the same, watching and analyzing individual frames. This reiterates that time-lapse and regular video share the same delivery.

results in the illusion of movement as seen by our eyes in real life. Time-lapse video is essentially the same as a regular video in its final construction, but the initial capture is very different. You could capture one frame every second, every minute or even every hour. So the speed at which time appears to pass by when you watch a final time-lapse video is much quicker. Essentially, regular video shows time passing by as we see it and time-lapse speeds it up.

We can use time-lapse to effectively compress time. One example of this would be a building being constructed over a three-year period. We could capture the entire construction for three whole years but depending on the capture and edit, we would be able to show the construction in just two minutes. This enables us to witness events that could not be seen in real life. It wouldn't be possible to stand and watch the building being constructed for a three-year period, but watching a two-minute video is a quick and easy way to demonstrate the build. Time-lapse is a powerful and effective tool and is used in areas such as scientific research, entertainment, teaching and art, so apply it to the areas you love and enjoy it.

Individual frames make up video and time-lapse

Many years ago it was discovered that if a moving subject was captured with still photographs in quick succession, we could play back the frames at the same speed as the initial capture and create the illusion of movement; this is basically how video works. The minimum number of frames to show movement naturally is 24 frames per second. If you play back the frames slower than the initial capture, the image appears more choppy, or almost animated looking. This effect is sometimes seen when a clip has been slowed down to get slow motion video. Generally speaking for video, less than 24 frames per second is not desirable, so always use this as the minimum playback frame rate.

Because time-lapse video is a popular area for still photographers and videographers alike, it is quite possible for either party to translate everything they know about colour, composition and subject matter directly into a time-lapse video. This is fantastic because although you may be slightly anxious about learning a new area, you probably have more knowledge than you think which is directly applicable to this visually exciting area.

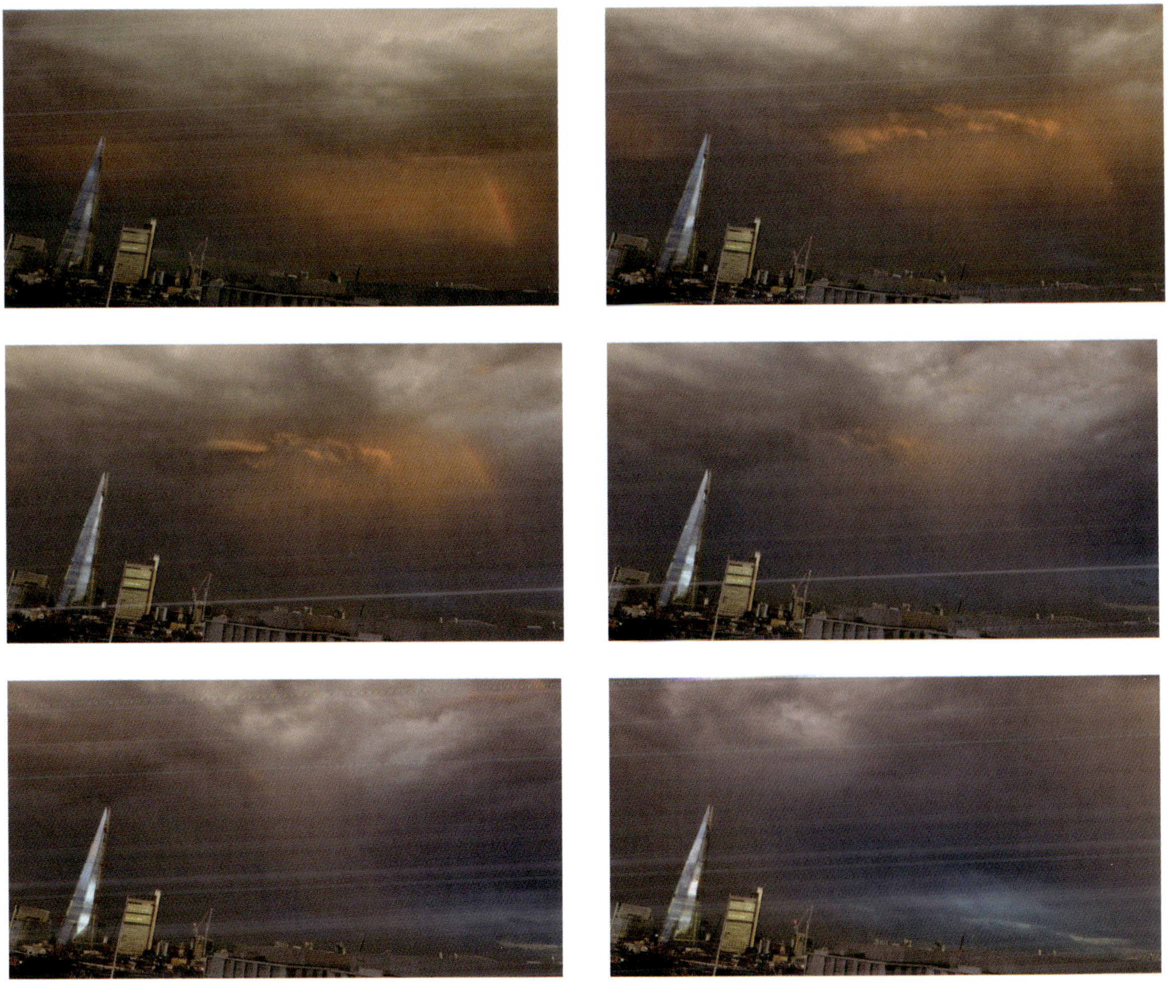

▲ These individual still photographs are taken from a time-lapse video, demonstrating how well movement can be communicated with time-lapse photography. Camera settings: 1/1.3s, *f*/22, ISO 100.

TIME-LAPSE IS HALF-WAY BETWEEN STILLS PHOTOGRAPHY AND VIDEOGRAPHY

Time-lapse is a half-way house between two very exciting worlds: stills and video. Both photographers and videographers can learn a lot more than they bargained for when exploring the subject of time-lapse photography, as there is natural crossover, and the line is getting very thin between practices.

Time-lapse is a natural progression for the meeting of the two areas, so use it as a valuable opportunity to explore another world that will inspire and excite you. It is becoming more common for either a photographer or a videographer to use terms such as 'image-maker' or 'content producer' to describe themselves. This is probably more applicable to professional image-makers because it is always preferable to represent your adaptability and not to pigeonhole yourself when image-making is your profession.

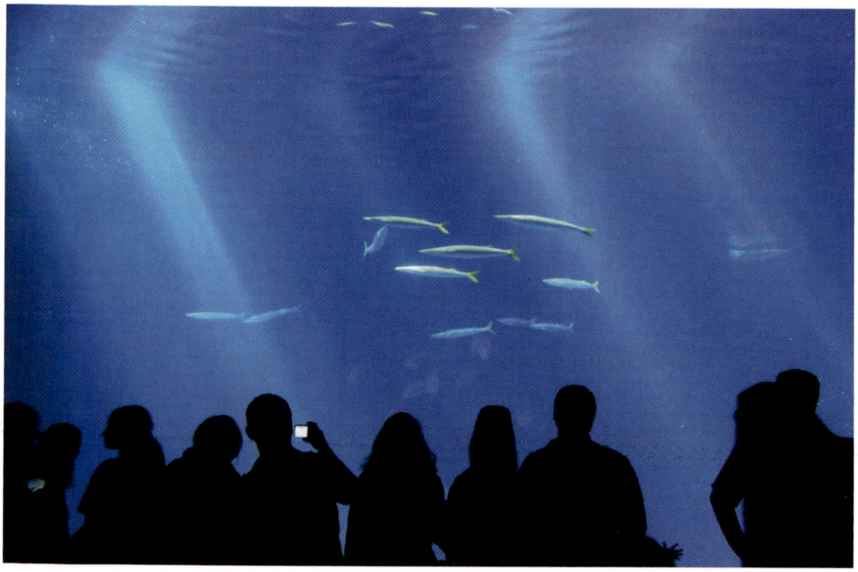

When searching for subject matter to use in your time-lapse videos, look for scenes that work well for regular still photographs. Once you have found a great image, bring it to life with time-lapse photography and give it movement. Camera settings: 1/8s, *f*/2.5, ISO 450.

For the stills photographer

You may never have recorded a video in your life as part as your hobby or profession, but please overcome any reservations you may have. You may not even be interested in video, but it is important to consider that much of what you learn with time-lapse photography is similar to, if not the same as, film-making. Many stills photographers are apprehensive about video, mostly because of the software used. If this is the case, please be assured that the video software is much easier to use than stills photography software, so don't let this hold you back. Video is simply still images with movement, and in certain circumstances can be a more effective communication tool than still photographs alone.

For the videographer

Even if you do not shoot much in the way of stills photography, and spend most of your time filming and/or editing to create videos, after exploring time-lapse photography you may find that you discover a growing interest in stills photography. There is much to be gained from learning about stills photography in terms of visual style and creative diversity. If you have not tried your hand at stills photography yet, please explore it and enjoy.

COMMUNICATING WITH TIME-LAPSE

One of the biggest reasons why time-lapse is such a rich and interesting area is because what it achieves visually cannot be created in any other way, so as a communication tool it is unique. With all image-making it is helpful to establish what you are trying to communicate before starting out; this could be something as simple as a sunset. If you are creating content to be shown as part of a movie, you will have a good starting point as the message to portray will have already been established. In this example you will need to decide how you can create something that will complement the main story line, as in this instance the time-lapse itself is not the main feature.

If your time-lapse is the primary piece, you might have more creative freedom to be able to build your idea from the ground up. Rather than just going out and shooting at random, make sure you have a clear idea of what you want to show and the message you want to get across. This process will aid your experience and also make it easier for the viewer to understand what your footage is portraying. You could, for

▶ Stunning landscape scenes with interesting cloud formations give us inspiring subject matter for time-lapse videos. Often landscape photographers will become interested in time-lapse to give their scenes movement, but time-lapse can also be a bridge for film-makers to expand their creativity. Camera settings: 1/250s, ƒ/8, ISO 100.

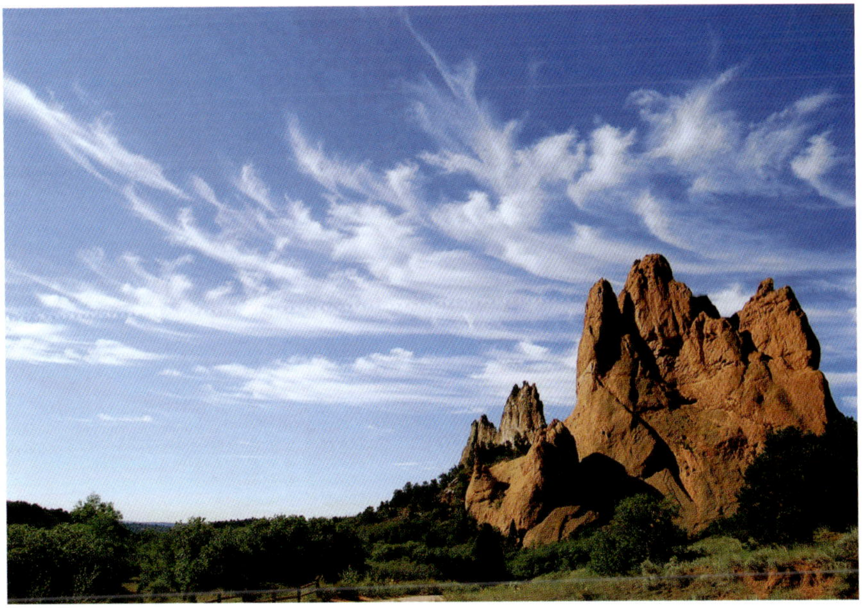

▶ Scenes like this will give subtle movement in the water as it is blown by the wind, adding life to an already breathtaking scene. Camera settings: 1/160s, ƒ/9, ISO 200.

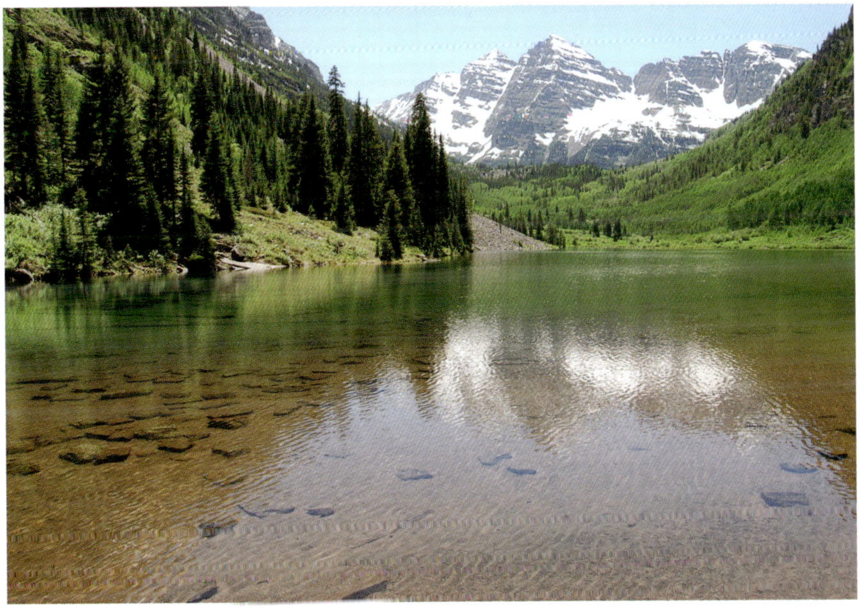

example, shoot city scenes to show how the crowd movement interacts with traffic and communicate a buzzing city centre. In contrast, you could choose a quiet park with people strolling around and feeding ducks in order to show the serenity of the location. Both of these contrasting examples will provide strong visuals and can communicate in a way that stills and video cannot. Exploring time-lapse and how it helps us portray the passing of time will produce exciting and unique content.

A study of movement and time

A great way to look at time-lapse photography is as a study of movement and the passing of time. If you would like inspiration for choosing subject matter this is a really effective idea to adopt. Start to

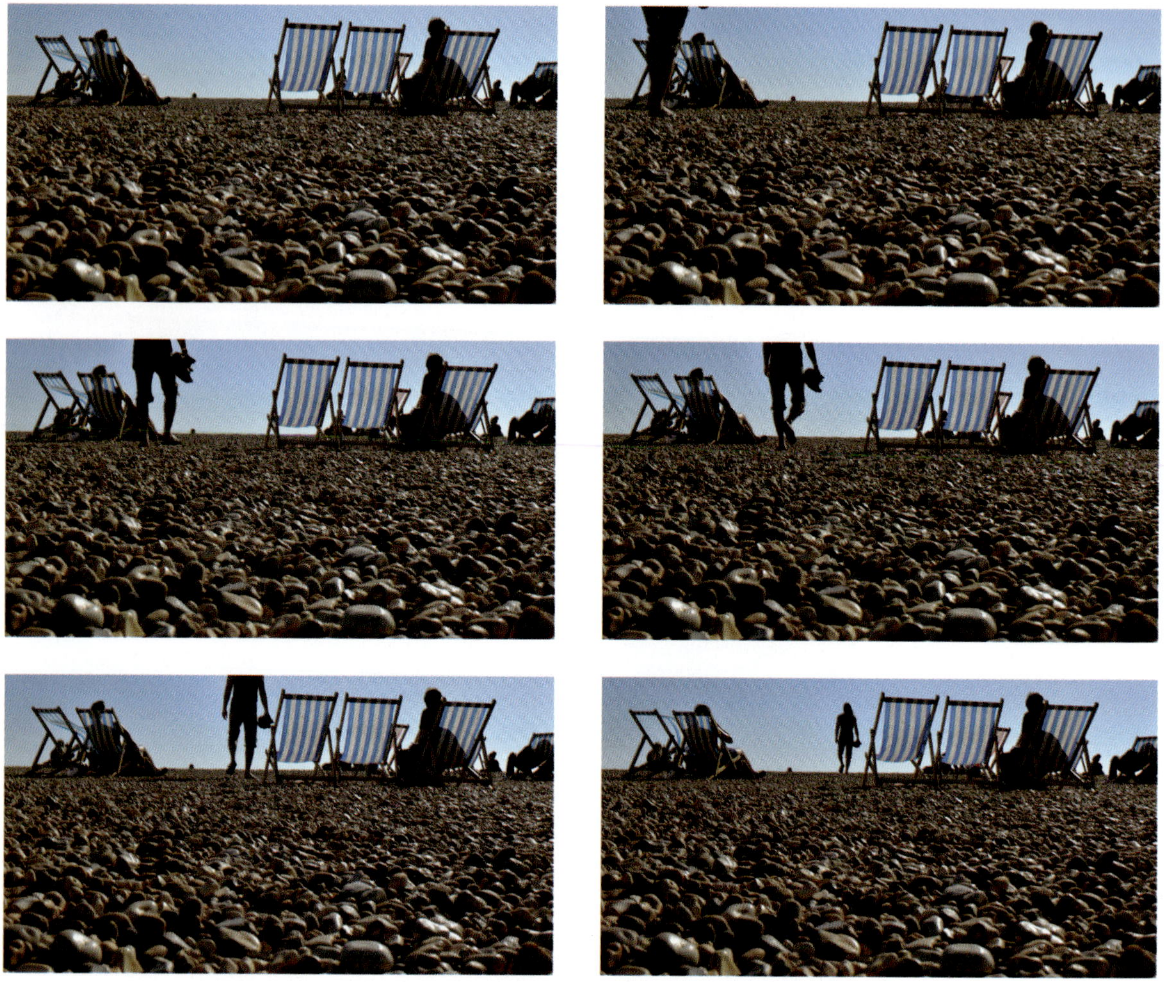

▲ Communicating time passing can be done in a number of ways. This example is simple but effective: someone is walking through the frame across the beach. When we see people walking very quickly, which is how it appears in a time-lapse video, we can tell straight away that time is moving at a different pace to reality. Camera settings: 1/80s, *ƒ*/16, ISO 100.

look around you and see how movement and time relate to each other. Observe clouds, traffic, people, rivers – anything that has movement and catches your eye visually. Finding different ways of defining an area of interest will always enable you to advance your work. Keep coming back to these two words – movement and time – they are key to capturing and producing time-lapse videos.

Useful questions to ask yourself

At many points during the creative process it is invaluable to come back to the initial reason why you were inspired in the first place. Always remind yourself of your target and what you are aiming to achieve. You can do this by asking yourself questions. Be honest and make sure you get answers that will be useful to the creative process. Here are some example questions, but this is not an exhaustive list and you may wish to create your own as well. It is

LOOKING AT THE WORK OF OTHERS

It's research time. Watch some time-lapse videos on television or online and ask yourself what you think works and what doesn't. Think about what catches your eye. For example, you might find you particularly like time-lapse videos of landscape scenes with dramatic clouds. Look at how long the video is and how it is edited together, making notes on what you like and getting inspiration from the work of others. Look at images that you have already taken and think about how they could be made into time-lapse videos. Make sure you record your research and ideas. Keep a notebook because any small notion could end up becoming an inspiring and important piece of work.

useful to ask yourself these questions at the beginning of the process, but also to bear them in mind as you work.

- What are you trying to communicate?
- Is your subject appropriate for time-lapse?
- What inspires you about your subject?
- What kind of time-lapse do you want to make?
- What do you want the end result to look like?
- Do you want your playback speed to be fast or slow?
- What is your time-lapse for?
- How long do you want your time-lapse to be?
- How is your time-lapse going to be shown?
- Who is looking at your time-lapse?
- Why are you making the time-lapse?

You can apply some of these questions when shooting a still photograph or a movie too. A good analogy for this process is a car journey: if you get in your car to drive, you want to know what your destination is. Without a clear idea of your destination you will get lost and drive around in circles. Make sure you navigate your journey successfully by knowing your end point. This systematic approach can help build confidence and it is amazing how far it can go to help you achieve your goal.

TAKING YOURSELF OUT OF 'AUTO'

Many photographers miss out on great content because they are still in 'auto'. We are not talking about green camera auto on the mode dial of the camera, but about a mindset that the photographer adopts when he or she is working. If you are in 'auto' it means that while you are working you are just recording what you see with no real thought about composition, shooting position or how the image looks aesthetically; we are in effect putting a photocopier against the world and simply recording how it looks. We might be doing this without even realizing it, but it means our work may lack personality and individuality.

Try to change your viewing height. Most people see life at eye level and even though this height varies, most pictures we see are taken like this and therefore can start to look similar. Free yourself up and stand on something and look down or lie down and look up; suddenly you totally change the perspective and feel of your imagery. This is a great approach that will change your image-making and, after practice, you will find that any area you are interested in shooting will start to improve in a short space of time. If you take yourself out of 'auto' you will reap the rewards.

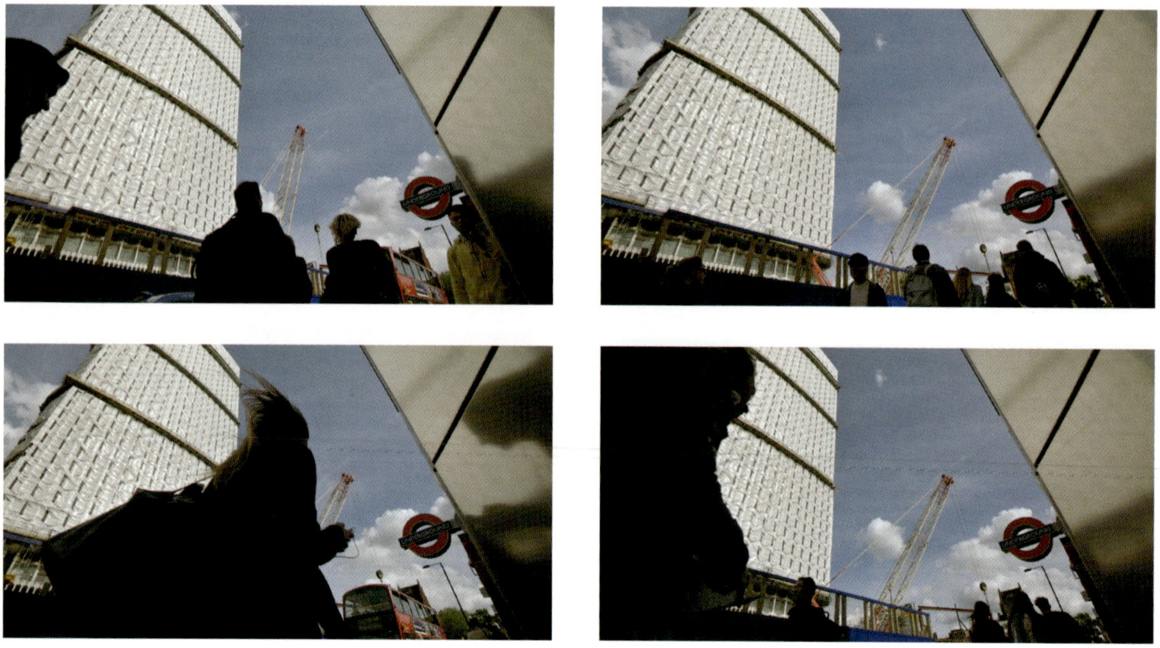

▲ Taking yourself out of auto means moving the camera around and experimenting with different angles. This time-lapse was shot outside a busy train station from floor level looking up. By choosing this angle we are able to capture people, clouds and a moving crane. Sometimes the strangest angles work really well when accompanied by movement. Camera settings: 1/250s, ƒ/9, ISO 100.

ALWAYS LOOK AROUND BEFORE SHOOTING

Pick up your camera and, whatever your location is, give the following a try. First, look around you and notice how much you can see: look left, right, up and down. You can almost see completely behind you without having to actually turn around. Afterwards, look through the viewfinder of the camera. Notice how much less you can see with the camera in front of your face. This will of course vary depending on what lens you have on the camera. The lesson here is that if you are in a situation where there is a lot to see, there might be things that you miss by only looking though the camera's viewfinder. Don't miss shots; look around you first and then set up the camera.

DIFFERENT APPROACHES WITH TIME-LAPSE PHOTOGRAPHY

Using time-lapse capture for stills photography

Time-lapse photography is a strong medium in its own right but time-lapse-related functionality on your camera can be used to capture individual still photographs. If your subject is traffic, for example, and you want a good set of images to choose from, rather than setting up the camera and taking one picture every so often manually, you could set the camera up to shoot full resolution still photographs for time-lapse. This means you would not have to keep pressing the shutter release button on the camera. Sit back and let the camera do the work.

KEEP BOTH EYES OPEN WHEN SHOOTING

This technique is generally appropriate for shooting stills or video and not time-lapse because you could well be set up on a tripod, but even so it could be a game changer for other areas of your work. Try looking through both eyes, whilst looking through the camera. Some sports or wildlife photographers train themselves to keep both eyes open whilst shooting because there is so much action taking place and they do not want to miss anything. This is a great approach because if something happens and your lens is not facing towards it, the moment could be missed for ever if only the eye looking through the camera is open. Some will find this physically easier to do than others; it may feel unnatural at first. It will also depend on which eye you use to shoot with and how big your camera is. If possible, try to shoot with both eyes open for a whole day and see if it works for you.

THE TEN SHOT RULE

Try the ten shot rule. Start by choosing a shooting position. It could be anywhere, maybe at home or at a location that you would normally shoot in. See if you can take ten different images that you really like, without moving your feet. This will help you to think about how to take yourself out of 'auto' because it forces you to look around rather than look through the viewfinder of the camera all the time. It will also encourage you to explore the parameters of what your lens is capable of.

Time-lapse for movies

Time-lapse photography is used for video all the time, whilst shooting television series, documentaries or even blockbusters. It can be used to either show the passing of time or to add visual interest. Most people see time-lapse videos on a daily basis without even realizing it because video content in general is becoming more prevalent within advertising, social media and news apps. Keep an eye out for time-lapse content at the beginning of programmes or during them. Generally speaking time-lapse content will end up as a video so a film-making approach will be hugely advantageous.

Adding visual diversity

When time-lapse is used as part of a movie, it can act as a visual tool to enhance the viewer's enjoyment and to give the look and feel of the film more diversity. Most film-makers will want to make their production look as visually exciting as possible and give the viewer a memorable experience. One of the many reasons why people become interested in time-lapse photography is that it's stimulating visually and different from the look of regular video clips. As image-makers we should always be searching for ways to add diversity to our work and to push ourselves creatively.

Compressing time

With video, there is sometimes a need to show time passing quickly to serve the storytelling. It could be someone repairing a car or a crowd gathering at an event. If shown in real time this might take hours and would be incredibly boring and of no interest to the viewer. If we capture a long period of time with a view to communicating it quickly, we can also choose which sections to omit, therefore leaving the most interesting and relevant parts in the final video. Our patience with looking at all types of media is becoming progressively shorter, so time-lapse enables the photographer or videographer to communicate quickly and efficiently.

Subject matter

Time-lapse photography generally communicates time passing and to do this we need to show

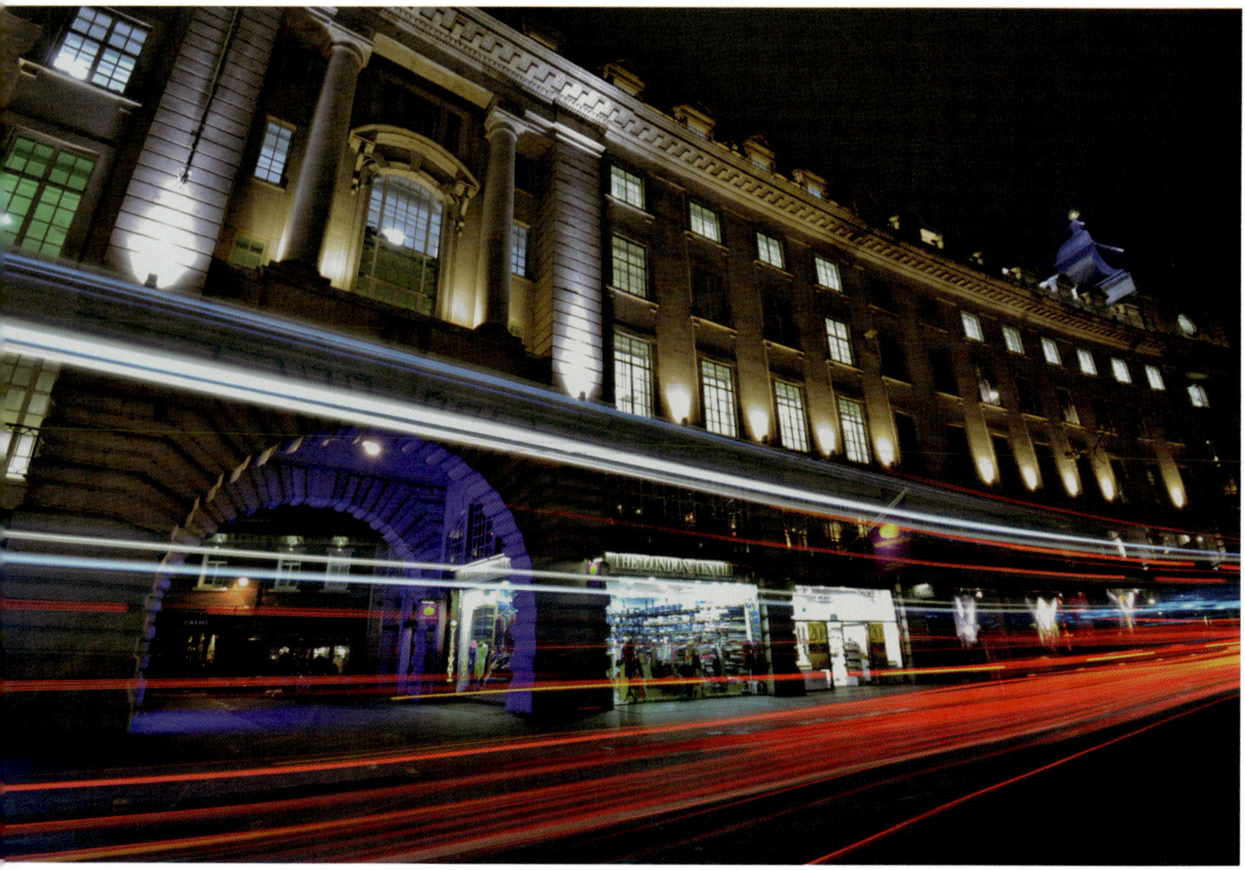

▲ When capturing fast-moving subject matter, sometimes we miss the moment, so why not let the camera capture multiple images and then choose your favourite still image afterwards? This photograph was captured using the interval timer function. There were around twenty pictures captured, but this one had the best motion blur with the traffic. If the interval timer had not been used, this shot would never have been captured. Camera settings: 25s, ƒ/14, ISO 100.

movement. Some examples that will work well are water, scenes at the beach, crowd movement, traffic, clouds, funfairs, sunsets and sunrises. Different lengths of time can be recorded and a time-lapse can be captured in ten minutes or over a much longer period of time, even years. Think about how different subjects might require different shooting durations. Consider how playback speed might affect how certain subjects are communicated.

Montage

The montage is used in movies to compress time, much like a time-lapse, so it can be helpful to take inspiration from these and use ideas from them. You may recall an action film where a montage is used. These are usually presented with backing music that matches the tone of the piece and is fast paced with quick cuts between different shots. You can create a montage with a theme or use more random subject matter, depending on how you want the end result to feel or what you want to communicate. Take inspiration from movies you watch and things you see on television.

You may well end up with a number of test or first draft time-lapse videos when you start finding your feet with the subject. You might not think that they fit together, but these test videos are important to review in order to see what has worked and what

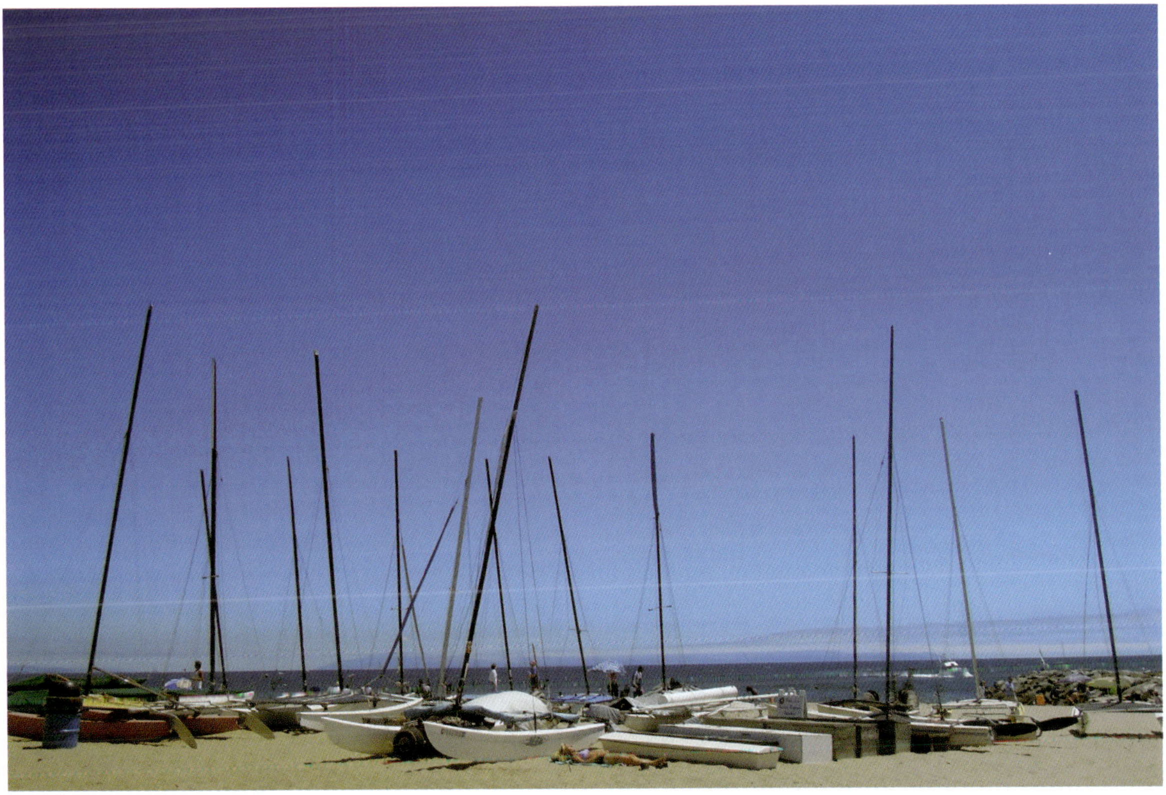

▲ This image taken for a time-lapse video uses a slightly different approach. The movement in this video is provided by the people right at the bottom of the shot, behind the boats. Despite being a very small part of the frame, our eyes are drawn to the movement. Camera settings: 1/1600s, ƒ/5.3, ISO 160.

hasn't. It is a good exercise to watch all of your test videos together, rather than playing them individually. Gather some of these together and make a montage. This will be good practice with video editing and also ensure that you review your work. Reviewing your work in a montage format will help with creative direction and technical practice.

Creative areas that are related to time-lapse photography

There are many areas, old and new, that are related to shooting stills and video, and also some that combine the two. If you are getting more creative with your photography and/or video-making it is rewarding to look at other areas. Some of these areas are: slow motion, time stacking, stop frame animation and hyperlapse. Always keep your mind open to different ways of communicating with your image-making. Here are some of these examples explained in more detail.

Stop frame animation

An area that is very close to time-lapse photography is stop frame animation. These are movies that are created by shooting separate still photographs just like time-lapse. To create the illusion of movement a model or figure with moving parts, usually of a fictional animal or person, is posed in a scene and a still photograph is taken. The model is then moved slightly and another frame is taken. This process is repeated resulting in many still photographs that are then played back quickly. In the final movie the models are animated and appear to move by themselves. This technique is generally used for children's programmes and is often used for feature films. This is a painstaking process, requiring a lot of patience.

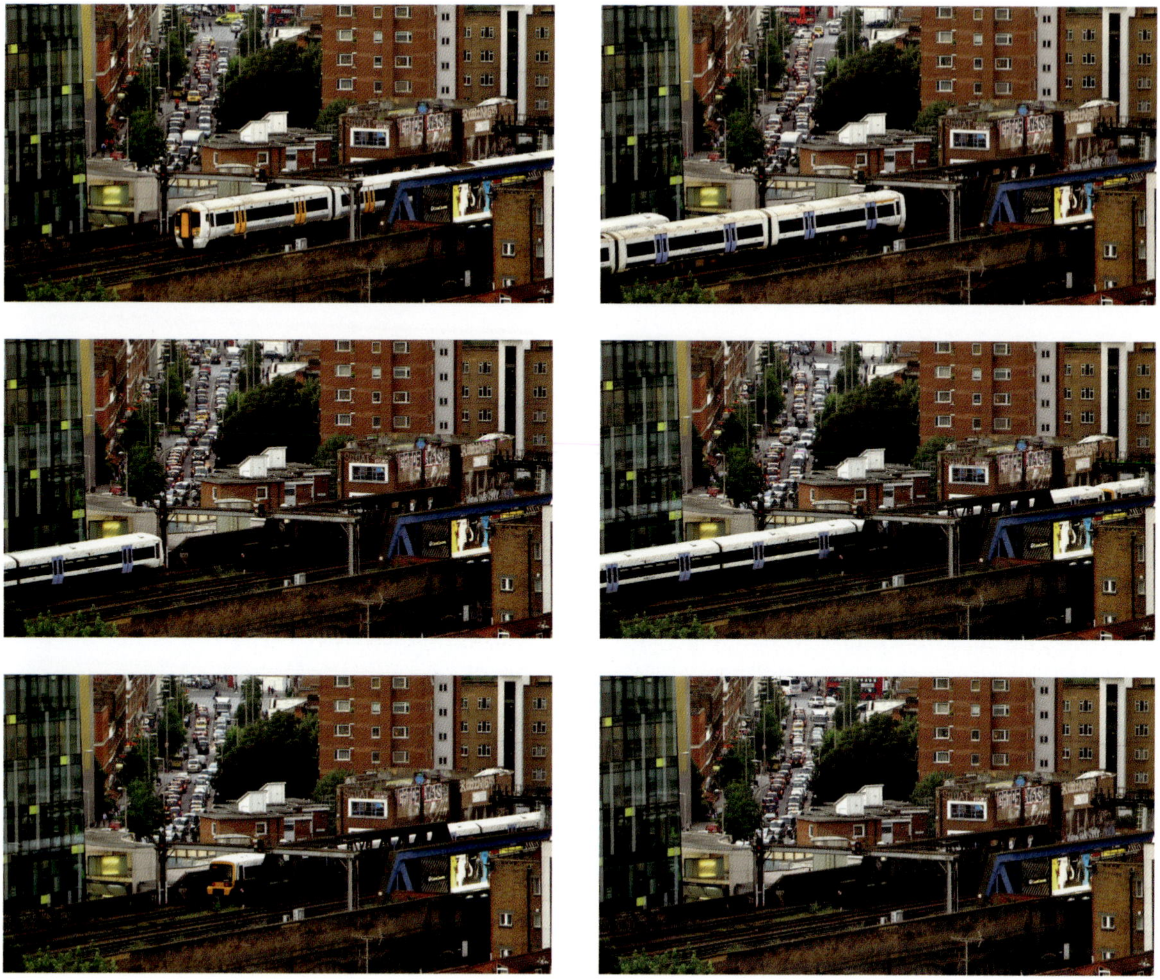

▲ It is often the case with time-lapse that giving the viewer a lot to look at works well, which sometimes means filling the frame with plenty of interest. In this example we have a complete cross section of a built-up area. There is movement of traffic, trains, and people, including inside the buildings. Camera settings: 1/200s, *f*/4, ISO 1000.

It is likely that if someone is interested in time-lapse they have a healthy curiosity about animation. Watch some animated films and get inspiration; it may not seem like the most obvious place to look but you could be surprised.

Hyperlapse

This new hybrid of time-lapse photography is achieved when the camera itself is moving whilst it is capturing a time-lapse video. The camera's lens can be zooming in and out during the video and sometimes there is a point of interest that is focused on during the camera's movement. The great thing about hyperlapse photography is that anyone can do it and it does not require any expensive equipment to move the camera around, which would normally be required for this kind of video. Hyperlapse is created when the photographer is moving, usually at a small, even distance between each shot. An easy method of doing this is to take a step, shoot an image and then continually repeat the process whilst moving in any direction. The end result will be a series of stills that when put into video software for video playback gives a shaky looking hand-held

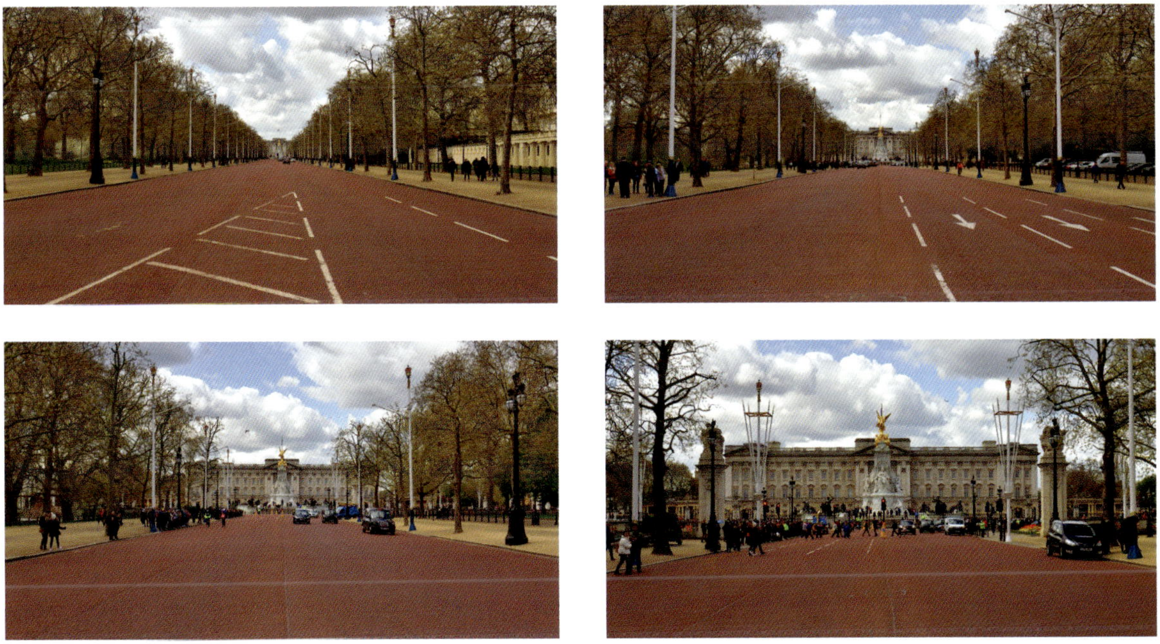

▲ These are still images taken from a hyperlapse. This shows how the camera is able to move, rather than being one static shot for the duration of capture. Camera settings: 1/200s, ƒ/9, ISO 100.

look, but it will essentially be a moving time-lapse.

To reduce the natural camera shake and movement, a Steadicam correction tool is used in video-editing software to make the movement steady. For the editing software to work effectively, make sure that a clear reference point is visible in the frame, such as a building or tree. The result looks like it is shot using a very expensive rig, but it doesn't cost the photographer any more than they have already spent on a camera and the computer software. It is always worth being aware of evolution like this in areas related to time-lapse photography; often the most exciting developments are just around the corner.

Time stacking

A time stacked image is constructed from different frames of the same scene. The capture is very much like time-lapse in that you will have many images of the same scene, but captured over a long period of time. The time-lapse camera features can therefore be used to help the initial capture for time stacking photography. In editing software the images are then stacked together, or superimposed. You might use parts of the sky from a sunset in your scene, but the foreground will be from mid-afternoon, for example. It can look eye-catching when all of the interesting-looking times of day are represented in one frame.

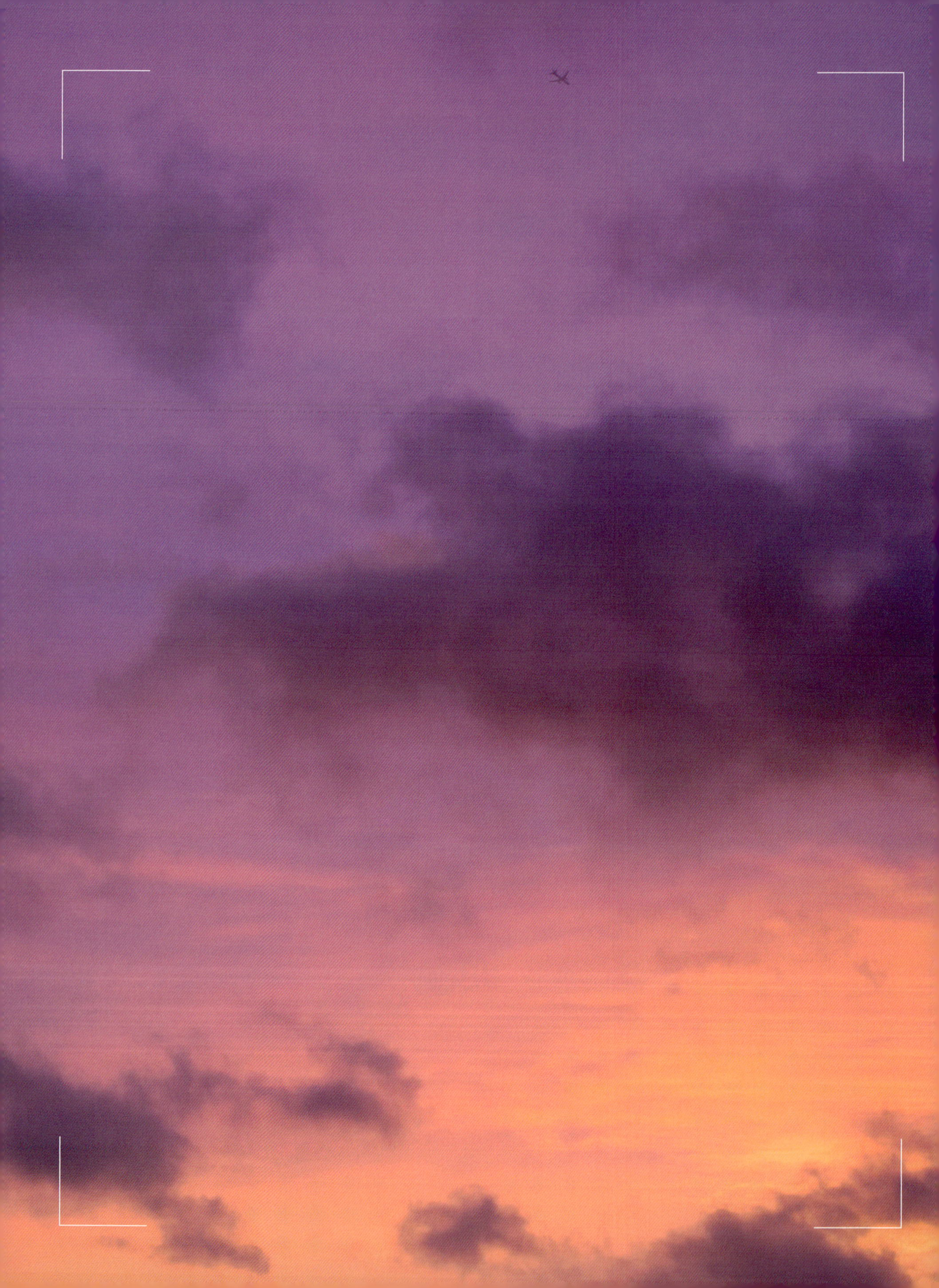

Chapter 2

Time-lapse basics

In this chapter we take a look at the technical side of digital imaging in the context of time-lapse photography. Information covered in this chapter will be applicable for both stills photography and shooting video, as well as our main subject area. We will look at the key settings available in our camera to help us create time-lapse video content. With a good understanding of the technical aspects we can ensure that what we are visualizing can be achieved.

Equally, by knowing the parameters of our camera's technical properties, we can plan around this, whilst applying our creative input. There is nothing worse than almost capturing a fantastic time-lapse, only to discover that the settings were incorrect and the content ultimately unusable. It is always advantageous to have a good balance of both creative and technical knowledge because these aspects complement each other and together help you become more efficient and develop your work more quickly.

RESOLUTION

Every image or video you create with a digital camera is made up of many small squares (pixels) that are lined up together in rows, almost like bricks in a wall. Each square records light and converts it into digital signals. When millions of squares are put together to make up an image you do not see the individual squares but an image that looks like what you see with your own eyes. By zooming right into the image on the back of the camera or on a computer screen you can see these individual pixels that make up the image.

A common misconception with resolution is that the higher it is, the better the picture quality; however, the quality of the image is mainly down to the glass in front of the sensor (the lens). If you want to improve the sharpness and clarity of your imagery it might be better to look at a new lens rather than a higher resolution camera – more about that later on.

The first thing that will come to mind for most people when the word resolution is mentioned is 'megapixels'. This is a marketing label that refers to the number of pixels you are using on your sensor to make up the image. If your camera records 24 megapixels, it means that your image will have 24 million pixels in it. Video format is mostly how we view our time-lapse photography, so it is important to know what resolution means in the context of video as well.

The term 'megapixels' is not used for video: instead we use terms such as HD (High Definition), Full HD or 4K. Sometimes video resolution is referred to as 1080p or 720p. These references are useful, as they tell us the actual number of pixels along the short edge of the frame that we are recording. Listed on the next page are the terms by which we refer to them, alongside the actual resolution. The two numbers shown are the pixel dimensions. This is the number of pixels that make up the long edge and the short edge of the frame of the image or video. If you multiply one number by the other, the total number of pixels can be calculated and therefore

◀ When you spot that amazing sunrise be sure to get straight out and capture it. The clouds passing through the frame gives the time-lapse movement that is beautifully complemented with the range of colours in the sky. Camera settings: 1/60s, *f*/3.5, ISO 280.

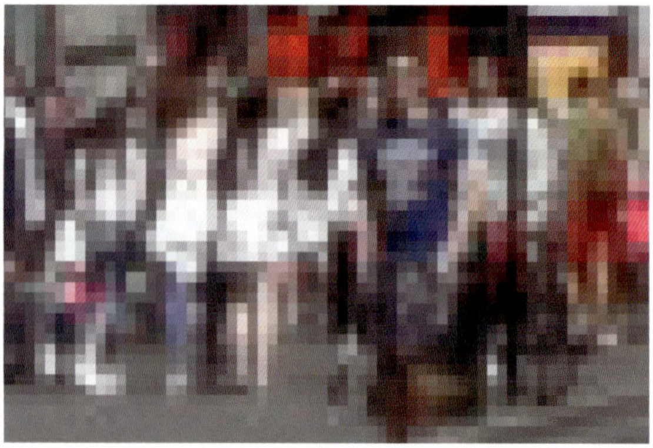

▲ A small section of a still image that has been blown up in order to see the individual pixels. You can see that each pixel has one colour and is a square shape.

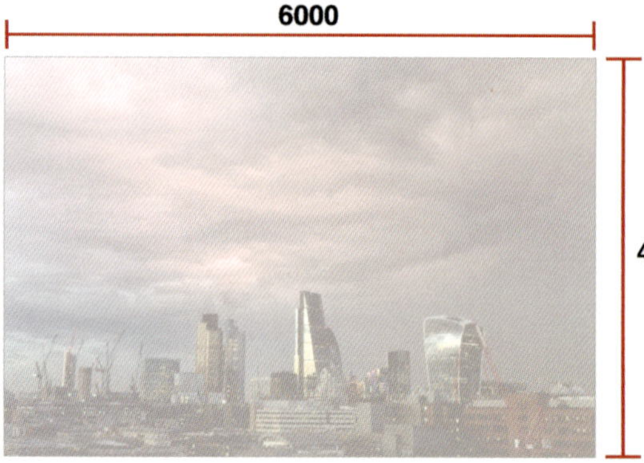

▲ This example shows how the pixel dimensions relate to the actual image. The horizontal edge has 6,000 pixels and the vertical side has 4000. To find out how many pixels there are overall, multiply 6000 by 4000 and this gives us our total surface area. In this example the result is 24 million pixels or megapixels.

the total resolution. For image-makers, the most useful numbers to look at are the pixel dimensions. Looking at these values tells us how many pixels we physically have in our frame, which helps us when we need to re-size images for our output.

These pixel dimensions are approximate dimensions and may vary slightly depending on the camera's sensor. The number of megapixels is usually rounded to the closest whole number, for example, if a sensor technically has 12.2 megapixels, we just say 12 megapixels for ease of use. 4K is a different way to refer to video resolution: 4K means that there are approximately 4000 pixels on the top edge of the frame. (Market research is frequently carried out by manufacturers to find more memorable ways to sell and remember the latest and greatest equipment and resolution. Another way to refer to Full HD is '1080' and this refers to the short edge of the frame. With 4K it was decided that '2160' was not catchy enough, so 4K was used to market this resolution and generation of technology.)

Examples of video resolution options

4K = 3840 × 2160 pixels
Full HD = 1920 × 1080 pixels
HD = 1280 × 720 pixels

Examples of stills resolution options

50 MP (megapixels) = 8688 × 5792 pixels
36 MP (megapixels) = 7360 × 4912 pixels
24 MP (megapixels) = 6000 × 4000 pixels
16 MP (megapixels) = 4928 × 3280 pixels

How do stills and video resolution relate to each other?

To answer this question we will take Full HD video resolution (1920 × 1080) as an example. To find out the total number of pixels we multiply one value by the other, which gives us a total of 2,073 megapixels. If we approach this number from a photographer's perspective, this appears very low compared to what we are used to with individual still photographs.

Full HD, also known as Blu-ray, if marketed on the basis of the resolution figure in megapixels, would be unlikely to sell so successfully. This is why marketing terms have been cleverly developed to make resolution for video sound more impressive than perhaps it is (when considered from a stills photography perspective). Compared to a 24 MP or 36 MP digital stills camera, video has a much lower resolution, but don't let this put you off because Full HD video still looks great to watch. Fewer pixels are required for movies because there are at least 24 frames being shown per second and our eye only

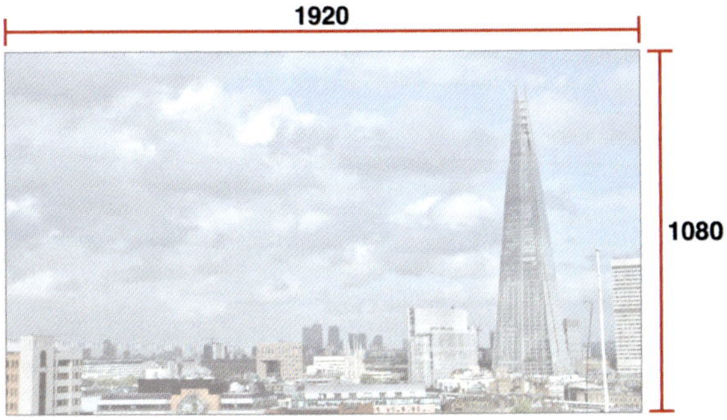

▲ This example shows Full HD video resolution. Just like a regular still image, to work out the total surface area i.e. the resolution, we multiply one value by the other to get the total number of pixels in the frame.

needs a small amount of resolution to see detail with moving image. Even though it sounds low in resolution, the number of frames is high and we also have audio added to the file as well. Altogether, this makes the file bigger than you might think.

Aspect ratio

Aspect ratio is essentially the shape of the frame of your video or still photograph. With most DSLR cameras the shape or aspect ratio of a still photograph is 3:2. This means that if the long edge is divided into three equal parts then the short edge is two of these parts in length. There are lots of different aspect ratios that you can choose from, one example is 1:1 which is a square. Lots of people like to use square images on social media because of the way the shape fits into news feeds.

It is always important to be aware of what you are shooting for. Your final delivery might need a specific aspect ratio; this may well affect how the image is shot in the first place. With HD or Full HD video the aspect ratio is 16:9. This is more of a letterbox shape than the still images produced straight out of the camera. If you have a flat screen television in your living room, the likelihood is that it will have a 16:9 aspect ratio.

Care has to be taken when alternating between stills and video because if we take a still image and put it straight into a video then the aforementioned

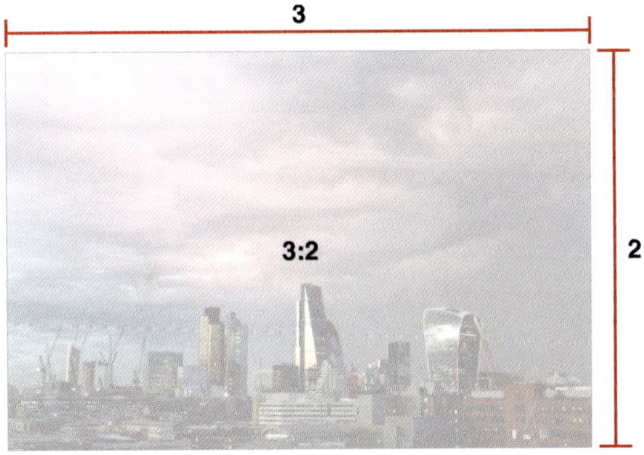

▲ Aspect ratio is basically the shape of the frame. This example shows how the 3:2 aspect ratio relates to an image. If the long edge is divided into three equal parts then the short edge is the length of two of them.

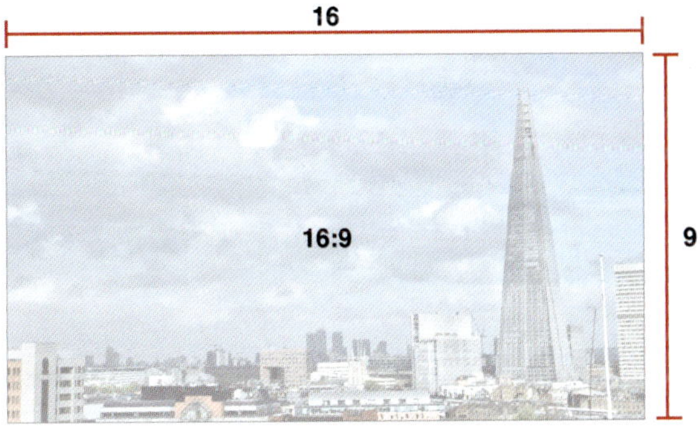

▲ The format for video is more of a letterbox shape than that of a regular still photograph. We have to be careful when going between stills and video to ensure that we don't lose part of the frame through cropping.

shapes will not fit into one another. For example, placing a 3:2 shape into a 16:9 ratio will crop the top and the bottom of the image, and this can completely change its look and feel.

Another issue to be aware of is that the aspect ratio of your content may vary depending on what camera you are using. If we compare a DSLR to a pocket compact camera, the shape of the sensors will be slightly different. This will only affect the still photographs, however. If video is HD or Full HD, for example, these will always be the same shape. When producing a time-lapse, the final delivery will generally be video and therefore a 16:9 aspect ratio. Being aware of the different shapes produced

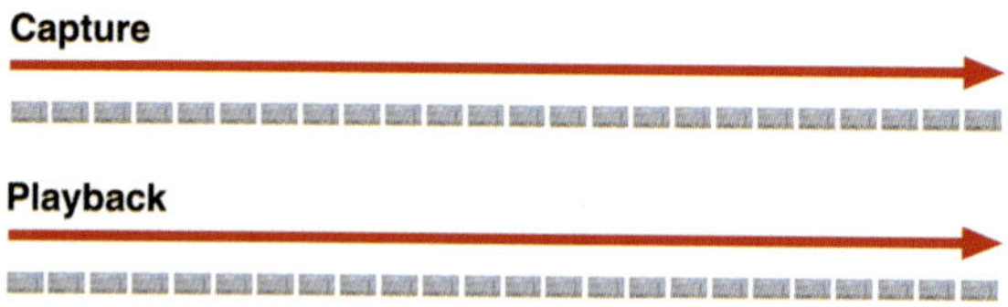

▲ This diagram represents one second of time passing for capture and delivery with shooting regular video. Both capture and playback are at 24 frames per second which means the video will be the same speed as real life and the result is therefore no faster or slower than reality. Not all frame rates are at 24 but this is the minimum required to get natural-looking movement.

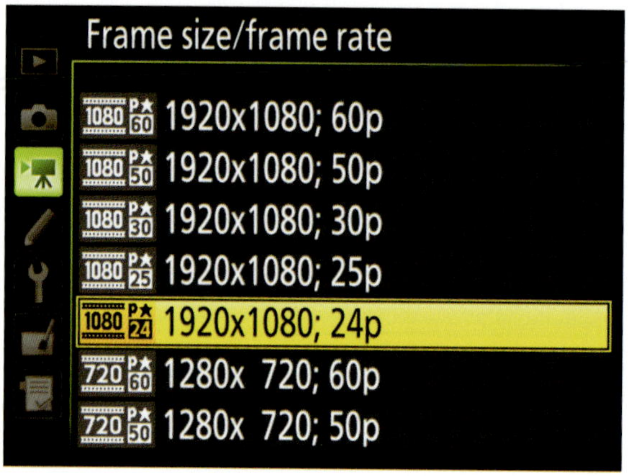

▲ Your camera should show you the pixel dimensions and frame rates that are available in its menu system.

by different resolutions and sensors will ensure that you don't inadvertently end up with unwanted image cropping.

DIFFERENT WAYS TO CAPTURE TIME-LAPSE WITH YOUR CAMERA

1. Shooting video for time-lapse delivery

One way to make a time-lapse is to film a video clip and then speed it up afterwards. Most cameras will shoot video these days including pocket cameras, professional DSLRs and mobile phones. Time-lapse is about playing with the perceived passing of time, so we can capture a regular video showing time passing by as we see it and then experiment with the playback by speeding the video clip up.

An example of this is traffic moving on a motorway, which you could film for ten minutes. If you watch the video back straight out of the camera, it will be pretty underwhelming; if you speed it up to double or even up to eight times faster, however, it becomes much more interesting visually because it shows us time passing by quickly and the traffic moving along the road will suddenly become quite mesmerizing. You may be able to speed up the video clip in camera for a quicker preview, so check your manual to see if this is possible. If not then you will be able to do it on your computer. Most computers now come with free video-editing software that will do this.

It is preferable to speed up a video clip using software as opposed to a camera because it offers a choice of playback speeds, which will enable you to change the way the video looks, feels and communicates time and movement. Some packages allow you to choose to speed the video up by percentages, whilst others let you choose timing – either way it is usually very easy to find and use this function. A pitfall of shooting regular video for time-lapse delivery is that it is relatively limiting in terms of what you can achieve visually. If you shoot stills for time-lapse photography, it will free up your creativity and enable you to explore new areas of visual communication.

2. Shooting stills for time-lapse delivery

Video is generally the end delivery with time-lapse; however, it is much more satisfactory to shoot separate still photographs initially, and make the final movie from these stills, as we shall see below. There are different modes that can be found on advanced stills cameras that are available to us. We will look at the most common settings that are found on DSLR and compact cameras. Titles and names do vary between brands, but the ideas will be the same.

Interval-timer shooting

The interval timer (or in layman's terms, the 'automatic picture-taking timer') enables the camera to take still images automatically by triggering the shutter release button at an interval of your choice. If you were going to do this by pressing the camera's shutter button manually you would not only get a sore finger but you would get unwanted camera movement. You can set the interval timer, for example, to take a picture every four seconds. Simply press 'start' and let the camera capture your time-lapse for you. Afterwards you can make the time-lapse video out of the separate images using software on a computer. Although you will not be able to view the final time-lapse video in the camera straight away you can flick through the images and get an idea of what the final piece will look like. This mode is a built-in feature of most DSLR cameras. If this is not the case you will be able to purchase a remote trigger that gives you this function. Always refer to your camera's manual when looking at these options to check functionality.

One major advantage of using this function is that the pictures that are taken will be in whatever file format or resolution you have the camera set to for regular stills photography. This means you can get full resolution images from the camera even though you are shooting for time-lapse delivery. This would be particularly useful if there were a still from which you wished to produce a large photographic print or if you wanted to do a lot of editing to an image.

When using the interval-timer function, make sure that you have set the time and date correctly on your camera. Sometimes if the clock is not set this function cannot be used, as the camera uses its internal clock to operate the timer. If you are using an external trigger with interval timer functionality this is normally not quite so important.

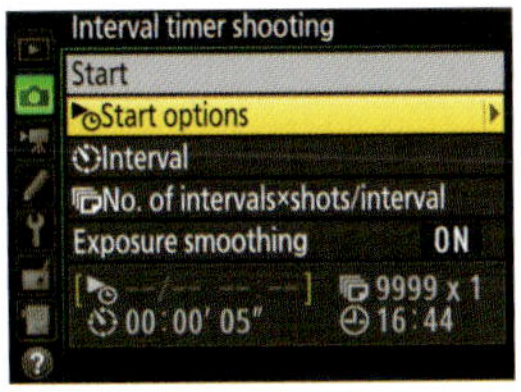

▲ The interval timer function on your camera or remote will enable you to choose how often you want the camera to take a picture.

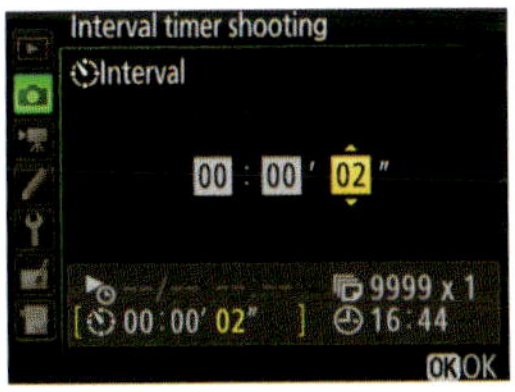

▲ This image shows an example of a menu which enables you to control how often the camera takes a picture. Here we can see that two seconds has been programmed; this means one still image will be taken every two seconds.

YOUR FIRST TIME-LAPSE

Whether you are using the camera's interval timer or a remote trigger, put your camera on a tripod and set the camera up to capture a view of moving traffic, people passing by or clouds in the sky – anything with plenty of movement. Shoot at an interval of one frame per second for ten minutes. Afterwards, look at the individual frames and the movement between each photo. Find how to build the images into a time-lapse video using the software on your computer. This could well be one of your first ever time-lapse videos, so show it to family and friends or post it online. See what people think; every time-lapse you create is an important part of the learning process. Any problem that you encounter during this process will be invaluable to you. We need to find the challenges of the overall process to understand it and subsequently overcome these trials.

Interval timer for stills photography

The camera's interval timer can be used simply to take many still photographs, with the intention to choose one image from a set. An example of this is where you may be taking pictures of a sunset, and you might not be sure exactly where you want the sun positioned in the final frame. You could take a set of images in quick succession, which can be

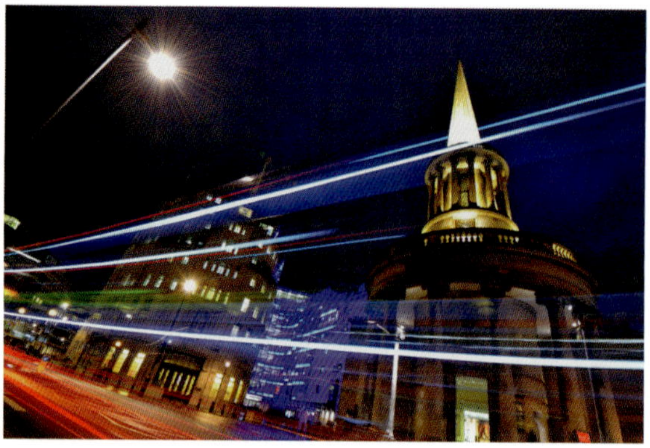

▲ This image has been captured using the interval timer function. The motion blur in the traffic has been timed perfectly by the camera whilst the photographer stood guard and let it take pictures automatically. Camera settings: 13s, ƒ/11, ISO 100.

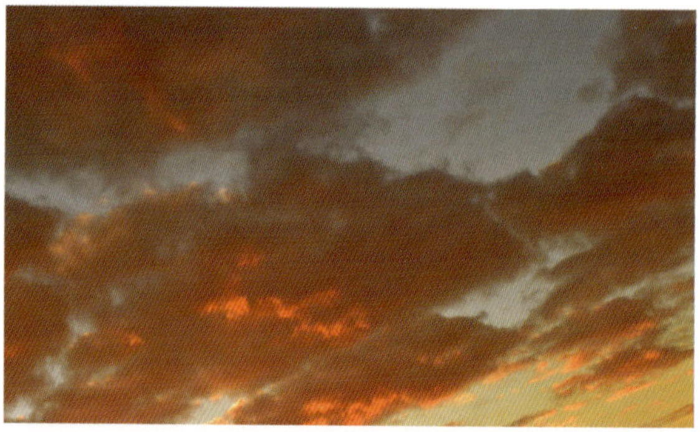

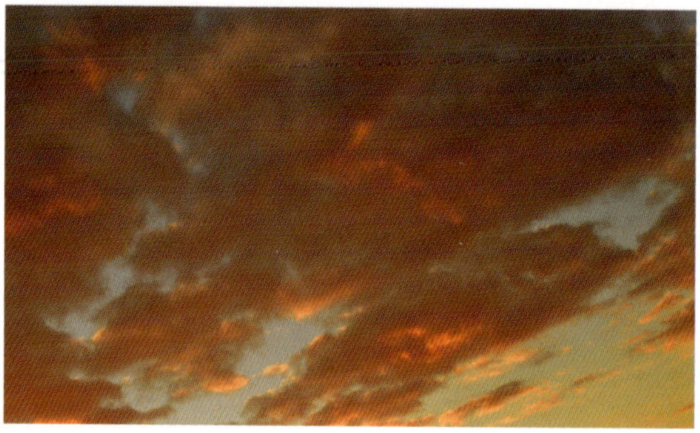

▲ This sequence of images is from a time-lapse video that has been captured with the interval timer mode. This shows how sometimes you only need to point the camera out of your window at home to get a stunning time-lapse video. Camera settings: 1/5s, ƒ/16, ISO 100.

done by pressing the button on the camera every few seconds and capturing images as the sun moves. Alternatively you could let the camera do the work by using the interval timer to automatically take a picture every two seconds for example. You will then be able to choose from a number of still photographs afterwards and you haven't had to press the shutter manually for each image.

This may on the surface appear to be a lazy option but if you have paid a lot of money for a camera, why not utilize the functionality available and let it do some of the work for you? Whilst the camera is taking still images you can be on guard making sure that the equipment is secure and maybe put your feet up and have a bite to eat. It is also advantageous to have a range of images to choose from. After shooting, you might choose a different image from the one you liked best at the time of capture.

Interval timer for creating time-lapse videos

After capture, you will need to put all of the stills into a folder on your computer. There could be hundreds or even thousands of images depending on the length and frequency your capture was set for. Drop all of the still images into the video-editing software; most packages will give you a slideshow, in which the still images will be played back one by one in order. The next job is to make sure each still is shown for 1/24th of a second so that you get playback at 24 frames per second. The result will show the individual stills being played back very quickly like regular video, but this video will be a time-lapse.

Most video-editing software packages will have this functionality as well as some stills-editing software. Check the program you already have before purchasing anything. You may find that you already own free software, which came with your computer, that will make time-lapse videos from still photographs. Eventually you may find that you want to purchase a more advanced video-editing program, if you do not have one already, but you probably won't need to do this immediately; you can create fantastic time-lapse videos with very basic software.

Resolution and file formats for interval-timer shooting

The two most common file formats on an advanced camera are RAW and JPEG. We will briefly look at these file formats before assessing how they are relevant to interval-timer shooting for time-lapse and stills photography.

JPEG

This is a universal, but highly compressed, file format that will be compatible with every piece of imaging software available. Designed to be heavily compressed to reduce the file size, this format is the most common file for general stills photography. It is, however, not ideal for post-production and editing because of the limited options available. This file format always gives a good picture as seen on a screen but does not capture the full colour that the camera's sensor is capable of. If you need to rescue your images and have shot JPEG, you are much less likely to be able to retrieve than if you are using RAW.

RAW

The industry term for this file format is RAW because it is the information directly from the camera's sensor, without any aggressive compression, and therefore the raw information. This file format will give the best image quality available from the sensor and is much better for editing or rescuing the image post capture. To edit with these files you do need to check they are fully compatible with your software, however, as they will only work with specific packages. Sometimes RAW is referred to as the 'safety net file' because it is easier to salvage if you have made a error with exposure or colour. A huge advantage with RAW is that it uses what is called 'non destructive editing'. This means that when you make a change to the file you can actually go back, undo it and reset the image to how it was captured originally.

▶ The choice between JPEG and RAW will have a huge bearing on what can be done to your images in post-production. RAW lets us do far more to our image than JPEG. The JPEG is a smaller file, however, and tends to be a popular option for time-lapse photographers because of this.

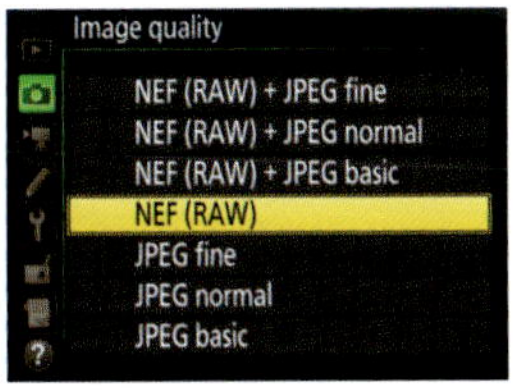

Which file format should I choose for interval-timer shooting?

If you are using the interval timer to get individual still photographs to print, for example, and not to collate into a time-lapse video, it is best to shoot RAW. This will take up more storage space on the card but will give you better colour and detail in the image. You are able to do much more to these files in post-production, giving greater flexibility and a number of options to choose from. Be mindful of storage, work out how many images you will be taking and check that the card is able to fit this amount of information on it. If you decide that you want to make a time-lapse video from the RAW files captured, it is best to convert them to JPEG before importing them into video-editing software.

If you are shooting with the interval timer for a time-lapse video delivery then it might be more practical to shoot JPEG files in the camera. You will also be able to fit a greater number of images on the card and therefore shoot for longer. You will be able to drop the files straight into the video-editing software you are using. The main reason for using JPEG for time-lapse, however, is because in terms of resolution, we do not need a great amount for video delivery. You can reduce the size of the JPEG files in your camera and shoot maybe 8 megapixel still photographs for your time-lapse. This particular example is popular because 8 megapixels is approximately the same resolution as 4K video. This means that you are able to create a stunning time-lapse video and be more future-compatible with your content. If you shoot at the highest resolution your camera has to offer, you could future-proof yourself

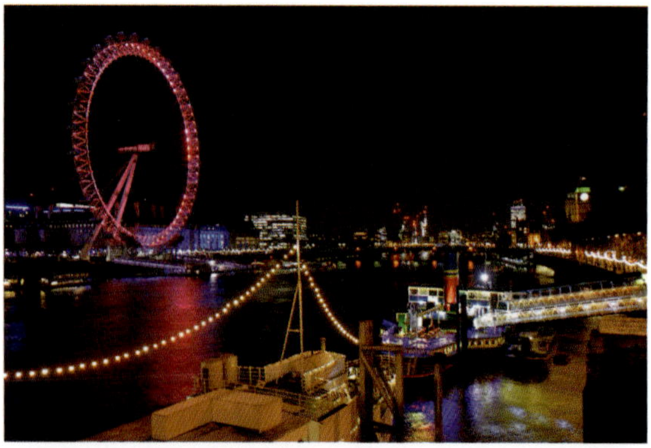

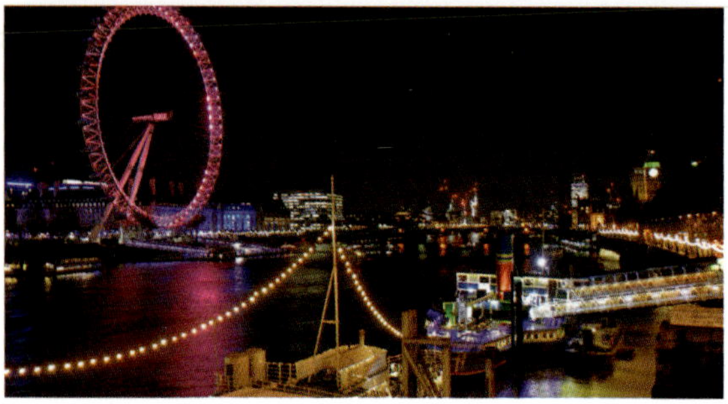

▲ This comparison shows how you can easily be caught out by the difference in aspect ratio if you are unaware of the different frame shapes between video and stills. The 3:2 image (seen here at the top) is framed nicely with plenty of space around the subject matter. When the 16:9 aspect ratio is applied, the top and bottom of the image is cut off. In this example (the bottom image) it has a negative effect on the composition of the image. If you change your aspect ratio, make sure that you recompose your frame accordingly. Camera settings: 1/1.3s, *f*/5.6, ISO 320.

even further as all digital screens are progressively becoming higher in resolution as technology moves forward. Also, shooting at a higher resolution will enable you to zoom in and move around the final time-lapse video in video-editing software.

Aspect ratio and interval-timer shooting

Interval-timer mode essentially takes still photographs, and the aspect ratio of stills on most advanced cameras is 3:2. If you are making a video then the aspect ratio will be 16:9 (more of a letterbox shape than that of still photographs, as described earlier). This means that the two media will not fit seamlessly together. We can fit the still photo into the 16:9 shape, but this might result in some of the image being cut off. Most people will probably not notice this, but it can completely change how your image looks. If you have to fit these shapes into each other, make sure the image fills the frame as fully as possible, thus giving the video more visual impact. Sometimes your camera will show a guide to help you see what shape you are working with at any given point; either way, you will get a good feel for this technicality after shooting both stills and video content. It sometimes helps to put some tape across the back screen of the camera to create a 16:9 shape and then you can make sure you compose the image with this in mind. This will ensure that you do not lose anything important when shooting stills for time-lapse using the interval timer.

Advanced interval-timer shooting

Once you have experienced using the interval-timer mode you can take it one step further. Most advanced cameras with this function will allow you to choose how many frames can be taken at each interval. An example of this is to set the interval to trigger every second. You could then set the camera to take two frames at every interval. This means the camera will take two frames every one second. The result will be more choppy and almost animated looking, not as smooth as a one frame per second capture. Don't explore this technique until you have fully understood shooting with one frame at every interval and made a few time-lapse videos. The ability to trigger multiples will enable you to create different visual styles with your time-lapse work.

Recording a time-lapse to a finalized video in camera

On some cameras this is called 'time-lapse photography mode' and some call it 'time-lapse to video'. This option enables the camera to take still photographs for time-lapse using the interval timer, but the camera puts the stills together into a video as you shoot, resulting in a completed time-lapse video

▶ Your camera might have the functionality to choose how many images are taken at each interval. In this example the menu shows 9999 x 1 which is 9999 images in total and one image will be taken at each interval. If you dialled in 9999 x 2, then the camera would take two images at each interval and the total number of frames that will be taken is doubled.

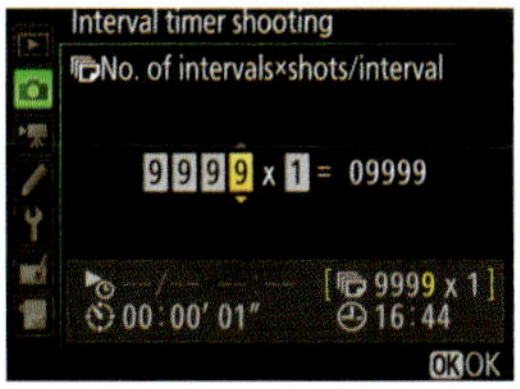

ready to use. This negates the need for a computer to create the video clips, but video-editing software could still be needed to edit the different clips together. This is a good option for convenience as you could make a time-lapse in camera and upload it straight to a website. If your camera has this option it could make your workflow much more manageable.

This option is not, however, for people who want full resolution still photographs from their time-lapse videos. It is possible to capture still photographs from the final video but they would be the same resolution as the video. One example would be Full HD: if we pull still photographs from this the images will be 1920 x 1080 pixels, which is not a great deal in the stills world, but will be good enough for website use. We are also limited with the file format that we can use when taking stills from video. Most technology will only enable you to make JPEG files, so you will not get the advanced functionality of RAW files.

With time-lapse to video mode, the playback speed of your time-lapse video will be finalized during capture. Because of this, you need to make sure the timing has been thought out fully. The frame rate of the playback will be whatever the camera is set to for normal video shooting, so if you choose 24 frames per second for regular video then the time-lapse will be 24 frames per second also. You will need to take 24 photographs when you are capturing the time-lapse for 1 second of playback. If you choose 60fps video playback then you will have to take 60 frames to get one-second of playback. This will take longer to capture when you are shooting, but the playback will be faster. Different playback speeds will suit different subject matter. You will get a feel for what you prefer after a bit of experimentation.

TIME-LAPSE TO VIDEO IN CAMERA

If you have a time-lapse to video mode on your camera, choose the highest resolution at a frame rate of 24 frames per second. Set the camera up on a tripod so that it is viewing a busy area with lots of movement – this could be in a park, train station or by a road. Set the interval timer to shoot at one frame per second and leave the camera running for about ten minutes.

Review the video and look at what is happening with the movement in the video. Notice how much faster things appear than in real life. Repeat the same time-lapse but at different playback frame rates. You will see that the playback speed changes and makes time appear to travel forward at different paces. If you repeat this process with your area of interest you will see what kind of playback speeds suit different situations. If your camera does not have this function, use the interval timer and try the same things out, play with different playback speeds. Experiment and enjoy.

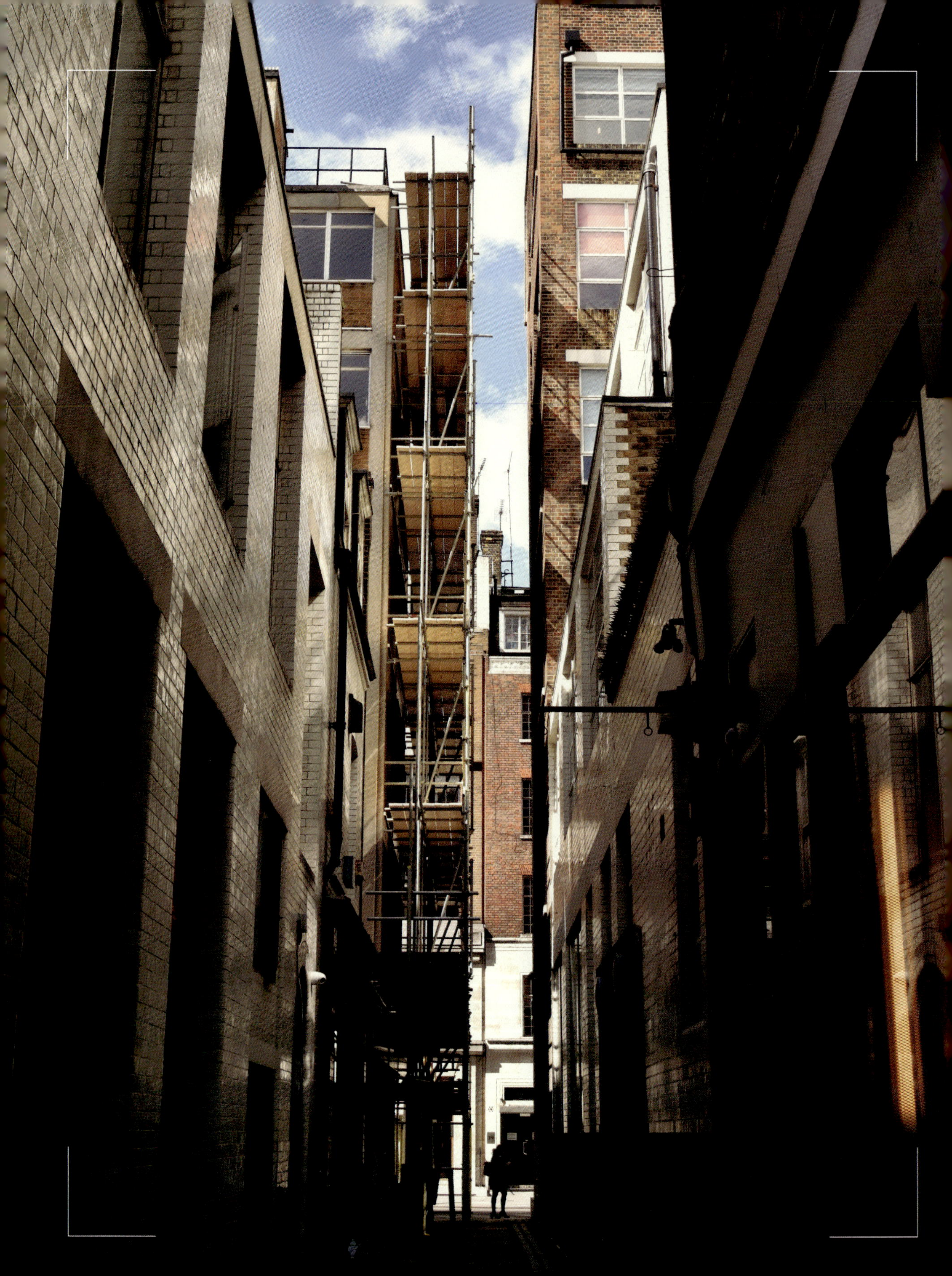

Chapter 3

Equipment

In this chapter we will take a look at equipment that will help you with your time-lapse photography, exploring ideas about what to take with you to a shoot and what can be used to make your set-up more efficient. You can pick and choose the contents of your kitbag according to personal preference and the job in hand. We will start by having a look at the camera itself, then other items in and around the kit bag.

IMAGING DEVICE

An imaging device can be a mobile phone, tablet, compact camera, or a DSLR (Digital Single Lens Reflex) camera, to name a few. We will look at different devices and discuss advantages and disadvantages of each. It is becoming increasingly common for a photographer or videographer to use at least two of the devices that we will talk about. Even a professional photographer who uses a high-end DSLR camera will always use a secondary device such as a mobile phone or a compact camera for research purposes or to be more discreet in certain situations.

There can be some snobbery or elitism surrounding which device an individual chooses to use. There is really no need for this, since image-making with any device should be embraced and all technology should be evaluated as a potentially important tool for use in different situations. As technology evolves, so does time-lapse photography and the surrounding areas; it would be foolish not to investigate all that is available to us.

Mobile phones and tablets

Most people already use mobile devices to produce photos or video, whether or not they are a photographer. They are simple and easy to use and whenever most people want to record a moment in time, they will reach for the device that is closest to hand. More serious photographers don't consider using a phone or tablet as their main imaging device because the quality of the images and control of the device is limited, but even so, explore your phone and see what it is capable of. Phones can be a great tool for capturing initial ideas or making notes relating to your subject. If you see or think of something that could make a great time-lapse video and you don't have your main camera with you, a device like this will record the idea so you can come back to it later, rather than forgetting about it. In this way portable smart devices are invaluable to us.

Advantages

Phones and tablets are generally portable, compact, light and easy to use. Some say, 'the best camera is the one you have on you' and most people carry their phones around with them at all times. Smart devices are basically small computers and can be used as such. When it comes to getting a weather forecast, finding out your GPS location or what direction the sun is going to set in, a smartphone with the right software or apps installed will tell you all of this, so even if it is not used for taking the pictures, it can be a very important tool to assist you. Another advantage of a smart device is that the

◄ Bold tower blocks can often be used as great subject matter for time-lapse videos. You will get movement in the sky with clouds as well as people, traffic and reflections on windows. Camera settings: 1/800s, *f*/8, ISO 500.

SHOOTING TIME-LAPSE ON YOUR PHONE OR TABLET

Download a time-lapse app on to your smart device. Some are free and some you may have to pay for; either way you will be able to capture a time-lapse video fairly easily. Lean the device up against a solid item on your window sill. Frame the image so that there is something moving, such as clouds or traffic on a road. Set the time-lapse app to capture one frame every three or four seconds, if the option is given, and let the app record for at least twenty minutes. Make sure that you do not move the device when it is shooting.

Once the time-lapse has been captured, have a look at the quality and colour that the device gives you. Maybe explore using the device as a time-lapse tool at different locations. It is better to do this during the day because these devices are not great in low light situations. You can, however, learn a great deal about what works with time-lapse photography using a phone or a tablet like this.

equipment is capable of making no sound when a still image or video is taken. There are endless photographic, video and time-lapse applications as well as editing programs that we can download onto a phone or tablet, opening up a huge world of options. We can also upload content to the internet quickly and easily.

- Portable
- Readily available applications
- Access to the internet
- Ability to make calls
- Connectivity to larger cameras

Disadvantages

Photography is all about light and therefore it is better to use a device that controls light effectively. With a mobile phone or tablet the ability to control light is very limited, which means that your creativity is restricted. Although the image quality of smartphone devices is advancing, we are restrained by the size of the sensor that can be fitted into the device. A small sensor is never going to be as good as a large one contained in a DSLR or sizeable compact camera. The dynamic range of the sensor (i.e. the amount of information and detail the sensor captures) is also minimal on a smaller sensor.

The quality or sharpness of your image is also mainly down to the lens, and a smartphone has only a very small lens built in. Phone and tablet manufacturers do not generally make additional lenses for their devices. You can purchase small 'third party' lenses to attach to a phone, but this can be very impractical. Another big disadvantage with smart devices is that if someone calls or messages you it could stop your time-lapse or video being recorded. The shape of the capture can also be limiting. On most phones you get a vertical rectangle when recording using the built-in digital camera; therefore it is always best to hold the device sideways if you want to use the content from a phone next to any content captured on a dedicated device.

- Image quality is not ideal
- Limited control
- Battery life
- Not easy to replace battery if needed
- No choice of lenses

Compact and mirrorless cameras

Any small camera, whether it is a sports, compact or an advanced mirrorless camera, is a dedicated device for photography and video, rather than a multi-functional item like a phone or tablet, and can provide a big step up in performance and quality. Compact cameras are getting better all the time and some have interchangeable lenses, which means that you can be much more creative.

The sensors in these cameras are much better than in phones and tablets because they are bigger in size. Some advanced compacts will give you the same options as larger DSLR cameras and therefore can give you advanced control with a smaller camera. A well-chosen compact camera can give you surprising results because of the technology inside; they punch well above their weight and are fairly inexpensive compared to bigger DSLR cameras.

Advantages

Compacts are lightweight and reasonably high quality, whilst usually inexpensive. Neither compact nor mirrorless cameras (as the name would suggest) have internal mirrors, and this has clear advantages. Mirrors are found in DSLR cameras; they move up and down inside the camera and contribute to the clicking noise when a picture is taken. This noise cannot be turned off in a DSLR camera because of the physicality of these moving parts. With a compact, however, the click can be turned off, making image-taking completely silent. With the absence of a clicking noise you can create content and be discreet whilst you are doing it. Because these cameras are small, you can also use them without attracting the same attention you would if you had a large DSLR camera – the bigger the camera, the less subtle it is. Most manufacturers are releasing advanced compact cameras, which are what many image-makers are looking for as they want performance without having to carry a lot of weight around with them.

- Lightweight
- Discreet
- Relatively inexpensive
- Better quality than a phone or tablet
- Some models have interchangeable lenses

Disadvantages

Compact cameras without interchangeable lenses are becoming less popular because of the increasing quality of phones and tablets, and many manufacturers are reducing their product ranges as a result. This means that this kind of camera could potentially become difficult to get hold of. Most compact

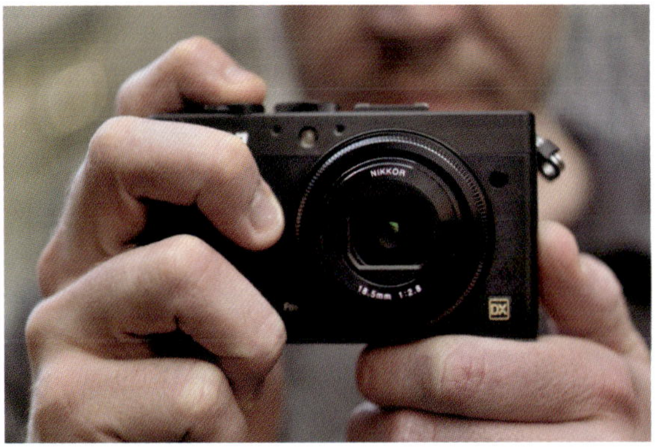

▲ Compact cameras are very advanced and the quality that we can achieve is getting better as time goes on. This example is a compact that has electronics from a larger, more advanced camera but is small and portable.

cameras are not built as well as DSLR cameras which means the life span can be significantly shorter than a more expensive camera.

The small size of a compact camera can make it more difficult to use; of course this is personal preference, but the smaller the camera the fewer buttons that can be built into the device. These cameras also usually have a smaller battery than a bigger camera and therefore can run out fairly quickly. A lot of compacts actually have very limited time-lapse options, and depending on the product, sometimes there is no time-lapse option at all.

- Battery life
- Build quality
- Functionality
- Some don't have interchangeable lenses
- Small sensors

DSLR (digital single-lens reflex) cameras

These cameras are ultimately the best tool for time-lapse, for many reasons. If you want one device that shoots high quality stills and video there is no better option available. A DSLR will have more longevity than a compact camera or smart device because the build quality is much better – this will be a key factor if it is used on a regular basis. These cameras will rarely be replaced by the user for reasons other than being broken or superseded by new technology.

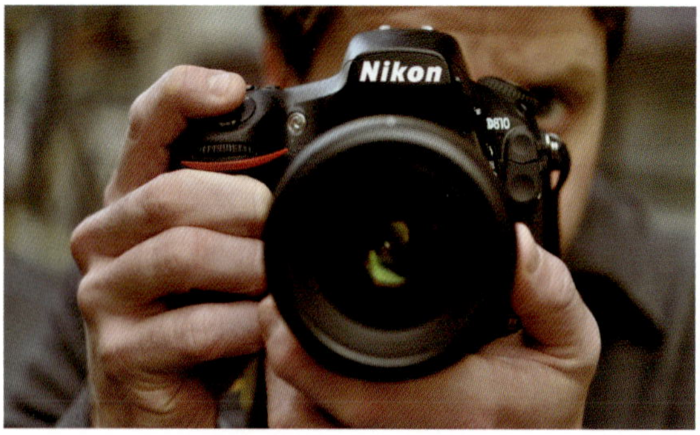

▲ This camera is a fully fledged top-of-the-range professional camera. This kind of imaging device will give outstanding quality and advanced functionality.

When learning about photography and time-lapse, it is better to buy a camera that you can grow into because as you explore you need a tool that can keep up with your developments. Any recent DSLR camera by any of the leading brands will be a good workhorse. Most camera manufacturers will have entry-level DSLR cameras to get you started, advanced prosumer cameras which are in the middle of the lineup, and the flagship professional cameras right at the top end. Ideally a DSLR that shoots video, stills and has an interval timer will be the best tool for time-lapse photography. If you get a higher-end camera, you will be able to explore the advanced performance whilst developing your knowledge and you are much less likely to find you want to do things that the camera doesn't offer.

There are different sensor sizes on DSLR cameras but the most popular and highest quality size sensor is known as 'full frame'. This sensor size is exactly the same as a frame from a roll of 35mm film. This is the kind of film we used to use in cameras before we had digital devices.

Advantages

These cameras are fast and responsive, which is important when you want to capture an image of a moment that presents itself suddenly. Some compact cameras are not as quick, which means you can miss the moment. With a DSLR it will take an image immediately when you want it to. DSLRs also have interchangeable lenses, which means you can gradually build on your lens collection and push your photography creatively. Lenses for DSLR cameras tend to hold their value if taken care of and will stay with you for life.

- High quality output
- Robust build
- Responsive
- Fast focusing
- Advanced menu options

Disadvantages

DSLR cameras and lenses can be expensive and this is sometimes a deterrent; the weight can also be too much for some. DSLR bodies can depreciate in value very quickly, especially once a new version has been released. This happens relatively frequently and can be frustrating considering that they carry a much higher price than a compact. If dropped, this kind of camera might give you a hefty repair bill. Good-quality camera and lens equipment is built with precision and if it needs repairing it can be labour-intensive and therefore expensive.

- Large
- Expensive
- Heavy
- Complicated at first

USEFUL ACCESSORIES AND OTHER EQUIPMENT

Having looked at the options when choosing a camera, we need to consider everything that goes along with it. Accessories can be just as important as the imaging device itself in contributing to the final result. Use this overview as a possible checklist to ensure that you have everything you might need for time-lapse photography. You may decide that some items are going to be essential whilst others may not be appropriate to your set-up and how you work.

Filters

Many landscape and time-lapse photographers use filters on the front of their lens. The two most common types are neutral density filters and graduated filters. Neutral density filters act as a light reduction device if a shooting situation is too bright. A graduated filter will darken only the top part of the frame to prevent the sky becoming overexposed, but it will have no effect on the bottom half of the image, which will essentially be your foreground.

Filters are often seen as quite mysterious, but they are really not that technical. There are hundreds of filters out there for you to experiment with. Most people tend to use filters simply to protect their lens, but be careful as they can affect the imagery in a way that you are unaware of. If you already have a filter on your lens, take a picture with and without it to test for this. Filters are also explored under Chapter 4: Light and Exposure.

Remote triggers

When we take an image with our camera we push a button on the device, and this can create unwanted movement. For time-lapse and regular stills photography, sometimes we do not want the camera moving when a frame is captured. Remotes enable you to trigger the camera without touching the device itself, which overcomes this issue.

Remotes can either tether to the camera or trigger the camera with Wi-Fi, infra-red or radio connectivity. Any solution will effectively do the same job in that the camera is not moved by your finger pressing the shutter release button. Do some research or go to a photographic dealer and see what options are available for your camera. If your camera has a built-in interval timer or time-lapse photography mode then this acts as a trigger. An external interval timer can, however, offer additional benefits such as better functionality and an increased number of options available.

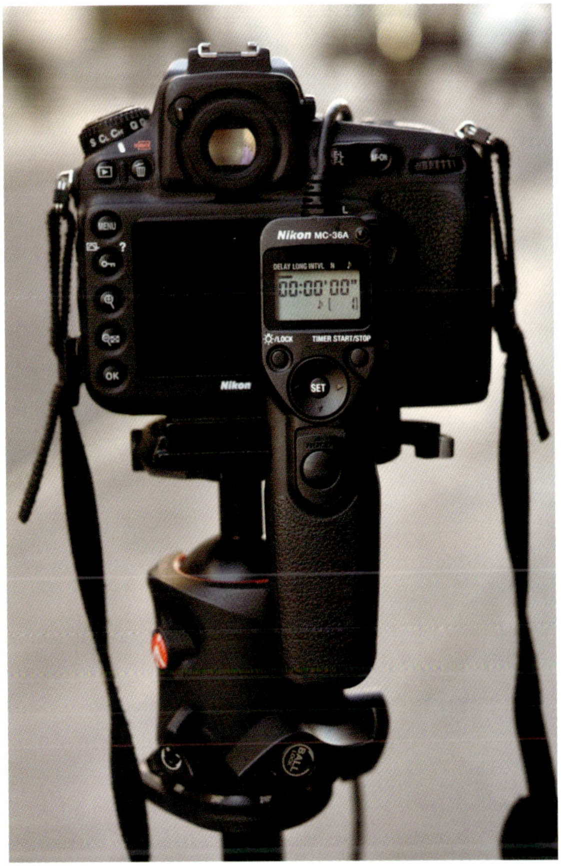

▲ This example shows a high-end external intervalometer. This enables you to access advanced time-lapse options that you do not get in the camera as standard. Many manufacturers have a device like this. So even if your camera does not have an interval timer you can still use it for time-lapse photography.

Using your phone or tablet to trigger your camera

There are some really useful apps that can be downloaded to your phone and used in conjunction with many cameras on the market. Functionality between systems may vary slightly and apps also advance quickly with changes in technology. To trigger the camera with the phone, the two are connected via Wi-Fi or Bluetooth and an app on the phone enables you to have a live view, seeing through the camera's lens without being anywhere near it. With this connection you are also able to transfer images from the camera to the mobile phone or tablet that you are using. Functionality of these systems is getting

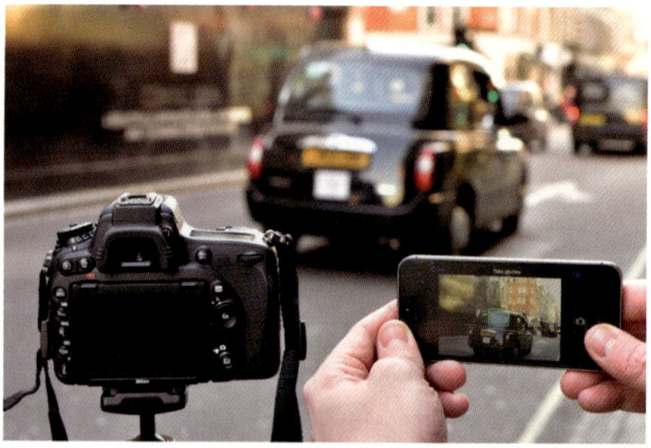

▲ Some cameras have Wi-Fi connectivity, which allows you to trigger your camera from a smart device as well as view through the camera and focus, as shown in this example. Functionality varies between manufacturers so explore the options that are compatible with your equipment.

better all the time and in many cases this solution is cheap or even free.

Using computers to trigger your camera

Most people have a computer and will use it for editing and viewing their work, but many are unaware of what computers can offer in terms of triggering a digital camera. A computer with the appropriate software is able to trigger the camera via a wireless or tethered connection, with the correct accessories. Try connecting your camera via USB to the computer and using software to trigger the shutter. Nikon's Camera Control Pro software is one example of a great package that enables you to have comprehensive control over the camera for shooting stills, video and time-lapse. When shooting to a computer we can shoot more, because we are only limited by the computer's hard drive and not a memory card in the camera; most computer hard drives have much more storage than a camera's memory card.

Most camera connection software for laptops enables you to use live view, and you also get the ability to focus and take pictures from the computer without even touching the camera. There are other obvious advantages to using a computer, such as having internet connection and direct access to editing software. If you want to make a time-lapse

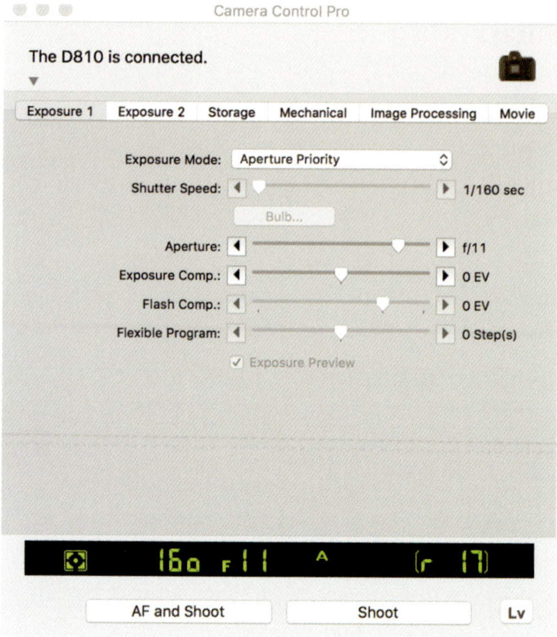

▲ This shows a software program that enables you to change the main functions of the camera from a computer; you do not need to be anywhere near the camera when you change settings or trigger it.

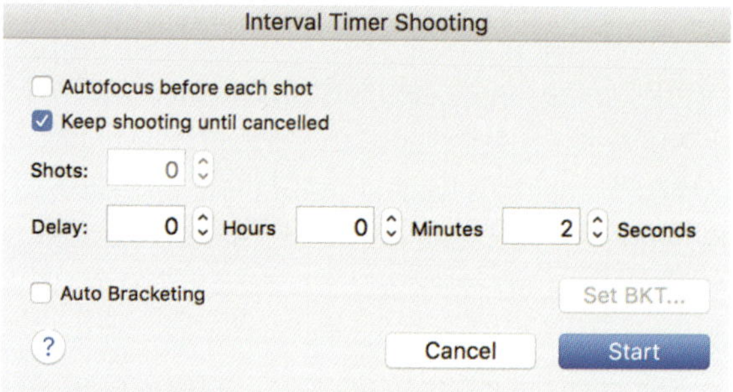

▲ This is from the same software program, showing the basic but effective interval timer that is controlled from the computer.

from inside your house and have the camera outside for a day, then this would be a great solution. You could stay indoors in the warm and watch the images transferring onto the computer one at a time, as the time-lapse is captured outside.

Batteries

Having a spare battery for your camera is essential. Always bring more than you need; if you think you will only need one battery take three. The last thing you want is to be setting up your time-lapse after driving two hours to get there and find that your battery has one bar of power left. Remember to bring a charger for your camera's battery and your mobile phone as well. You don't want your camera to run out of juice, but if your phone loses power then you could potentially be in a dangerous situation.

Think about where the nearest available plug socket is, as a back-up plan. If you are driving, your car can be used as a battery charger. There are charging kits that you can get to plug into the car's cigarette lighter and also portable power cells that can be pre-charged and taken along to a shoot, as well as solar-powered batteries. Just check at your camera dealer or look online for charging solutions. The batteries themselves are very important so beware of third-party copies. It is tempting to purchase cheap batteries because the price is usually a lot less than the manufacturer's own. You could end up with a very expensive repair bill, however, because cheap copies of batteries are more likely to explode or leak.

Memory cards

A very important part of the hardware in your equipment set-up is your memory cards. No one wants to run out of storage half-way through a shoot; you might need to delete something else on the card to make space, which you may regret. A good rule of thumb is to try and estimate how much storage you require for a shoot and then triple it – it is useful to have much more than you need.

Compatibility is also something that is usually overlooked but very important. Always check that the cards you have bought are listed as compatible with the device that you are using. Corrupted images and video are usually the result of a card that is old and needs replacing or is not recommended for use with that camera. In your manual there will be a list of officially tested cards; you should refer to this list before buying storage.

With time-lapse photography, it is much better to use one of the fastest cards listed in the manual to ensure that the camera's performance is matched and complemented. All cameras have what we call a 'buffer' – a place where the images rest after they are created before they are stored on the memory card. Sometimes the camera shoots so fast that the buffer fills up with images too quickly and then the camera will slow down. A fast card will ensure that the camera is performing at its optimum ability.

Sometimes a card might be too old for your camera, but it could actually be too new. If you have a five-year-old camera and you have just purchased the latest and greatest in storage, the compatibility might be a problem in this instance as well.

Card readers

It is common now for computers to have a built-in card reader, so that you can take the card out of your camera and plug it straight into the computer, which is a great solution. If you do not have this luxury you will need to obtain a card reader. Make sure you choose a device that is compatible with the cards that you are using; also check that the card reader is compatible with the USB port on your computer as well. The moral of the story is to check and double-check compatibility before purchasing to ensure that you don't find yourself in a situation where your hardware does not work together.

The back-up plan is to use the camera's built in USB connection so it can be connected directly to the computer. Either way, you can manually drag the folder over from the camera or use the native software that comes free with the camera. Most manufacturers provide software to transfer images over quickly and easily.

LENSES

If you are a DSLR or advanced compact user, furthering your understanding of lenses is almost more important than the camera knowledge itself because the lens is where the quality and look of the image can be changed dramatically. In this section we will take a comprehensive look at lenses and their role within time-lapse photography, and demonstrate how they can help to expand your creativity. Use this as an opportunity to learn more about the lens that you have or what you may be looking to purchase.

Your lens is the most important part of your camera. The camera itself is like a computer in many ways: it does many things now that a computer is able to do and you can get a lot for your money; the performance with most is incredible and many cameras do a lot more than you are likely to ever need. Cameras get replaced in the marketplace quite frequently as new technologies are developed, and accordingly can depreciate in value relatively quickly. The camera itself is proving to be a temporary item in a photographer's kit bag these days; a lens however, will stay with you for life, if it is chosen wisely.

The beauty of DSLR lenses is that there is such a wide variety of lenses to choose from. Most manufacturers have a massive range going back many years: the two big companies, Nikon and Canon, have produced literally millions of lenses. This does of course make choosing a lens tricky, and a good knowledge of them is needed in order to improve and understand our image-making.

An important point to make is that there is no such thing as one lens that does everything. Manufacturers are only able to design lenses around the laws of the physics of light, and to do different jobs we need different lens designs. Of the vast number of lenses out there, some are very cheap and others are more expensive than your car, so the wrong decision could be costly as well as creatively limiting. This chapter will de-mystify the language of lenses and make clear the practical uses of the different types. It is hoped that your confidence with lenses will also grow, enabling your image-making to progress.

Taking the correct lens for the job

When attending a shoot, the process will be much more efficient and enjoyable if you bring the most appropriate lens for the job. If you have the wrong lens it's quite likely that you will not achieve what you anticipated and that you will have to come back to your shooting position another day with the correct lens. Sometimes one lens will be sufficient, and at other times you will need more than one.

This section explores all aspects of lens selection, together with all the relevant terminology, so that rather than being perplexed by the jargon, you can use it to your advantage.

Focal length

The focal length is written on the lens and this indicates how big or small the frame around your image will be. Some lenses have one focal length written on them, such as the 35mm lens; others have two, 16–35mm for example. Getting a good feel for what this means in practice with your image-making is advantageous. You will find that after a while you will start to get an instinct for what focal length you need for any given job. The only way to get to that point is to learn and this just requires experimentation and hands-on experience.

Focal length and time-lapse

Focal lengths between around 10mm and 70mm are generally popular for time-lapse photography because the most common subject matter tends to comprise landscape-style shots, and these focal lengths are favoured for landscape photography. Do not limit yourself to these lenses, however. The more you explore different lenses and new ways of using them, the more interesting your photography becomes. Even though there are focal lengths that are often used for time-lapse, try everything that you have at your disposal. Consider hiring or borrowing different lenses you have never used before. There is a tremendous amount you can learn

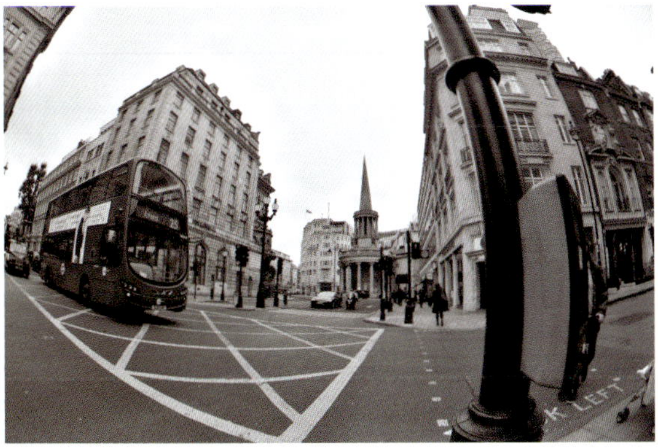

▲ 16mm.

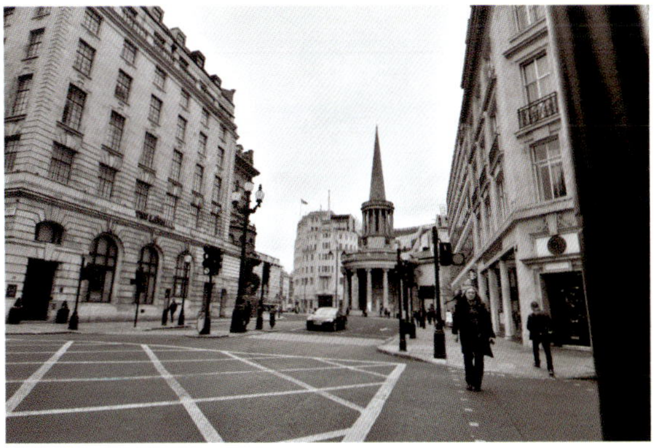

▲ 24mm.

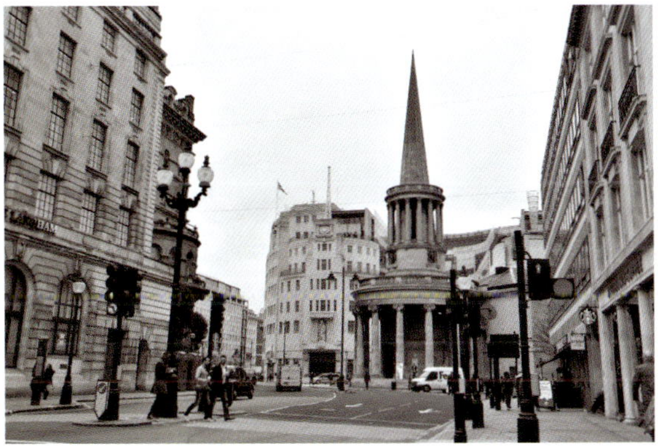

▲ 50mm.

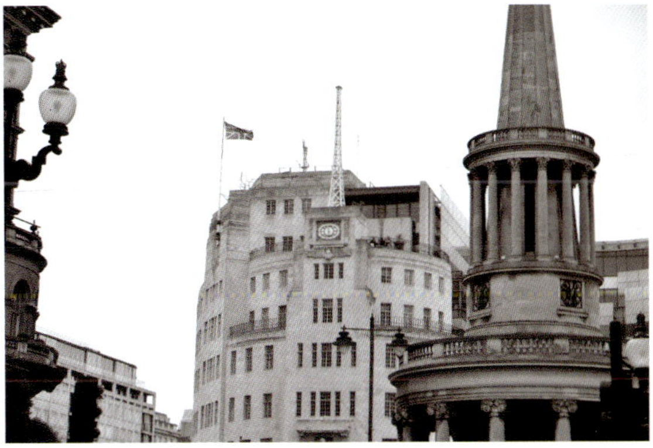

▲ 80mm.

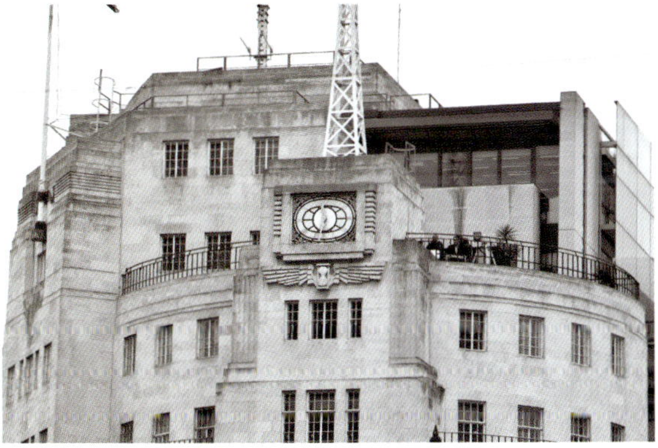

▲ 200mm.

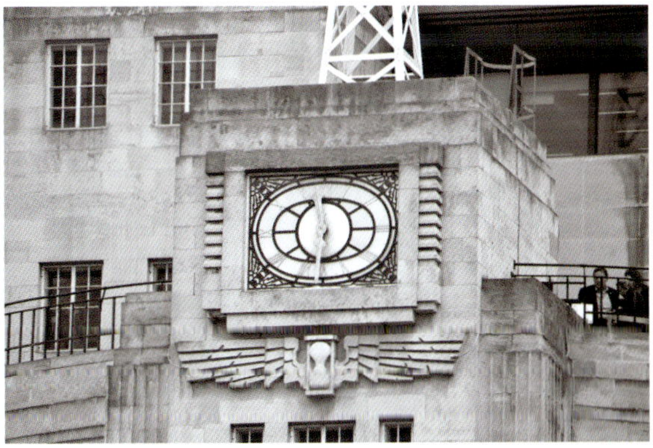

▲ 500mm.

about photography through experimentation; keep in mind that the lens is the most important part of the camera.

The 50mm prime lens

Often photographers will talk about their beloved 50mm prime lens and how it is the best lens they own, but why? Apart from being compact and effective in low-light shooting situations, what is all the fuss about? A key factor in why this lens is such

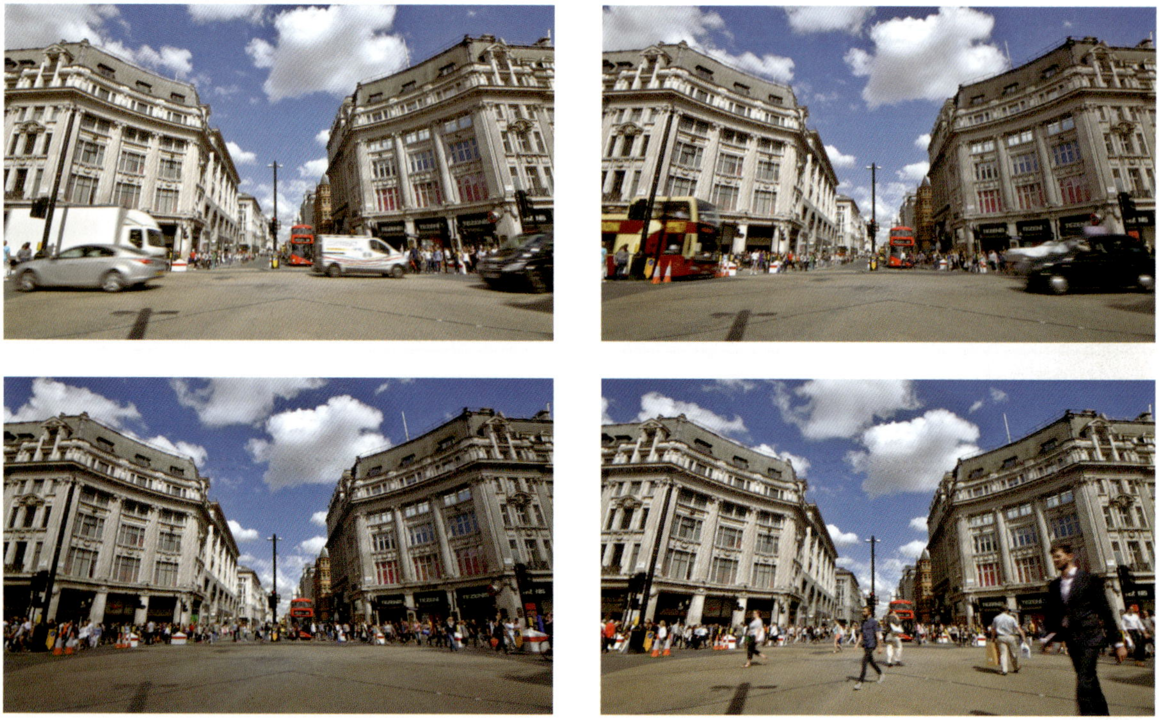

▲ This time lapse sequence was shot with a very wide-angle lens at a focal length of 16mm. This enables us to get a large scene in the frame even though we are unable to stand back a great distance. Sometimes you cannot stand further away from your subject matter because of restrictions with traffic, people or walls so a wide-angle lens is a great solution for this issue. Camera settings: 1/25s, ƒ/22, ISO 100.

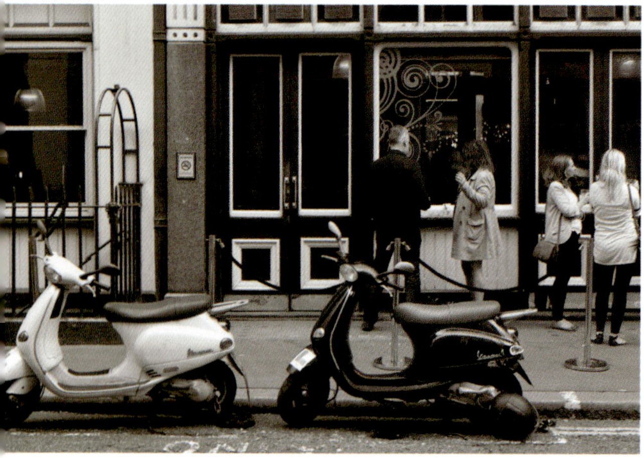

▲ This frame would work well as a time-lapse video as well as a street photography image.The 50mm prime lens enables us to frame a subject on the other side of the street with ease, making it quick to take a snap shot of anything that is happening. Camera settings: 1/160s, ƒ/5, ISO 250.

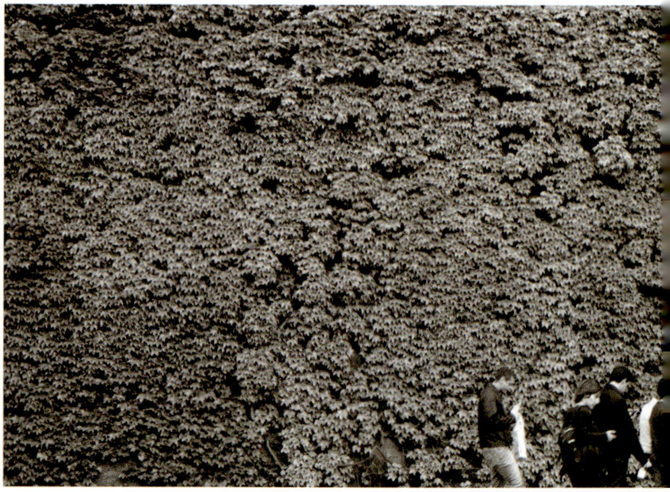

▲ With street photography and time-lapse it is a great idea to frame your shot first and then wait for people to move within the frame. This approach is a great way to build the image and get a better hit rate. Camera settings: 1/50s, ƒ/14, ISO 1250.

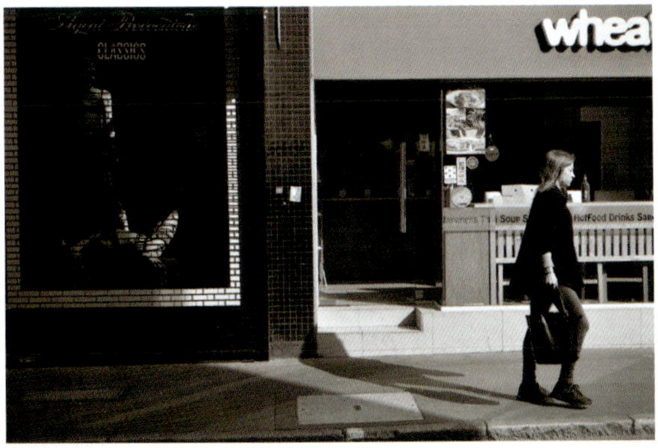

▲ Using harsh shadows in your frame works very well when capturing street scenes. Be careful of the camera's settings as it is difficult to get a good exposure in these conditions. Camera settings: 1/4000, ƒ/2.8, ISO 400.

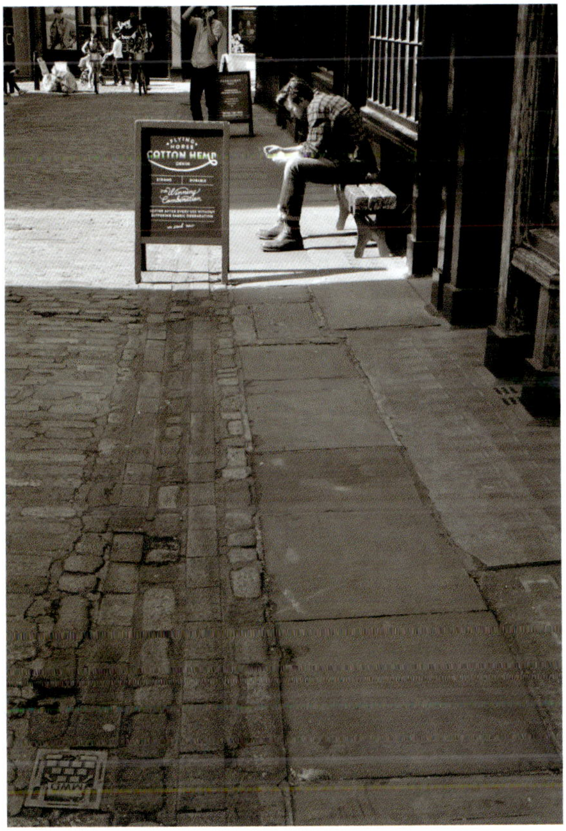

▲ Look for rays of sun shining through buildings when capturing your imagery. Remember over time the light will move, so consider this when shooting time-lapse. Camera settings: 1/400s, ƒ/16, ISO 900.

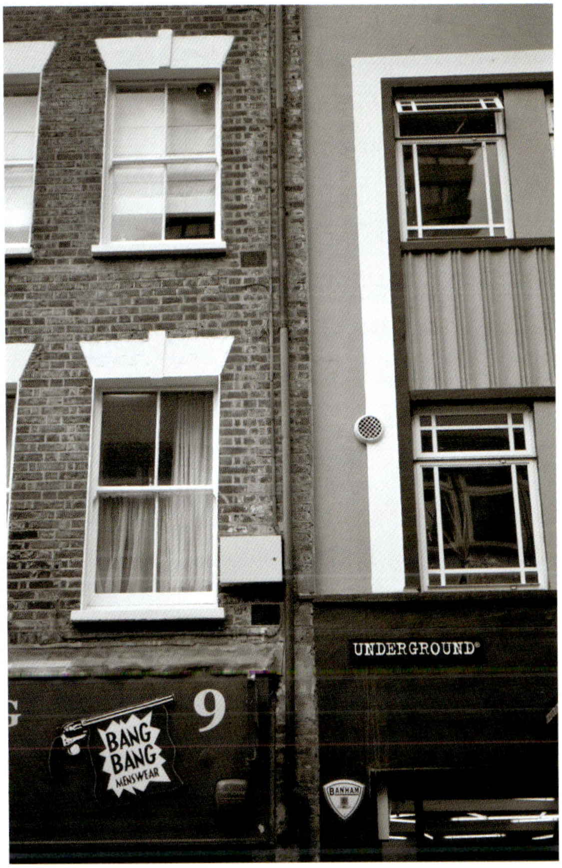

▲ Looking up before you shoot enables you to see more. Most people tend not to look up in built-up areas, but sometimes this is where the most interesting detail lies. Camera settings: 1/2500s, ƒ/1.8, ISO 250.

a popular choice is that it will represent your subject how you see it, with your own eyes. Obviously we do not see the world through a rectangle like the camera does, but the distance and perspective of the subject appears the same through a 50mm as it does when you look at your subject without viewing it through the camera. Think of this lens as the 'eyesight lens' – it imitates what your eyes see.

What focal lengths suit you?

Some people have a clear idea of what focal lengths they like for certain shooting situations; others will still be learning and may lack confidence, not knowing where to start with the seemingly endless number of options available. If you want to find out

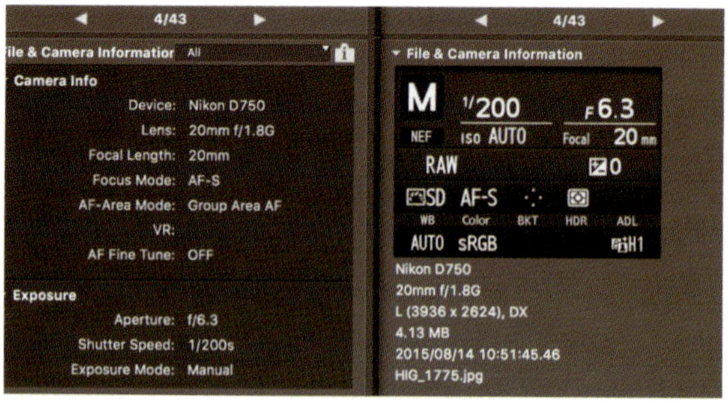

▲ These are examples of how your shooting data might look on the software on your computer. There is a wealth of information to help you understand what settings you had when you were using the camera at the time of shooting.

LEARN FROM YOUR SHOOTING DATA

Look through your archives at the images that have already been taken and look at the shooting data of the images. This information can be found on the back of the camera after capture or on photographic software on your computer. Usually software that comes free with the camera will show this information, or you might already use other photographic software that will show this data as well. If you are unsure about where to view this, you will find it in the camera's manual or the 'Help' menu of the software.

By reviewing the focal length of your images after shooting, you are able to take note of what kind of numbers you use most often. You may find, for example, that you use 20mm a lot for landscape photography and 70mm for portrait photography. Knowing the numbers that suit you will enable you to speak to other photographers in their own language and choose and use lenses more effectively.

what focal lengths suit you, it can be much easier than you may think. Look back at imagery that you have already captured and see what focal lengths you have most commonly used. You can do this by viewing the shooting data on your files.

Metadata or shooting data

Every time you take a picture, the camera and lens information is recorded within that file, as well as lots of other details about the camera's settings. This data is called metadata or shooting data, amongst other things. We will refer to this as shooting data for now because this term is more self-explanatory. If you look back at the focal lengths you have used previously, the data will provide you with an insight into your own shooting style, which you may not have picked up on before. Some people read recommendations and case studies about what other people use, but why not find out what you actually use in your own photography?

Zoom lenses

A zoom will enable you to rotate a ring on the lens or press a button on the camera to adjust how far away or how close your subject matter will appear through the camera's viewfinder by zooming in and out. This is generally quite a flexible tool and if you are unsure how far away you will be from the subject, this type of lens is a sensible choice. Zoom lenses can cover different ranges of focal lengths, but the key is to choose the range that suits you.

Often people speculate why there is not one zoom lens that has all of the focal range covered. The reason for this is that if one lens was 6–600mm, for example, then it would probably be the size of a small elephant. Accordingly, manufacturers consciously decide to keep the size and weight of lenses down as much as possible.

A lot of research is done into what parameters of the focal range will appeal to different types of photographer. One example is the Nikon 200–500mm lens, which is designed for bird-watching and sports photography. For time-lapse photography, wide-angle zoom lenses are generally more popular because they can capture a big scene, such as a large landscape, and get everything in the frame. One example of an appropriate lens for time-lapse would be the 16–35mm zoom lens. You may also already have a wide-angle lens, something like an 18–55mm or a 24–105mm, which commonly comes with the camera when you buy it, and these focal lengths are perfect for time-lapse.

Fixed and prime lenses

When a lens has a fixed focal length it means that you cannot zoom in or out with the ring around the lens. Although this may at first seem restricting, these lenses have huge advantages that really do outweigh the disadvantages for most photographers. These lenses are also referred to as prime lenses, because they are generally sharper than a zoom lens. The reason for this is that the construction can be simpler because of the lack of moving parts that would otherwise be required for zooming the lens in and out. When you are shooting a time-lapse it is rare that you will be zooming during capture, making a prime lens a very practical option.

The tricky part is choosing the right lens for any given job. If you make the wrong decision with a prime lens and you only have the one, then you might not get what you were after. If you decide that primes make sense for what you shoot, it is best to get a good feel for what kind of focal length suits you best. If you have a 24–70mm zoom lens and on reviewing your images you see that many of the pictures are taken at 24mm then that's an easy decision. Get a 24mm prime lens and you will have a lighter lens to carry, as well as the appropriate focal length. Remember, if you ever need to zoom in and out with a prime, you can always walk forwards and backwards.

Telephoto lenses

Telephoto lenses have higher focal length values. The kind of numbers you will see on these lenses will be around 100mm up to 800mm, and maybe even higher. These lenses are physically longer in length than wide-angle lenses and can get quite heavy because of the amount of glass inside them. If you find it difficult holding a heavy lens like this,

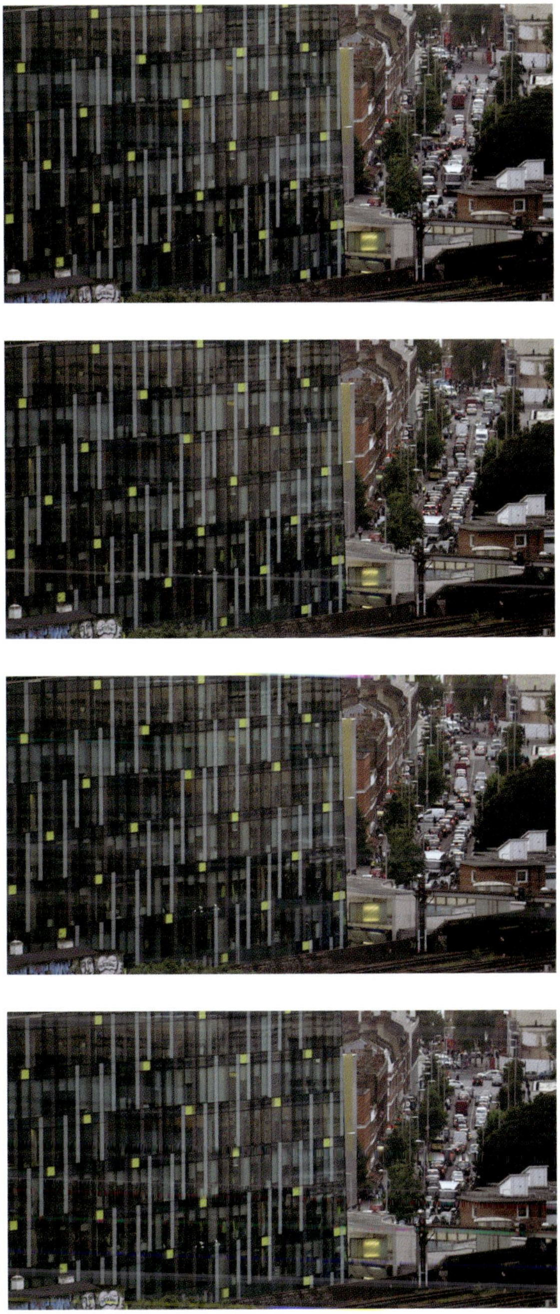

▲ Using a telephoto lens we can capture time-lapse videos of subjects that are far away from a high vantage point. This shot put the movement to one side of the frame, which works very well in the final video. The movement in your frame does not always need to be in the middle; try experimenting with composition. Camera settings: 1/320s, *f*/4, ISO 1000.

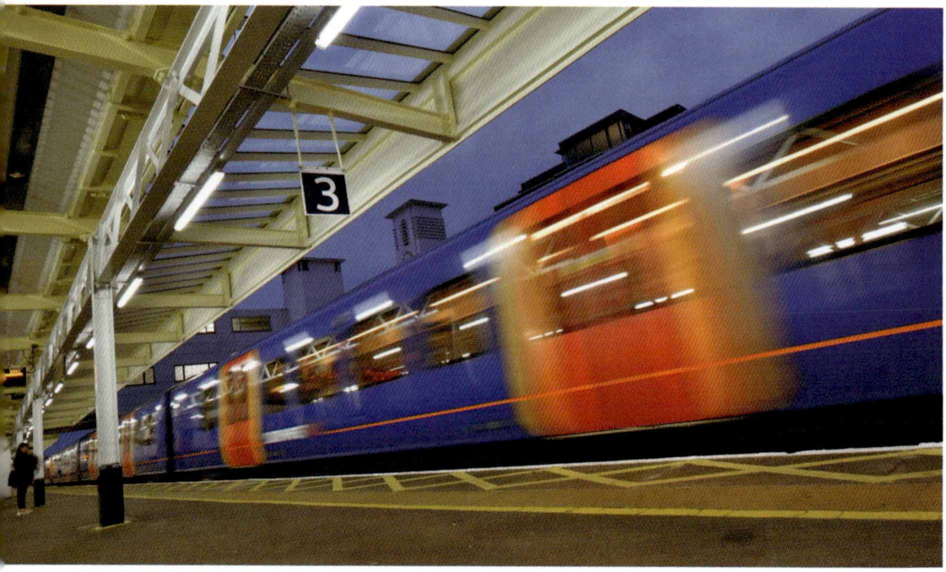

Try working with a wide-angle lens on your camera, using a low vantage point, and tilt the camera up at the subject. This point of view enables us to accentuate scale and the wide-angle lens is able to capture a large scene successfully. Camera settings: 1/2.5th, ƒ/8, ISO 100.

a monopod or tripod will take the weight away from your arms. For time-lapse photography a tripod will probably be the best solution as it holds the lens and camera much more steadily than a monopod. A telephoto lens is normally used by wildlife or sports photographers, but it can also be used by portrait photographers, landscape photographers and of course time-lapse photographers and videographers. These lenses add an effective solution for picking out detail in a scene and capturing something that is small and very far away.

Teleconverters

A teleconverter does exactly what it says on the tin: it converts a telephoto lens. What it actually converts is the focal length of the lens, which enables the photographer to get closer to the subject. A teleconverter cannot be used as a lens in its own right and will need to be mounted between the camera body and telephoto lens to do its job. This pushes the lens away from the body, which effectively increases the focal length and frames the subject more tightly, so you appear to be closer to it.

We will use an example here: if a 2x teleconverter is used in conjunction with a 400mm lens, it would double the focal length and result in 800mm. This would enable us to get closer in to the subject without buying a completely new lens, therefore saving a lot of money. Sports or wildlife photographers will typically use these to photograph subjects that are at a long distance away from the camera. It is much lighter to carry one lens and a teleconverter than it is to carry two separate lenses, which assists greatly when carrying a bag of equipment on your back.

A small disadvantage is that most teleconverters will let less light into the camera, which can darken down the image and possibly make focusing slightly less effective. The technology in newer DSLR cameras does make it very easy to get around this, however. Teleconverters are not meant for every lens out there and might not fit each lens you own, so always check the compatibility before buying one. Manuals for any lens or converter can be downloaded from the manufacturer's website so you can refer to it before purchase.

Wide-angle lenses

A wide-angle lens can frame a very large scene easily and therefore capture the entirety of your subject matter. The focal length of these lenses can start from around 6mm and go upwards to approximately 50mm. The approach with time-lapse and landscape photography is usually very similar in terms of focal length and so a wide-angle lens will generally be used an awful lot. You may not need to look very far to find one of these lenses because most cameras come with one when purchased. If you are thinking about using a wide-angle prime lens then be aware of the exact focal length that will suit your situation; you will find this in time and with experience.

Sometimes the lower focal lengths on a wide-angle zoom or prime lens can get distortion or stretching in the corners. Some people really like this effect, whereas others will strive to avoid it. This generally happens at very small focal lengths, such as 14 or 20mm. It is best to decide for yourself as to what you like the look of, and the best way to do that is to experiment.

Variable and constant aperture lenses

Every lens you own will be one of the two types of lenses described below. Understanding this terminology will help a lot with the practical aspect of how you use your lenses and, even though it is quite technically advanced, it will help you grasp what different lenses are capable of and also why lenses can vary in size so much. If you are not confident with what aperture is and how it affects your imagery, then it may be worth reading the Chapter 4: Light and Exposure and coming back to this section afterwards.

Variable aperture lenses

These lenses are generally smaller, lighter and cheaper than constant aperture lenses. Most cameras will come with a variable aperture lens as the kit lens when you buy it. An example of this would be the 18–55mm *f*/3.5–5.6 lens. The widest aperture available will vary depending on where the zoom is on the lens. If the zoom is at 18mm, then the widest aperture available will be *f*/3.5. If the lens is zoomed in to 55mm, then the widest aperture available will be *f*/5.6. This is why it is called a variable aperture lens; the widest available aperture varies as you zoom the lens.

Your picture might be darker at 55mm than it will be at 18mm because *f*/5.6 is darker than *f*/3.5. If you are shooting in low light situations it will therefore be a hindrance if your lens is zoomed in to 55mm. The best way to get around this is to zoom out, which enables the aperture to open up and let more light in, then walk closer to the subject.

Of course the aperture will have a direct impact on your depth of field as well, so if this is important to your imagery you will need to keep an eye on it. It is worth noting that if you are using mid or high aperture values such as *f*/8 or *f*/11, these apertures will not vary when zooming. This is because the only aperture values affected on a variable aperture lens are the ones listed on the outside of the lens – in this case, *f*/3.5–5.6.

Constant aperture lenses

A constant aperture lens is a zoom lens which enables you to zoom in and out without the widest available aperture changing and therefore it can remain at a constant aperture. For example, a popular lens is the 24–70mm *f*/2.8 constant aperture zoom lens. Notice that this lens only has one aperture value listed: *f*/2.8. You can set this lens to *f*/2.8, zoom the lens and the aperture will not change. This kind of lens tends to be bigger and therefore more expensive because it has more glass inside. (High quality glass is very expensive to manufacture and the more there is, the more the price goes up.)

A big advantage with this kind of lens is that it is really good for low light photography. If you zoom in with a constant aperture lens it will not reduce the amount of light coming into the camera, making it easier to focus in low light situations and also for you to achieve bright looking pictures in dark conditions. Although constant aperture lenses are more expensive and heavier, they will help you work when it is darker.

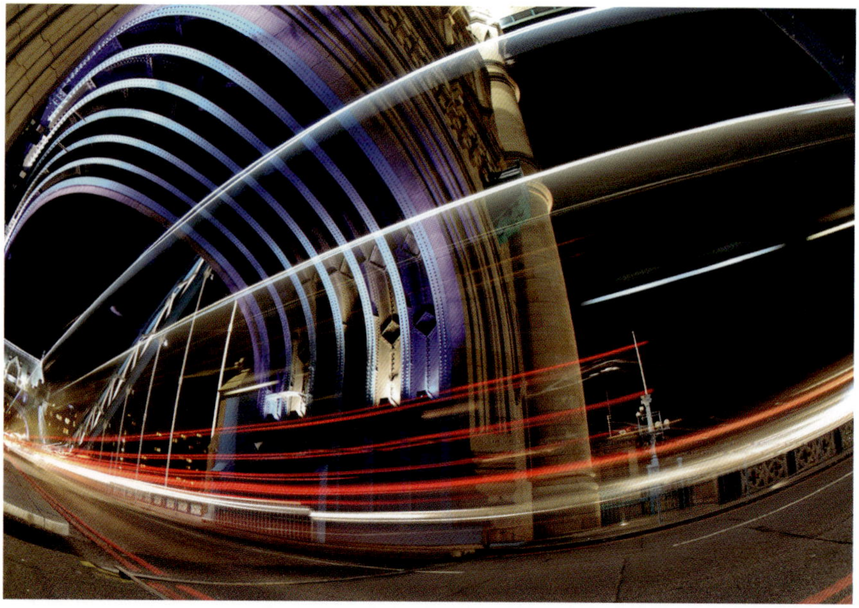

Using a fisheye lens will always be visually exciting. This example is taken from a low vantage point looking up and is capturing the motion blur of moving traffic. Camera settings: 13s, ƒ/8, ISO 100.

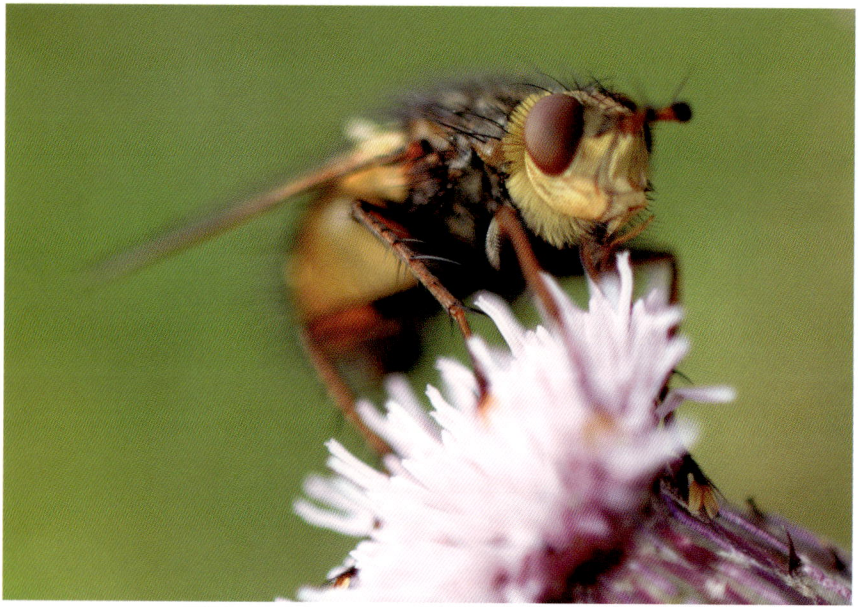

Using a macro lens gives you a passport to explore another world. This example shows that you can capture small detail and fill the frame with it. Camera settings: 1/1250s, ƒ/3.8, ISO 720.

Fisheye lenses

If you want to add another string to your bow then a fisheye lens will make for some great shots. This lens is called a fisheye simply because it appears that you are looking through a round fish bowl or a spherical fish eye and the image you get is very distorted at the corners. It is safe to say that these lenses are a bit of a one trick pony, but it's a trick worth having.

If you are thinking of using this lens for time-lapse then it is helpful to get used to the parameters of using one in the context of shooting standard stills first. One thing that you realize very early on is that if you want to make the subject fill the frame you need to move very close to it. These lenses will also be good for landscape or architecture photography because you are able to squash a huge scene into your frame. The lens gives such a wide coverage that sometimes you will get your own feet in the shot, so enjoy but be careful.

Macro lenses

If you have ever tried to take a picture of something very close with the standard lens that comes with your camera, you may have noticed that at a certain point you are actually unable to get the lens to focus and take pictures. This is because standard kit lenses are designed for general use and, because of the design, they are usually unable to focus that closely to a subject.

Macro lenses are designed specifically to operate at extremely close range; sometimes you are able to take a picture only inches away from what you are capturing. With the ability to get this close to what you are shooting you will be able to fill the viewfinder with every tiny detail, even that which you cannot see with the naked eye. With close-up photography we are able to step into a world of amazingly small detail that is unobtainable to us with any other type of lens. With a little practice you will be able to get some amazing time-lapse videos of flowers opening over the course of a morning, or insects moving around, for example.

Also consider that the working distance and sharpness that you get from macro lenses will lend itself well to portraiture and can also be an amazing lens for shooting video. Once you start using a macro lens a world of detail that can be unlocked; this can be addictive, so please be warned.

Tilt and shift lenses

This type of lens is a mystery to many people; they appear exotic and confusing. The lens itself looks very odd with buttons and knobs sticking out on all surfaces. It might look like some kind of strange plumbing device but it is actually an extremely diverse lens and has many uses, some of which are unique.

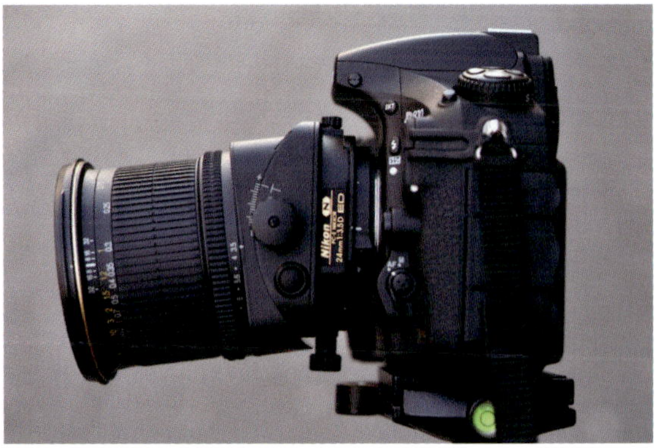

▲ Here we see a tilt and shift lens being tilted downwards with the controls on the outside of the lens. This is an exciting lens and enables us to achieve unique imagery.

Generally these lenses have two movements that can be adjusted with the switches and knobs. The two main types of movement found on these lenses are tilt and shift, hence the name. These devices are also referred to as perspective control lenses, because you are able to change the perceived perspective of your subject; this effect is usually used for architecture photography.

For time-lapse this kind of lens will enable you to create some exciting imagery that simply cannot be achieved in any other way. We will look at the two most common uses of these lenses, one of which is to control perspective and the other of which is a creative use of depth of field.

Controlling perspective with a tilt and shift lens

When you look up at a building from street level the lines of the building disappear into what is called the vanishing point. If you drew imaginary lines along each vertical line on the building then they would all meet at one point. This illustrates that the perspective from street level does not correctly represent the building because it does not appear to be straight, even though we know it is.

The reason we see it this way is because of distance; the bottom of the building is nearer to us and therefore looks bigger and the top of the building

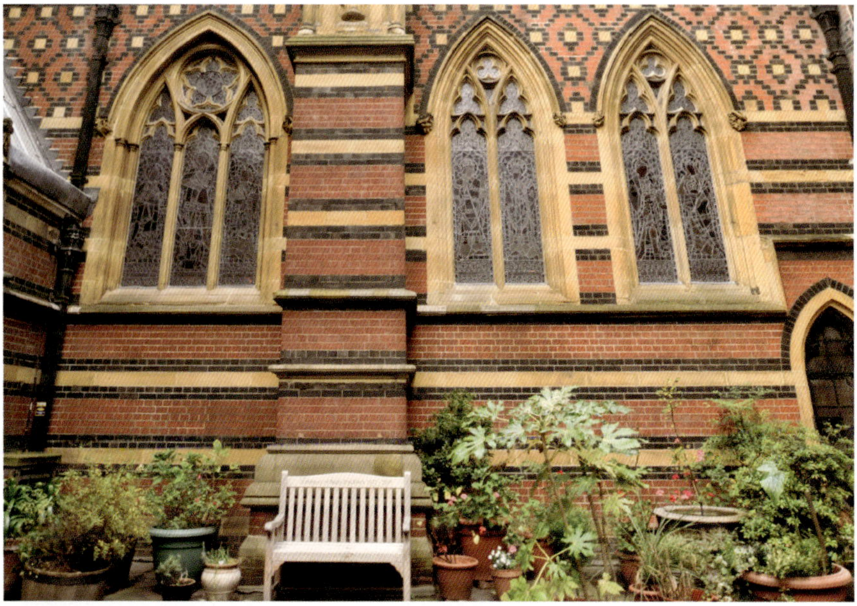

This example shows a regular image taken of a wall which represents how we see it when we look up at it. The lower part of the wall is closer and therefore looks bigger.

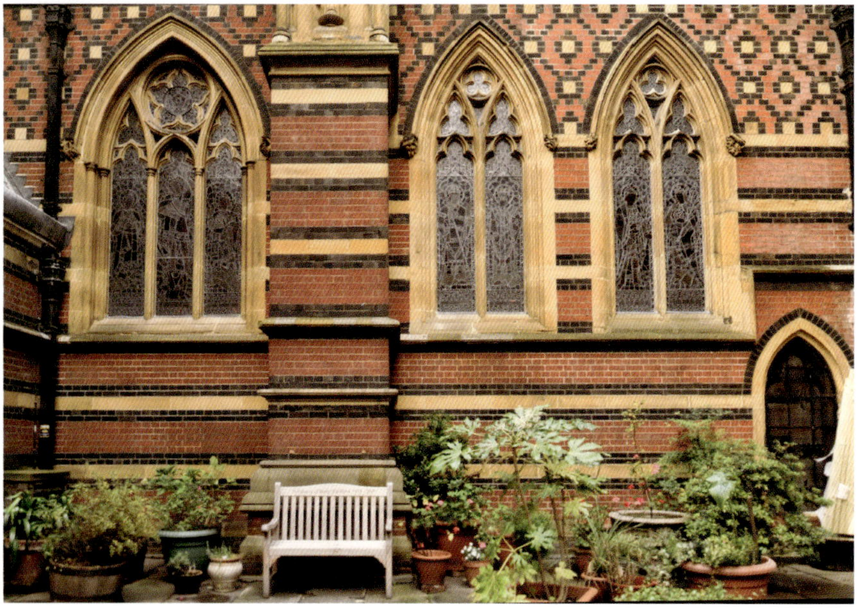

This is the same view but the perspective has been corrected with movements on a tilt and shift lens. The camera is in exactly the same place as the previous image, but the perceived perspective has been changed by moving the lens.

is far away and appears to be smaller. If you wish to correct or control this effect then a perspective control lens comes in very handy. By adjusting the movements on the lens we can adjust the perceived view point of the camera without actually moving. Once the perspective changes it appears to correct what we see with the naked eye, meaning the lines in the building will appear to be straight.

Changing perspective in your imagery can be done either with one of these lenses or with software in the camera or on a computer. Software is a much cheaper solution than buying a lens, but a lens will produce much better results. If you play with the perspective with software you might lose the edges

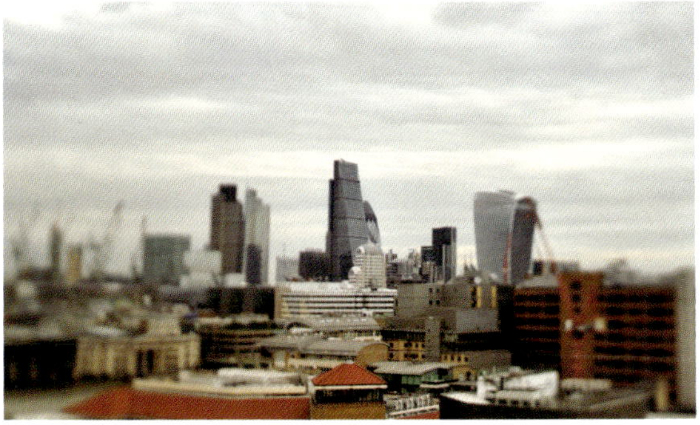

▲ This is a still taken from a time-lapse video showing that tilt and shift lenses are able to make different parts of the image sharp and others unfocused. This is not achievable with any other lens.

of your image as it pulls and stretches the file to emulate what the lens would be doing optically. These lenses are particularly useful when shooting time-lapse near anything tall such as buildings, trees or mountains.

Creative depth of field with a tilt and shift lens

It might be useful to read about aperture and depth of field in Chapter 4 and come back to this section, unless you are already familiar with both. Using a shallow depth of field in your imagery is something you may already be doing and if you want to advance your use and understanding of depth of field, a tilt and shift lens will enable to you do so.

If you set the 'f' number to the smallest value possible and then move the tilt part of the lens into full tilt, the depth of field moves from its usual plane, which is parallel to the sensor, and you will be able to place it wherever you want in your frame. You can move your shallow depth of field horizontally, vertically or even at an angle within your frame. Visually this will enable you to achieve exciting results.

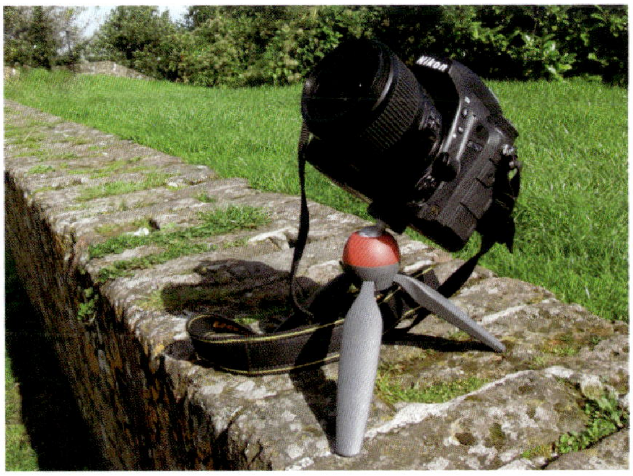

▲ This is an extremely useful pocket tripod that holds the weight of a full frame DSLR camera. Full sized tripods can be too big and heavy so we tend to leave them at home and not get a great deal of use out of them. This kind of tripod is a great solution because it is not heavy or bulky to carry and we can still get height by placing it on a wall or bench.

OTHER USEFUL ACCESSORIES

When you go out to shoot your time-lapse videos, the camera and lens are not the only items that you will need. Depending on what you are doing, there are many other components that can make your life less stressful and safer, especially when working out in the middle of the woods in winter, for example. Some of the items listed are common sense, but it's easy to forget the obvious when concentrating on the technical side of photography. The key with every shoot is to make yourself a checklist so that you cannot forget anything; be safe and methodical.

Tripods

Using a tripod is usually a necessity with time lapse because the camera needs to stay still during capture. Sometimes it is not as simple as just putting up a tripod and starting, however. If conditions are windy, the wind can move or vibrate the tripod and camera so that when playback of the time-lapse is viewed the video appears to jerk from side to side slightly. A good solution for this is to get a tripod that has a hook underneath. This will enable you to hang your bag on the hook – this will weigh your tripod down to reduce movement.

Sometimes the camera's strap can be caught by the wind and cause unwanted camera movement as well. The easiest way to solve this problem is to remove the strap completely or just wrap it around one of the tripod legs to stop the wind catching it.

If you put the tripod up on muddy ground or on an old wooden floor, think about the potential movement that can be created by the weight of the tripod leg or your feet standing right next to it. Some people use a bean bag and put it on top of the camera, to weigh the camera down and help reduce possible movement.

Other items

Gloves and hats

It is common sense to wear gloves on a cold day or night, but usually a pair of gloves will be the first thing you forget! There are fingerless gloves you can get that are made for photographers that will leave your fingers free to press buttons or use a touch-screen. Gloves can be used as a makeshift lens cover as well; maybe a spare set would be useful too, as gloves are easily lost. Consider taking a hat, to make sure you do not end up with terrible sunburn in summer or to keep your head warm in winter.

Food and Drink

Depending on how long you are planning to be out shooting time-lapse you may wish to consider taking food and drink with you. It is particularly important to take water with you on a hot day.

Suncream

With a healthy enthusiasm and passion for photography driving you to get going, the last thing you might think about is suncream. If you forget it and you go out on a hot sunny day, you will get burned. Apart from not being a great look it has obvious negative health implications.

Maps

Most people will use their digital devices to navigate with and that technology is incredible, but think about your battery life. If the battery on your phone runs out, it doesn't matter how fancy it is, it isn't going to help anyone. There is nothing like a good old-fashioned compass and map to get you around. Even though you can't browse social media or watch videos of cats running into glass doors with it, there is no battery and therefore it is failsafe, providing you can read a map.

Satellite navigation

Using satellite navigation in the car is an effective and safe way to get somewhere as quickly and as easily as possible. A lot of people are also using mobile phones, tablets or watches to navigate with as well and this is a great solution for walking to a destination that you are unfamiliar with. Please remember that the address sometimes does not get you all the way there. Use online satellite maps to familiarize yourself with where you are going before you depart. This way you will recognize when you have arrived, even if your navigation device does not take you right up to your final shooting destination.

Applications and websites

As we usually carry a mobile phone or a tablet with us all the time, we should utilize them to assist with our image-making. There are many applications that we can download to help us: some will assist with navigation and others could help with our time-lapse photography directly. We can find out where the sun is going to be at any time of day and there are time-lapse apps that can help you calculate how many images you might need to shoot for a given length of final video delivery. There are many apps that perform the same function, of course, so check to see what the reviews are like. One person may find an app very useful and another not at all; simply pick and choose to see what you prefer.

KEEPING YOUR EQUIPMENT CLEAN

After spending lots of money on a nice new shiny camera, keep it that way. If the equipment is treated with respect it will last much longer. Keeping the camera's body and lenses clean will reduce the chance of dust gathering in the camera and having to spend money on getting it serviced or cleaned. There are simple things that we can do to reduce the likelihood of getting dust on the sensor in the first place.

Your camera's sensor

Inside the camera's body there is a digital sensor. This is a light-sensitive device that basically converts analogue light into digital signals, enabling you to capture your images. The camera's sensor has millions of tiny square pixels on it and the total number of pixels on the sensor dictates the camera's resolution. If you own a 24 megapixel camera this means that your sensor has 24 million pixels, or tiny squares, on it. Essentially this is what records your image.

A dirty sensor

If any dust, dirt or liquid gets onto your sensor it can be a disaster and often shows itself on the images; a lot of post-processing is therefore needed to get rid of these marks after capture. If a spot of dust rests on your sensor, you might see a small black dot in the same place on all of the images and video content from the camera. If the spots are in different places on your images it means that the dust is moving because the air inside the camera is being pushed around by the moving parts every time a picture is taken. Worst case scenario is when liquid of some description gets onto the sensor. When moisture evaporates it will sometimes leave a fine residue that can be pretty difficult to get rid of. If any unwanted dust or residue is present, this can be cleaned relatively easily. Just take the camera along to a good camera service centre and get it looked at by a camera technician.

Cleaning your sensor

If you ever get dust on your sensor you will want to get rid of the mark as soon as possible. But don't give in to the temptation of trying to clean the sensor yourself, even if you get frustrated with the marks on your images. Unless you are a professional and clean sensors every day, it is very unwise to try to clean it yourself; if you don't know exactly what you are doing you could easily scratch the sensor. A repair bill to resolve this is often more than the camera is worth because the entire sensor will need to be replaced, and the sensor is one of the most expensive parts in the camera. You will also need to pay for the labour costs of taking the camera apart and putting it back together again, which adds up quite quickly.

Canned air

Compressed air in a can is commonly purchased in camera shops and can be used to blow the dust away from the outside of the camera because the pressure of the air can shift dirt quite well. If you try to use it for cleaning the inside of the camera, however, this can be really bad news. If the canned air is running low or if the can is held at an angle, chemicals can be sprayed out of the nozzle as well as the compressed air. These chemicals could stick to your sensor and stay there permanently. The sensor unit would then need to be replaced by a technician at a service centre. Do not use compressed air on the inside of the camera ever, unless you are a qualified technician.

Software and removing dust spots

If you have dust on your sensor and there are black dots on your images then all is not lost, as there are ways of removing the dust spots and rescuing the pictures. Many software packages have what is called a 'clone' or 'heal' tool, which will copy a small area next to a dust spot and stick it over the top of the blemish. This can take quite a while if there are multiple dust spots but can totally cover up the fact you had any dust on the sensor at all.

There are other options available too as some manufacturers enable you to create what is called a 'dust reference file'. This is a picture that you take at the time of shooting a set of images that you wish to take the dust away from. You then put the batch of images into the software that comes with the camera and it will use the dust reference picture to remove the dust from the batch of images. You could have 100 images with dust spots on them which can be sorted out in minutes with this process. Check your camera's manual and the 'Help' menu in the software to look for this function.

Keeping dust away from your sensor in the first place

We have established that it is not a good idea to attempt to clean the inside of your camera in any way. So here are some practical steps that can be taken to reduce dust on and in your equipment in the first place. These points are good practice but don't feel that you need to do all of it. You will know what applies to you and equally you may already look after your equipment adequately. Ultimately these steps can save you a lot of money and time in resolving issues with equipment.

Vacuum your camera bag

Although this might seem odd, vacuuming your camera bag is one of the best ways to reduce the chances of getting dust and dirt in the camera to start with. Your camera spends most of its time zipped up in the camera bag and when you travel the movement can shake dust and dirt around onto the equipment. Generally when people have problems with dust, you will find that the camera bag itself has bits of a forest sitting at the bottom of it.

Turn the camera off when changing lenses

When the camera is turned on, the sensor generally has a very small amount of electricity going through it and if you detach the lens it can gather dust. This same effect can be seen on your television at home – even though the front of the device is vertical, dust is still attracted to it because of the static charge. Accordingly, make sure that you turn the camera off when changing the lens. Sometimes when in a rush this is easy to forget, but over time dust can start to build up if you do not follow this rule.

Hold the camera face down when changing lenses

When you change a lens you open up the inside of your camera to the elements. Use gravity to reduce the chances of getting dust inside the camera by pointing the camera towards the floor when changing lenses. If your camera does not have a lens on it then don't leave it that way, as prolonged exposure to the air will introduce dust easily. Also, try not to change lenses unless you really have to. The less the inside of the camera is exposed, the better.

Don't change lenses in windy or dusty conditions

If you are on the beach on a windy day, it is pretty much the worst place that you can change a lens, no matter where the camera is pointed. Sand will blow into the camera and sand is a lot worse than dust: it can actually damage the internal workings of the camera. If you plan what lens will be best for your activities on that occasion, you won't even need to change the lens, which is the ultimate solution.

Sticky tape on your caps

Apply double-sided sticky tape to the inside of your body cap and lens protection caps. This can be purchased in most stationary stores and will prove to be a key item in your camera bag. If tape is stuck to the inside of caps then it can collect the dust that would otherwise fall onto your camera or lens. The great thing about this solution is that it is low cost and replaceable.

Keeping your equipment clean on the outside

Keeping the outside of the camera and lens clean is important for many reasons. If your equipment looks well kept it will be easier to market if you ever decide to trade it in or sell it second hand. If care is taken with the outside of the equipment, it is also much less likely that the inside, including the sensor, will get dirty. More importantly, the equipment is more likely to last longer.

Use a paint brush

If you visit a beach or a building site, for example, you cannot always avoid getting sand or dust on the outside of the camera and it can be difficult to clean this off with a cloth or with your fingers. A great way to remove anything external like this is to use a dry paint brush, because the bristles can get to parts of the camera that you cannot reach. The best kind of paint brush to use is one with hard bristles to make sure dirt is removed completely. If the brush has soft bristles it will not clean as well or may not make much difference at all.

Anti-static foam cleaner

This is a great cleaning tool (not a crazy indie band from the 1990s as the name suggests), which is used with a cloth or paintbrush to clean your equipment on the outside. It does a great job of cleaning camera and lens rubber grips, making the outside of the camera look almost new. The foam is generally squirted out of an aerosol can and then applied with the cleaning tool. This may not be something that you do often but is definitely advantageous if you work outside a lot.

Microfibre lens cleaning cloths

These cloths are designed generally for cleaning glass surfaces, so if you wear glasses you might actually already have a microfibre cloth. Sometimes when you go to pick a camera up, your finger squashes right up against the front of the lens or viewfinder and leaves a big ugly finger print. If you get anything on the glass surface of your equipment such as oil, moisture or dust then a microfibre cloth will usually shift it. To save hassle, buy about ten of these cleaning cloths and keep one in every camera bag and in every pocket of every jacket you own because you will always then have them to hand. The alternative is to use your sleeve or shirt and this could well scratch your new and expensive lens.

Deoxit

This is a cleaning product designed for cleaning electrical contacts. If you think the contact between your lens and the camera body or the camera's hot shoe contact for your flash gun is dirty, this is probably the best cleaning product available. It cleans but also improves the electrical contact. Deoxit can also be used for electrical household items.

BUILDING YOUR KIT BAG

Make a list of everything in this chapter you think you might need in your kit bag and go shopping. After using the items on a shoot, review the list and see if it can be refined. After a few shoots you will be able to compile an effective selection of equipment that serves you well and does the job for you. This will also ensure that nothing is forgotten when you are out shooting and you will have an inventory of what is with you. Formalizing your equipment in this way will give you a clear idea of what you have and need on a daily basis. More importantly it means you will not forget things; as the saying goes, 'Fail to prepare: prepare to fail'.

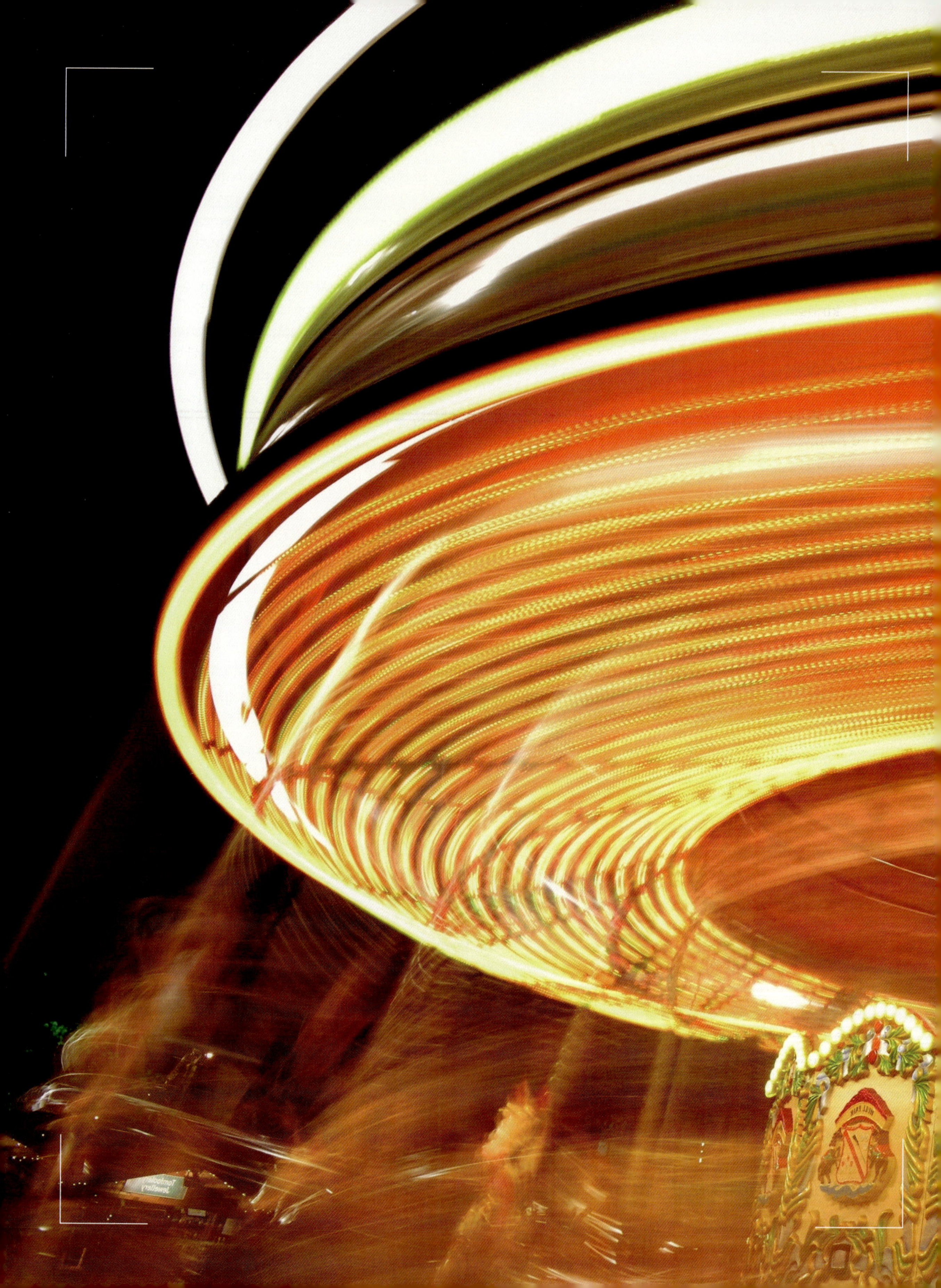

Chapter 4

Light and exposure

In this chapter we will take a look at the different kinds of light that we might be working with as image-makers. We will explore the world of exposure, which is about controlling light with the camera, both from a technical and practical standpoint. Light will be deconstructed and demystified, to help you find the best light source to work with whenever possible.

We will also explore ideas that will enable you to use your camera effectively under different lighting conditions. The information covered in this chapter is very important when using an advanced camera; learning about light will give you much more control of your work. Once you have developed an understanding of light and exposure, your confidence will grow every time you pick up a camera.

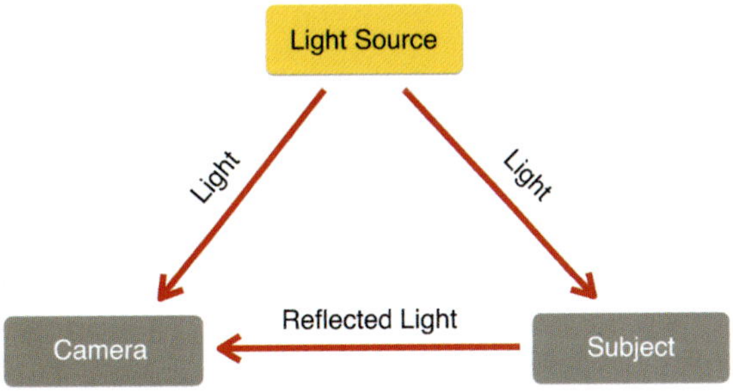

▲ This diagram shows how we are able to make an image of any given subject. When we take a picture of something we are recording reflected or direct light from a light source. This enables us not only to take pictures but also to see the subject with our own eyes in the first place.

THE IMPORTANCE OF LIGHT

Whether you are taking still photographs, making a video or a time-lapse, light is the most important thing to look at before anything else. When you record any subject matter with an imaging device, the only reason you are able to capture a picture is because of the light reflecting off it into the lens. If there is no light, you are not able to take pictures. The same theory applies to how you see with your own eyes. You are only able to see what is in front of you because light from the object you are looking at is emitted from the light source and bounces off the object and into your eyes.

◀ Being able to control elements such as shutter speed will give you a huge amount of creative control. This image of a merry-go-round is not something you could see with the naked eye. The camera's shutter is open for four seconds and in that time the ride has moved a lot, giving the final image plenty of blur. By using slow shutter speeds we can introduce welcome motion blur to our time-lapse videos. Camera settings: 4s, *f*/10, ISO 100.

Prior to grasping that light is the key to photography, many people find that they are limited as to what can be achieved. Many photographers get to a point at which they hit a wall and wonder why they are not advancing with their work. Most of the time the reason for this is that they have not realized that light is what you are actually taking pictures of and, therefore, is of primary importance.

You may have looked at a professional photographer's work at galleries, online, or in a book and wondered why their imagery has something striking about it. In reality, they might not necessarily be demonstrating technical mastery of the camera they are using, but they are experts in using light for image-making. If you concentrate more on light itself you will also start to look at the work of others and see why they have made certain decisions with their work. If you can see the light you will take a massive step forward.

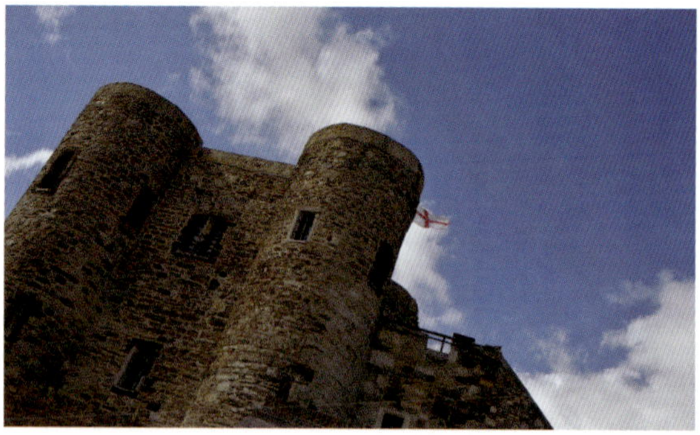

▲ This frame from a time-lapse shows how the light falling on the castle is diffused and the shadows are minimal, making the shape of the building look dark and shapeless. Camera settings: 1/2500s, ƒ/3.5, ISO 100.

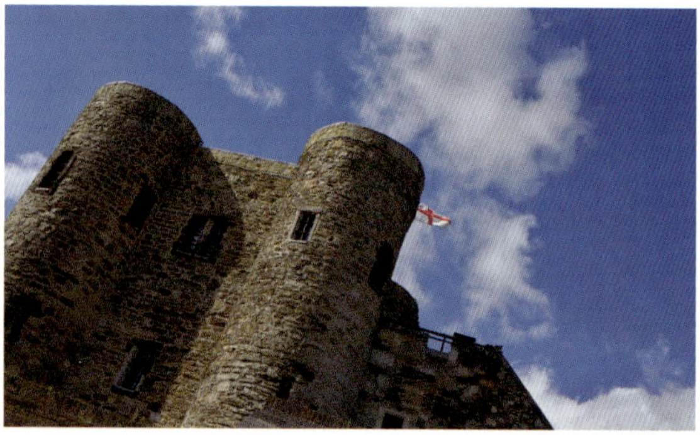

▲ The clouds have moved, letting direct sunlight through the clouds. This means that the quality of the light is now harsh and this helps lift the shape of the building and gives it some colour.

Learning about light

Before we break down the fundamentals of working with light, let us go right back to the beginning and ask a very important question: what does photography mean? The word 'photography' is derived from 'photo', meaning 'light', and 'graph', meaning 'drawing', so the literal meaning of photography is 'drawing with light'. This shows that light is not only the most important aspect to think about as a photographer, but it is what photography basically means in the first place.

The four main words to help you think about light are as follows: quantity; quality; direction; and colour. This is an invaluable way to assess any lighting situation in order to use it more successfully and improve your image making. We will look at each of the 'big four' individually and explore the relationship between them.

Quantity

The quantity is simply how much light there is in any given situation. If it's a bright day there is a large quantity of light and at night time there is a small quantity of light. Knowing how to react to different amounts of light is what most people struggle with when using their camera. One of the reasons why your camera has shutter speed, aperture and ISO settings is to control the quantity of light that you let into the camera and therefore how bright or dark the images appear.

If we are working with natural light, we are given the quantity and we have to work with what we have; we are unable to control the light but we can control how it looks in the picture with the camera's settings. If we use man-made lighting then we might have more control over the quantity of light available to us. One example of this is when you are using flash.

Quality

The quality of light can be defined as either harsh with heavy shadows or diffused with no defined shadows. If you have direct sunlight, for example, the quality of the light will be hard and the shadows created by any objects will be defined clearly on the floor next to the subject. In this instance there is a great deal of difference in the quantity of light between areas of direct sunlight and the shadow areas, and this can make it very tricky when dealing with the light.

If the weather is overcast, on the other hand, the sunlight is being diffused by clouds, making the light much softer and the difference between light and dark shadow areas not so abrupt. Consequently, diffused lighting is much easier to work with because the quantity is more consistent and the camera's exposure settings are easier to manage.

Harsh and diffused light can completely change

the mood and feel of the image and, for example, on a cloudy day the quality and quantity of the light can change in an instant. The quality of the light will change depending on the following:

- Distance
- Size of light source
- The path that is taken by the light
- Quantity

When you change the distance between the light source and the subject it can have a significant effect on the quality and quantity of the light itself. The reason for this is that light gets darker the further you are away from the source. The size of the light source will affect the quality; usually a small light source will give harsher light whereas a bigger light source will be more diffused because the light has a chance to spread out and break up.

The path that the light takes affects its quality and quantity. If the light is shining into your living room, for example, it initially shines through the window; at this point it is at its brightest. The light starts to bounce off walls and furniture and is then absorbed and reflected, depending on the surfaces. The path will change and break off into different directions and consequently will keep reducing in quantity as distance increases from the window.

Direction

When observing the direction of light, it is critical to note where it originates from. If natural light is your primary light source, the position of the sun will dictate the direction that the light is coming from. For example, during the middle of the day the light is falling downwards because the light source (the sun) is high in the sky. Shadows created during this time are small and don't tend to be particularly inspiring. If the sun is low in the sky, however, it will create long shadows that look fantastic in the movement of a time-lapse video. As well as understanding how light behaves due to its direction, you need to also observe the direction that the light source is taking,

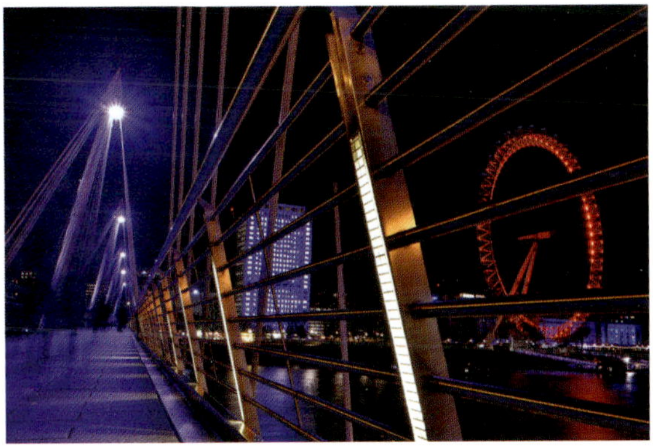

▲ There are at least three different types of man-made lighting in this image. When shooting with artificial lighting we need to consider how we use the available colour. Camera settings: 3s, *f*/16, ISO 320.

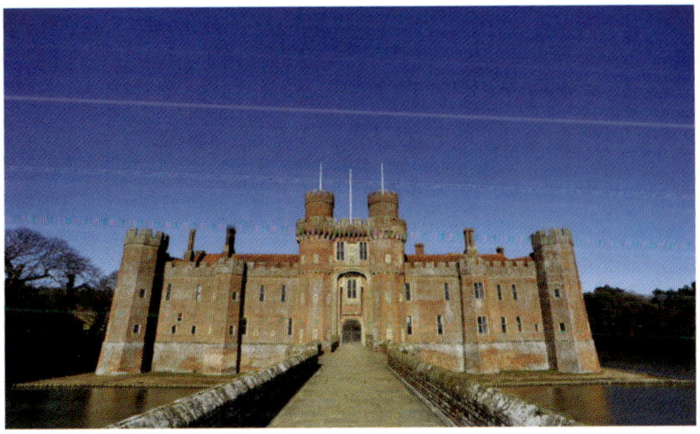

▲ During the day we tend to get natural light to work with and this can lack colour if we do not explore camera settings. Natural light can be inspiring one day and underwhelming the next. Changeable lighting conditions gives us a broad range of imagery to work with. Camera settings: 1/1600s, *f*/5.6, ISO 200.

and the speed at which it is travelling.

Colour

The colour of light can vary significantly depending on the source. There are two main types of lighting:

- Natural light
- Man-made light

Both offer an enormous array of colours that can be used to your advantage visually or, on the other hand, can provide you with a variety of problems. Either way, we need to be able to manage colour. With photography, we refer to the colour of light as the 'white balance'. The colour of the light as it appears in your imagery can be controlled by the camera's white balance settings. By going between

EVALUATING LIGHT AND THE HAND TEST

Knowing about quantity, quality, direction and colour individually is important, but you will need to use them all together in many situations, so it will help to be able to evaluate the light quickly before you shoot. Wherever you are right now, try the hand test. Hold your hand in front of you and look at how the light falls on it. You will be able to see where the shadows are falling and whether they are harsh or diffused, for example. Analyze the light and ask yourself questions like this:

- What is the quantity of the light – is it bright, dark or average?
- What is the quality of the light – is it harsh or diffused?
- What direction is the light coming from; is there one source or are there many?
- What is the colour of the light source (you might have orange, green, blue or neutral colours in your available light)?

Often there will be different light sources to contend with, which can make it very challenging. Try moving your hand around and seeing how the shadows or colour of the light changes.

the options that are available in the camera's menu we can change how the colour of the light source(s) appears in our imagery. We will explore the use of white balance to manage colour later on.

EXPOSURE

The exposure triangle

Exposure is about how bright or dark your imagery looks as captured by your imaging device. There is some simple terminology that we need to look at before moving on. If an image is referred to as 'underexposed' then it means it appears too dark. If it is 'overexposed' then it looks too bright. If an image shows the correct exposure then it looks approximately like it did when you were standing there looking at the subject. This is of course subjective and some people prefer to over- or underexpose their work, depending on their style and desired aesthetic.

It is generally more difficult to rescue an accidentally overexposed image because the lighter areas in the image go completely white, and details that would have been there if a correct exposure had been made will be lost. Some call these overexposed areas 'blown out highlights'. If you underexpose an image by accident, you are much more likely to be able to recover the detail because of the nature of digital photography.

Of course it's better to get the exposure correct in the first instance if possible, unless you are going for a specific effect or technique. To manage the exposure, we need to learn and understand in practical terms how the camera controls it. There are three aspects that enable us to control light with an advanced camera: shutter speed, aperture and ISO. The balance between these three elements gives us an exposure for the light that the camera is pointed at a particular moment in time.

Taking control of the exposure triangle

To take control of exposure, and get the images desired, we will need to learn how to change the shutter speed, aperture and ISO, and how to use them efficiently in different lighting situations. There are four modes on the camera that will give us different amounts of control of the triangle's balance. On some cameras these modes are M, A, S and P. On others the equivalent modes are M, Av, Tv and P. Advanced cameras by any brands should have similar annotations, if not the same. If you are unsure where these are located just check your manual. Mobile phones and tablets will generally not offer these modes, but they might be available

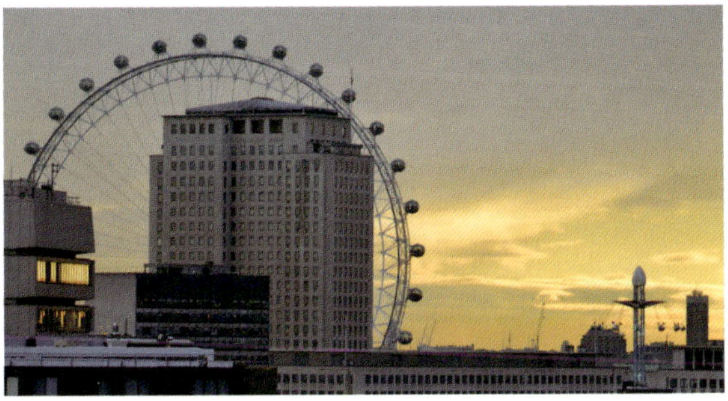

▲ This image has the correct exposure, which means it closely represents what the subject would have looked like when the time-lapse was captured.

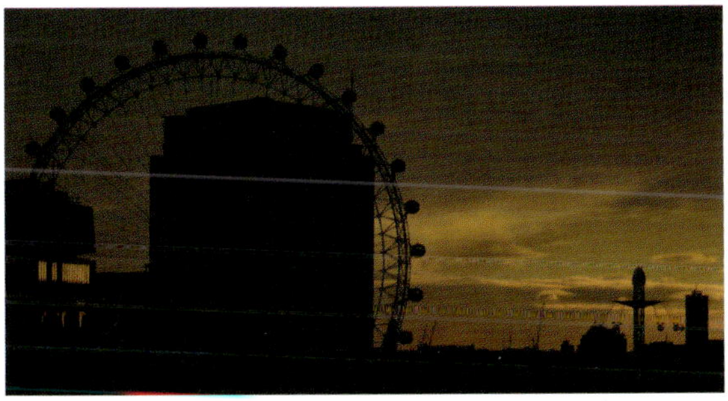

▲ Here we see an underexposed image. The picture is much darker than it would have looked at the time of capture. This darker effect is also referred to as 'low key' and is actually a very popular style of image-making.

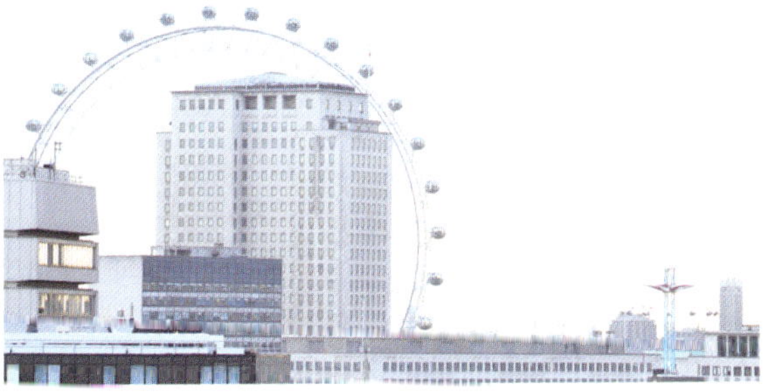

▲ This scene is overexposed. This image is much brighter than it would have looked at the time of capture to the human eye. It is dangerous to overexpose with digital photography because it is tricky to rescue details from an overexposed area. If we capture overexposed imagery for creative reasons it is called 'high key' photography.

▶ The exposure triangle is the most important factor to understand as an image-maker. By understanding how to use the triangle we take control of the way our images look by changing the three elements.

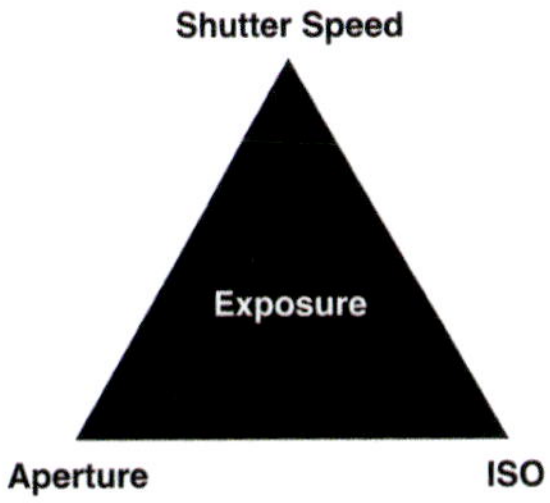

▶ Program mode is essentially auto mode. We do, however, gain some control over the camera, such as whether or not the on board flash is triggered. We are also able to make limited changes to the balance of shutter speed and aperture.

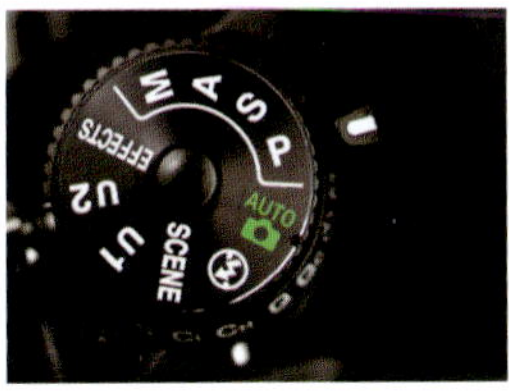

on an advanced compact camera. Ideally it is best to use a DSLR camera because they will have the four modes that we are looking at. If you fully understand the exposure triangle and how to control it i.e. what mode to choose at any given time, then you will take full control over how your imagery looks.

We will now cover all three items in the exposure triangle, whilst going through the modes on the camera. With time-lapse photography 'aperture priority' is generally used if you are using a tripod, but if the camera does not give the required results, then manual is the back-up plan. All four camera modes have their place; sometimes the way you choose to represent the light you have to work with at any given time and what visual effect you are trying to achieve are a matter of personal preference.

Program mode

This mode is very similar to auto in the way that it chooses the exposure for you, but it is much better than shooting auto mode. 'P' mode lets you retain a good level of control over the camera in general, including colour and focusing modes, whereas auto mode (the green camera icon) takes total control of the camera from you, and that is very restricting. If you ever need to use the camera in auto mode, think again and use P instead.

Program mode is the best option if you do not have any time to set up the camera properly and you desperately need to start shooting. The camera will give you a good exposure and therefore a fairly good

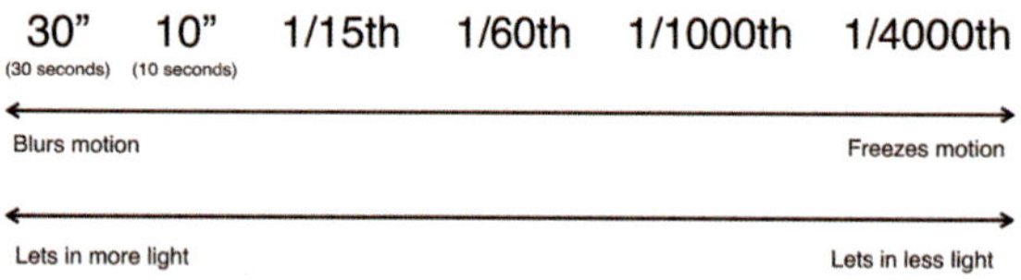

▲ This chart shows that the shutter speed changes the amount of light falling onto the sensor, but at the same time it also affects whether the image is sharp or has motion blur.

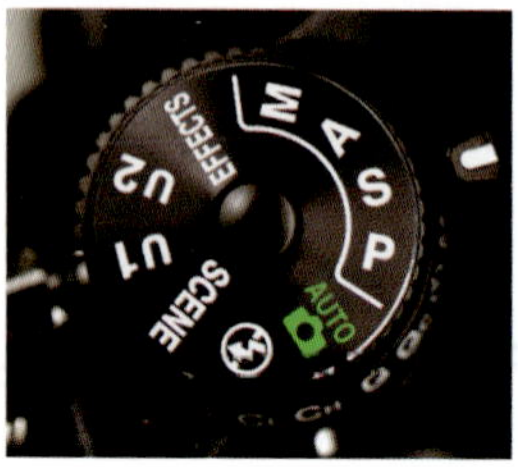

◀ When using shutter priority we take total control of the shutter speed manually. Other elements of the exposure triangle are then looked after by the camera so that we will get a good exposure in most lighting situations.

result. However, as we go through the other modes available, you will realize why it is not ideal in many situations.

With time-lapse photography you will want more control over how the image looks and with P mode you are very limited. In some circles P mode stands for 'point and shoot', and this is not far from the truth, but this mode does offer us more control over general settings and therefore is sometimes useful. In this mode the camera will choose the shutter speed and aperture for us, making the decision based on the light that the camera is pointed at. Try shooting with P mode and see what happens. You may find that it is a good mode for when you don't want to think about settings and you just need to get a shot.

SHUTTER SPEED

What is shutter speed?

The shutter is inside the camera's body; it opens and closes like a pair of curtains and lets light onto the sensor. By choosing the shutter speed you are choosing the amount of time between the shutter opening and closing. In the simplest way, shutter speed is how long you are taking a picture for, which in turn affects how bright or dark your image will look and also whether you get a sharp picture or a blurry one.

The shutter speeds are indicated by numbers, either on a screen on the camera, or through the viewfinder. Some shutter speeds have what look like inch markings next to them, for example 20", which means your shutter is open for twenty whole seconds. The camera's shutter will open, twenty seconds will pass, and the shutter will close again. The other set of numbers you will see will be displayed like a fraction, for example 1/20. This example indicates a shutter speed of one twentieth of a second.

Shutter priority mode

To take control of the shutter speed quickly and easily, shutter priority is the best solution. This mode enables us to choose the shutter speed whilst the camera determines other elements in the triangle, based on the light that is in front of it. You might say this is semi-automatic; we are choosing one element manually and the camera is choosing other factors for us automatically.

We are now going to look at terminology used by photographers when they are speaking about shutter speeds in order for us to understand them. The two terms we will consider are slow shutter speeds and fast shutter speeds.

Slow shutter speeds

When you use a slow shutter speed it means the shutter is open for a long time. The parameters that you will have in your camera which are generally deemed as slow shutter speeds are 1/50th of a second right down to around 30" (thirty seconds). If anything moves during the time that the shutter is open the movement will be recorded on the picture and will produce motion blur in your image.

When shooting time-lapse video we will be mostly using the camera on a tripod. Because the camera is not moving in this instance, we are able to use slow shutter speeds and get deliberate blur in

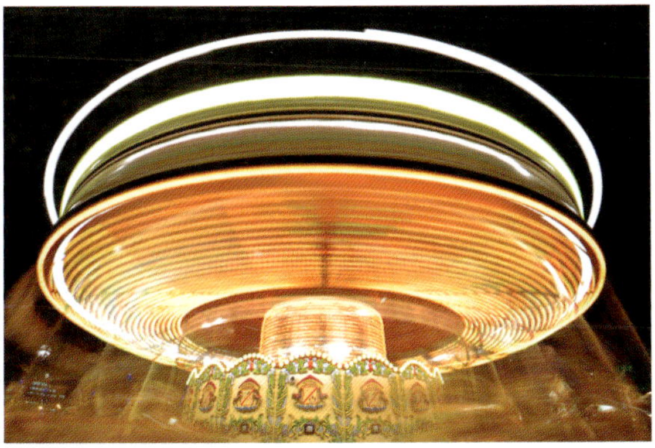

This fairground ride was captured at a very slow shutter speed of 4" (four seconds) to get motion blur. The camera was on a tripod to keep the camera steady whilst the shutter was open.

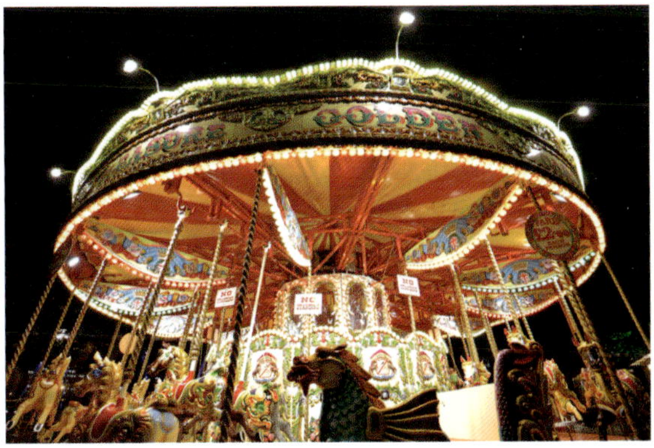

This image was captured at 1/200th of a second to freeze the movement of the fairground ride; this kind of shutter speed is also a good option for general hand-held photography to get sharp images.

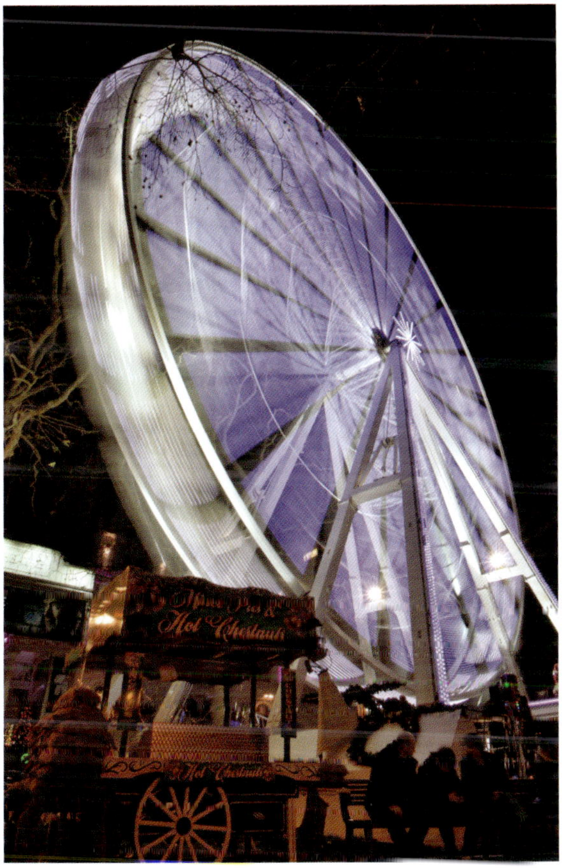

This image is taken with a 2" (two-second) shutter speed. In this example the ride has moved quite a long way in its circular motion. This gives the final image plenty of blur.

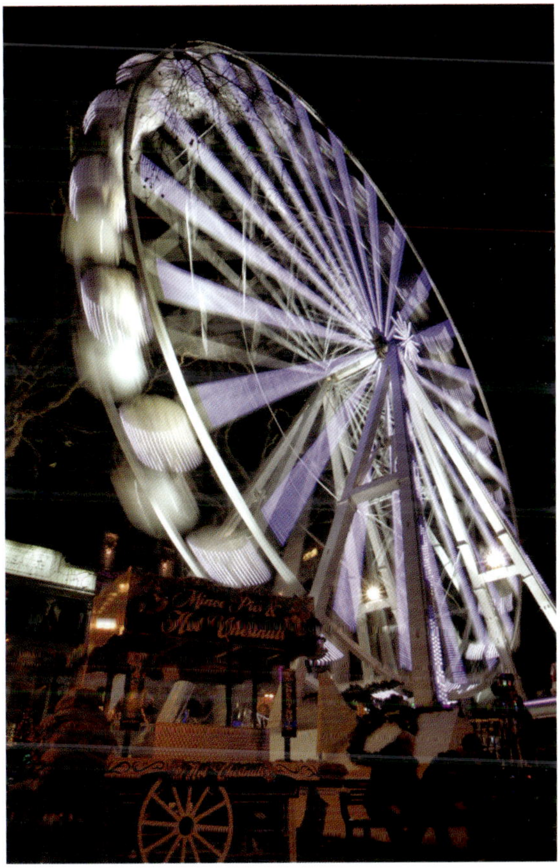

This image is taken with a 1/1.3 shutter speed. This still gives us motion blur but not as much as the slower shutter speed used in the previous image. This demonstrates how the amount of blur can be adjusted by changing the shutter speed.

TIME-LAPSE AND SLOW SHUTTER SPEEDS

Find a shooting location where you have traffic, boats, fairground rides, trains or anything else that moves that has bright lights on it. Shoot at night when it is dark in shutter priority mode on the camera. Experiment with around 4"–20". Make sure the camera is on a steady tripod and that it does not move during capture. The resulting time-lapse will show blur, but in this case the blur is deliberate and adds more visual movement to the video. This blur happens due to the length of time the shutter is open for; it records the moving lights as they travel along, creating directional blur. Remember, if you have a shutter speed of 4" for example, you can only take one frame every four seconds at least whilst capturing the time-lapse. This will increase your overall shooting time, but the results are well worth it.

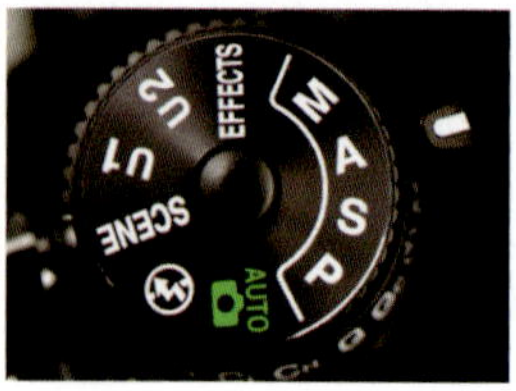

◀ In aperture priority mode you can control the aperture value manually. Other elements of the exposure triangle are then determined by the camera so that we achieve a good exposure in most lighting situations.

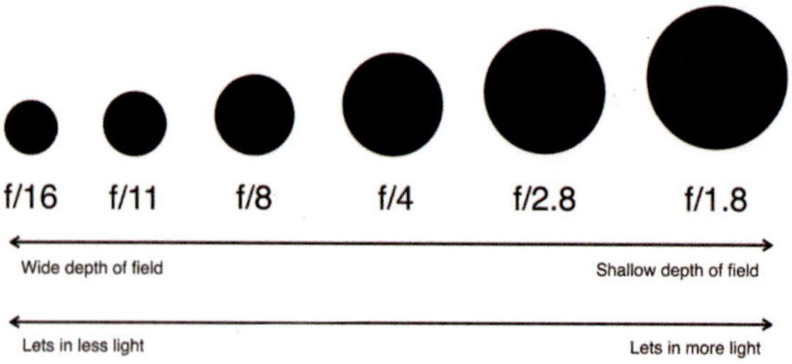

▲ This chart shows that changing the aperture changes the amount of light that is let in through the lens, but at the same time it also changes the depth of field.

moving subjects. In low light situations, being able to open the shutter for a longer duration of time will help us get a good exposure. If for example the shutter is open for four seconds it will let more light in than if the speed is set to 1/20th of a second.

Fast shutter speeds

When we use fast shutter speeds, the shutter opens and closes much more quickly. This will freeze any movement that is happening and achieve a sharp image, which is exactly what you want for normal hand-held stills photography. However, for time-lapse it is advantageous to have the choice between both fast and slow shutter speeds in order to achieve different looks with your work. The kind of parameters we are looking at with fast shutter speeds are around 1/4000th of a second, down to 1/125th of a second.

APERTURE

What is the aperture?

The aperture is a circular opening in the lens that is controlled by a dial on the camera or a ring on the lens. Because the aperture is in the lens, the parameters of your aperture settings will vary depending on what lens you are using. The aperture value is often called the '*f*-stop. This affects two things: firstly how much light is being let into the camera, which affects how bright or dark the image will be; secondly how much of the image is in focus, which is known as the 'depth of field'.

Aperture priority mode

This mode enables us to prioritize aperture, resulting in the shutter speed being automatically chosen by the camera. If we are on a tripod this approach will usually work very well. However, if we shoot hand-held we need to keep an eye on our shutter speed in order to avoid accidental blur.

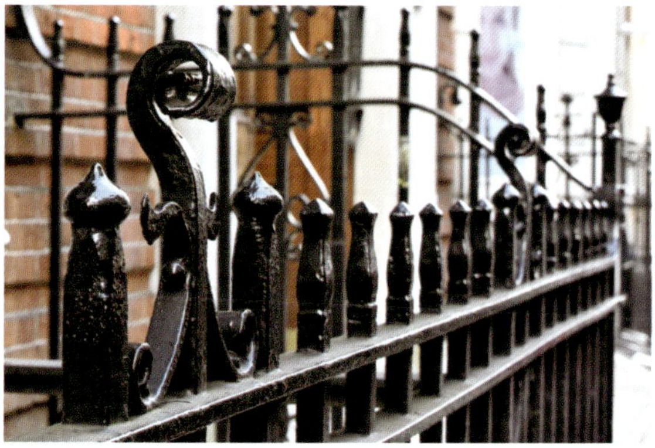

▲ This image is taken at $f/16$. This is a small aperture that gives us a wide depth of field. The camera is focused on the railing decoration to the left.

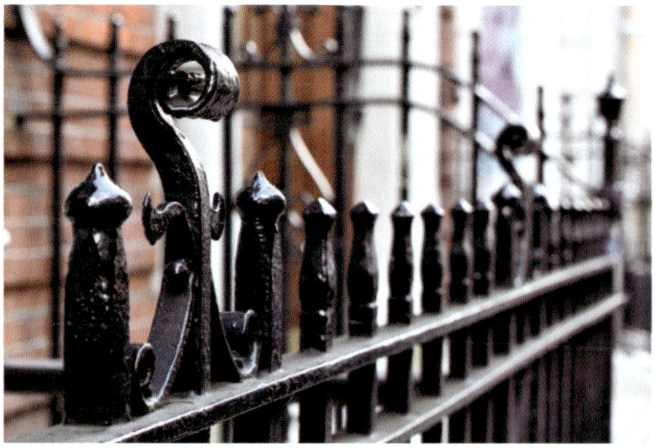

▲ Taken at $f/8$ this image shows the background starting to go out of focus, compared to the previous image, as the depth of field gets shallower.

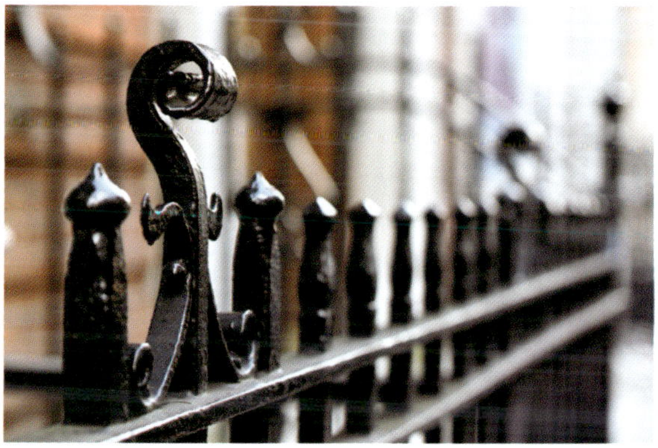

▲ An aperture of $f/4$ has given us a very small depth of field, thus making the background even less focused than the previous image.

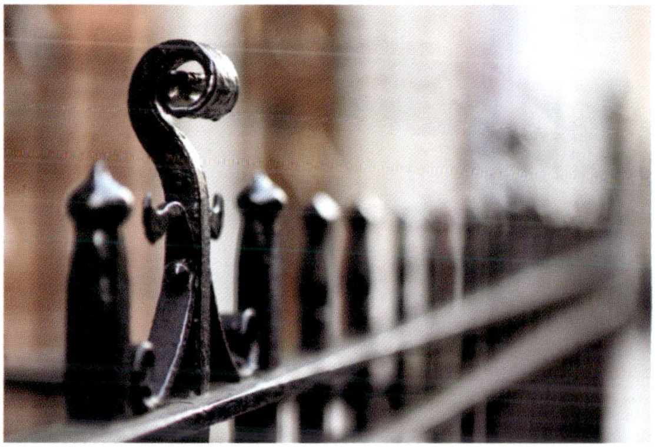

▲ A very wide aperture of $f/1.4$ has put almost all of the frame out of focus except for the area where the camera is focused. This image shows a very shallow depth of field.

Aperture value versus aperture size

Changing the aperture value will control how open or closed the aperture is inside the lens when a picture is being taken. The relationship between the 'f' number and the opening in the lens looks confusing initially (a small value gives us a big opening and a large value gives us a small opening), but an understanding of depth of field will help.

Depth of field

When you change the aperture you also change the depth of field. This dictates how much of the image is in focus. Whatever you focus on will always be the sharpest point in the image. You will notice that the image loses sharpness as you get further in front or behind where the camera is focused.

Another way to refer to depth of field is depth of focus; it is how deep the sharp area will be in your image. For time-lapse we will generally be using around $f/11$ to get a wide depth of field, which is a similar approach to landscape photography, but there are always exceptions. Experiment with depth of field and see what you come up with.

Remembering aperture and depth of field

Aperture and depth of field can be very confusing and this is the area where most people come unstuck. The easiest way to remember the relationship

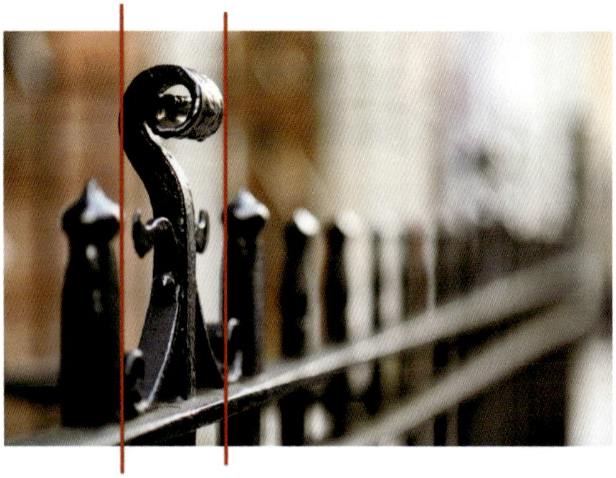

▲ Between the two red lines is the depth of field. This is the area that is in focus and outside of the lines is out of focus. These funny looking areas are called 'bokeh'.

between the two so that we can apply it practically when we are working is:

- A small *f*-number gives you a small depth of field
- A large *f*-number gives you a large depth of field

Advanced depth of field

After getting to grips with how to change your depth of field by using the aperture values, the next step is to get a feel for how the depth of field behaves depending on other factors. There are three elements that affect the depth of field:

- Aperture value
- Focal length of the lens
- Distance between the camera and your subject

Your understanding of how these factors come together to affect your imagery will become clear with experience, but being aware of these three elements is the first step. If you use a wide-angle lens, you will find the depth of field that you achieve is generally quite large. Even if we use a middle aperture value, it still gives us more depth of field than we might assume. With macro and telephoto lenses, you obtain the opposite effect. When we use these lenses, a very shallow depth of field can be evident. The distance between the camera and the subject also affects the depth of field greatly. For example, if you are mere

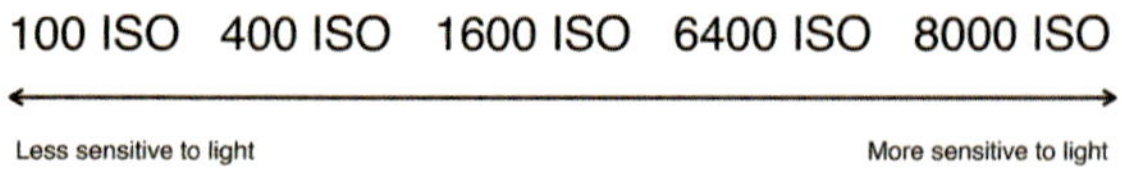

▲ When you change the ISO you change the sensitivity of the sensor to light. Low ISO values give you a low sensitivity whereas high ISO values give you a high sensitivity.

inches away from a subject when using a macro lens, the depth of field may be millimetres.

ISO AND SENSITIVITY

ISO is a measure of how sensitive your camera's sensor is to light. The ISO itself relates to the International Organisation for Standardisation. This company standardizes many systems, in this case the sensitivity levels on digital cameras. For example, if we had four cameras and set them all to ISO 400, they would all have the same sensitivity to light.

The lower values, such as ISO 200, are best used for bright days; we need this low sensitivity because otherwise the image could be overexposed. The higher ISO values, such as ISO 6400, are better for use in low light situations, such as concerts or at night. Basically, the higher the number, the more light sensitivity we have. A key point here is that ISO is down to the sensor and electronics in the camera, whereas shutter speed and aperture are moving parts inside the camera and the lens. ISO performance will vary depending on what camera model you own.

Digital noise

When you use high ISO sensitivity values you need to be aware of digital noise, which looks like small dots and can generally be seen in the darker areas of an image. The noise itself is a side effect of the camera's processor, which has to work harder at high ISO values. Generally speaking, the newer the camera and the more expensive it is, the less noise

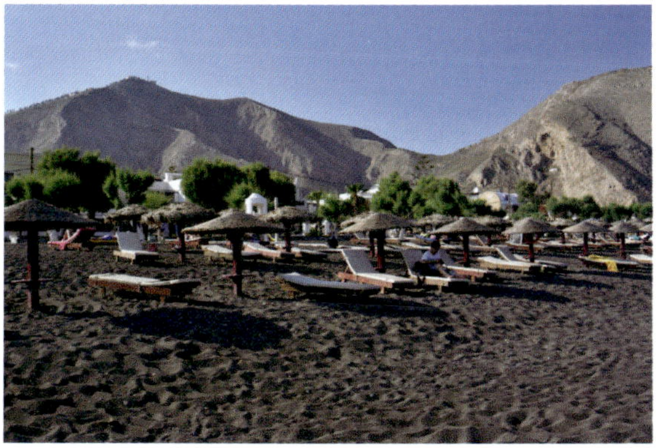

▲ This example shows where a low ISO value would be generally appropriate. The camera was set to ISO 400 because a low sensitivity is needed when there is a lot of light.

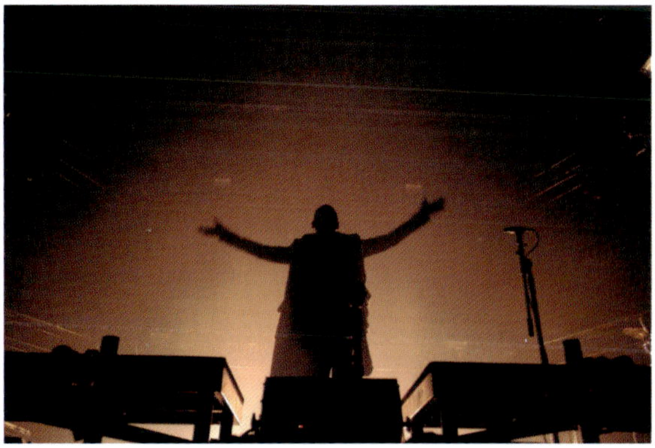

▲ When the ISO is set to an extremely high value you will get some digital noise. In a situation such as a concert we will have to use these values to be able to take a picture successfully.

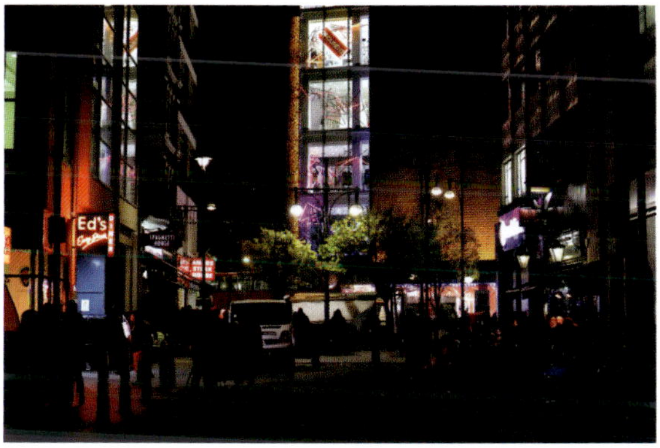

▲ In conditions where there are low light levels more sensitivity is needed. A very high ISO of 10000 was used for this image.

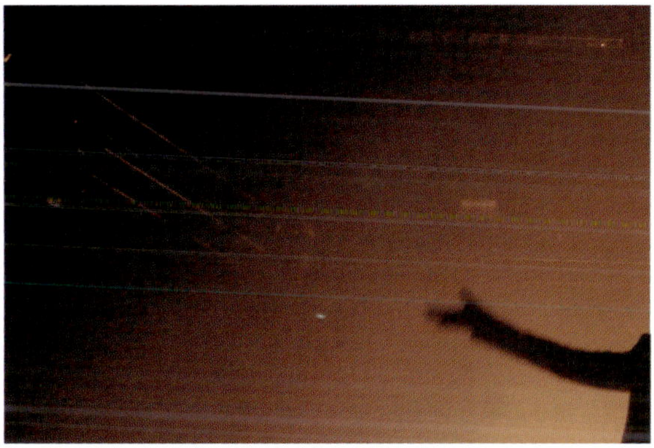

▲ This section of the image shows how digital noise can manifest itself.

you will get when using high values.

It's good to know the parameters of what your camera is capable of. See how high you can push the ISO on your camera before the noise kicks in when shooting in low light situations. The amount of noise you get will also vary depending on the subject matter. This effect is sometimes referred to as 'grain' because when film cameras were used before digital came along, we would get a similar effect, but it would be grain on the film that manifested itself on the image, rather than digital noise.

Auto ISO

Some cameras have the option to choose between manual and auto ISO because technology in more recent cameras give us noiseless images at high ISO values. This makes auto ISO a really useable option. You can use M, A, S and P modes with either manual or auto ISO. This effectively doubles the options available to us. Your camera might also have the option to choose the maximum value that auto ISO function will go up to. This further ensures you avoid the possibility of getting digital noise in your images, even when using the camera's auto ISO.

Time-lapse ISO settings

When creating time-lapse photography it is preferable to use the lowest ISO value possible. If the ISO value is at its lowest, you will get very clean images with no digital noise. If our shooting situation has a low quantity of light, we need to make sure the camera is on a tripod and we choose a shutter speed

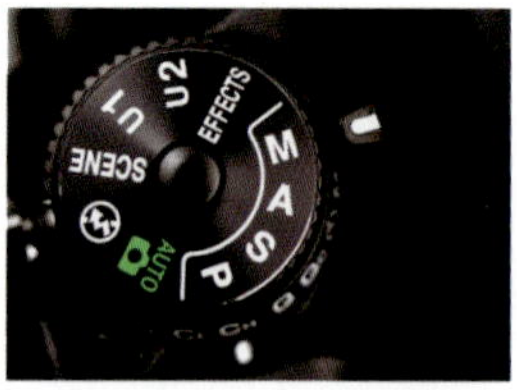

◀ When in manual mode, you are able to fully control the shutter speed and aperture. You can also choose whether the ISO is set to manual or auto, so you have choice of full manual or manual with auto ISO.

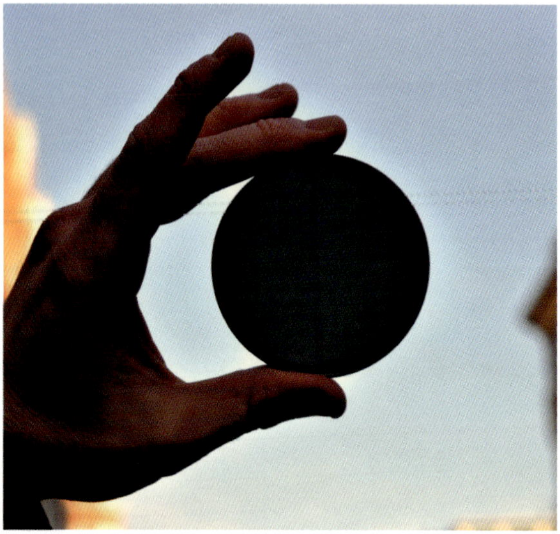

▲ This neutral density filter screws onto the front of the lens and reduces the amount of light falling onto the sensor. Here the filter is held up against the sky to demonstrate how much darker it could be.

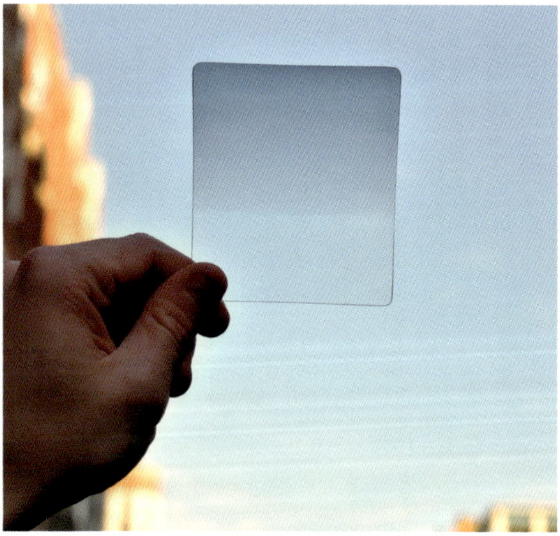

▲ This graduated filter slides into a holder in front of a lens. Held up against the sky we can see the darker section at the top of the frame darkens the sky in a landscape scene and the transparent bottom half leaves the foreground unaffected.

slow enough to let the right amount of light into the camera to get a good exposure.

Manual mode

This mode enables you to take full control of all three elements in the exposure triangle. If you do not want your shutter speed, aperture and ISO to change at all, then this is the solution for you. This mode is great if there is constant lighting and you want the pictures to be consistent. If we have changing light, however, we might want to consider if this is appropriate for what we desire visually.

One example of this is when the sun begins to set. If we get the correct exposure for the light levels during the day time, and the sun is going down, the light will decrease whilst the time-lapse is being captured and the images will get darker until they completely underexpose and go black. If you use program, aperture or shutter priority modes, the camera will attempt to let more light into the camera as it gets darker and the time-lapse will not fade to black, but will keep getting the correct exposure wherever possible. Always experiment with different modes to see what you are capable of achieving with them.

OTHER CONSIDERATIONS WITH EXPOSURE

Filters

There are two filters that can be used for exposure purposes that are quite often used for landscape and time-lapse photography: a neutral density filter and a graduated filter. (Filters are also explored in Chapter 3: Equipment.)

Neutral density filters are used to reduce the amount of light coming into the camera. The creative reason for this is that if there is less light coming into the camera on a sunny day, we will be able to achieve slower shutter speeds and get more motion blur. Without a neutral density filter a very slow shutter speed would get an extremely overexposed image during bright daylight.

Graduated filters are half dark and half transparent, which means that you can place the darker part of the filter over the bright sky and even the exposure out with the rest of the frame. This can be a great tool to get detail back in clouds which would otherwise have been overexposed.

Flicker with man-made light

When recording video or time-lapse, and even sometimes if you are taking still photographs, you can see either a change in the colour created by man-made lighting or a strobing effect. This is referred to as 'flicker' or 'banding'. This happens because most man-made lighting shows the refresh rate of the electricity running through it. Depending where you are in the world the electricity could run at 50 or 60 Hz (Hertz). You cannot see this flicker with the naked eye, but you can sometimes see it when using a digital sensor.

It is important to be aware of flicker so it can be recognized and eradicated. If you want to get rid of it, there are a few steps that you can take. Firstly, in the camera's menu there is often the choice between 50 or 60 Hz to match the local electricity refresh rate. If that does not work then try matching your shutter speed to the local refresh rate or make it slower. To match 50 Hz for example, try 1/50th of a second, which will usually stop any flicker completely. The last step to try if that does not work is to change the aperture setting. By closing the aperture down we will reduce the effects of flicker in the imagery. Most photographers will only notice flicker after a shoot and by this point it is usually impossible to take this effect out of your footage with the use of software.

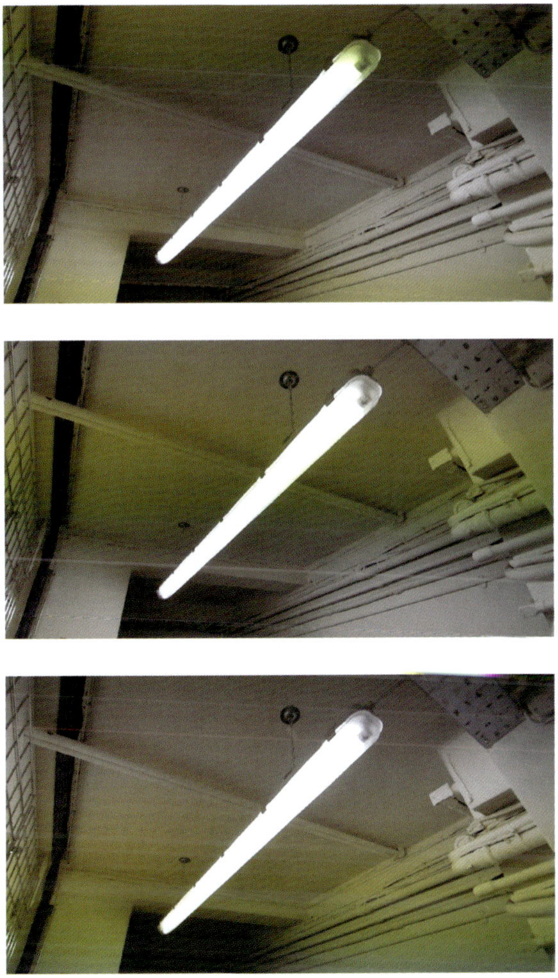

▲ These stills are from a video clip that was deliberately made to show how bad flicker can be and the kind of lighting that can cause this effect. The coloured horizontal lines that change location on each frame is banding.

METERING

Your camera's light meter

The light meter on your camera is one of the most important items to consider before anything else when image-making. This tells us if the exposure is too dark, too bright or just right. Most camera's meters are very simple: they have a zero in the middle, a minus symbol one side and a plus symbol on the other side. This meter can be seen on the back or top screen of the camera and through the viewfinder.

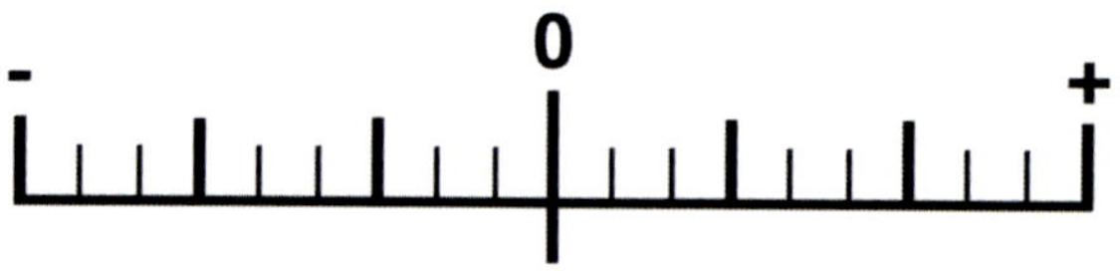

▲ Your camera's light meter will look something like this. This will tell you if the camera thinks your subject is too bright by moving towards the plus icon or too dark by moving towards the minus.

SHOOTING IN MANUAL MODE

Use the camera in manual mode, with ISO set to manual. Choose somewhere to take your picture; try shooting both inside and outside. Point the camera lens at what you want to take a picture of and change the shutter speed, aperture and ISO until the meter is on the zero. The shutter speed should be at least 1/60th of a second if you are hand held so that the image is sharp and without any hand shake. Once you have got the meter onto the zero, take a picture. Now you have taken an image in manual mode and your hit rate was 100 percent; no more spraying and praying. Practise going between different lighting situations and repeat this process. Although you might not choose to use this mode all the time, it is the best practice you can get. If you can use the camera in manual mode you will have complete control of your camera and all the other modes will be easy.

For example, if the settings in the exposure triangle are going to give you a picture that is too dark for the amount of light you are working with, you can see this from the meter as it will indicate towards the minus icon. If the picture is going to be too bright, it will be moving towards the plus. If you refer to the meter as much as possible before taking a picture it will really help reduce the number of mistakes you make.

Some people take ten pictures just to get one right, which is sometimes referred to as 'spraying and praying'. If you find yourself doing this it's probably not deliberate, but why not get it right first time by keeping your eye on the meter? Now you know about the exposure triangle and the meter, you will start to get a much better hit rate with your imagery.

Stops and exposure values

The terms 'stop', 'step', and 'exposure value' tend to be used a lot with photography, but they are not always fully understood. These terms actually all indicate the same thing; we will refer to 'stops' from now on. Stops relate to measuring exposure. Changes in exposure can be made with shutter speed, aperture or ISO. Using this terminology, you can say that one picture is 'one stop brighter' than another one, or 'two stops darker'. Most cameras don't have the word 'stop' in the menu, but instead they use EV (exposure value), which is exactly the same thing.

If you see EV+1.0 on the camera it means that you have dialled in to make the image brighter by one stop. Always look at the camera's meter when changing anything to do with exposure values on the camera. One 'stop' is either doubling or halving the exposure of your image.

An example of this would be the change between ISO 200 and ISO 400. That is one stop in exposure using ISO but we could use shutter speed or aperture also because all three elements in the exposure triangle work in stops. On most cameras the increments used are in thirds of a stop. Try going between 200 and 400 ISO on your camera and there are usually three clicks. This represents the thirds within a whole stop.

Please don't be put off by this language as there really is no need to use it if you don't want to; you can still get amazing imagery without it. Knowing this however can build your confidence when speaking to other photographers and also helps understand what they are talking about.

Your camera's metering system

Understanding what your camera's metering system

is programmed to do will enable you to decide whether to follow what it is telling you or ignore it, but use it as a reference. Coming back to the modes, the camera is ultimately choosing the exposure of your images if you are in program, shutter or aperture priority. The only time that you are fully in control is when your camera is in manual mode, with manual ISO set.

In manual mode you still have the camera's meter to tell you whether it thinks it is too bright or too dark, but you can choose to ignore it and sometimes you may have to. If you are getting images that you feel are too dark and the meter is on the zero, you will just have to change your settings and overlook the meter. The camera is programmed to do a job and it does it well, but it cannot be subjective like you can and it does not have a creative brain.

Middle grey and the grey scale

The metering system on your camera will always try to do the same thing: it will adjust elements of the exposure triangle, if the camera is controlling them, until most of the frame is middle grey. To understand how the camera is making this decision we need to look at the world in black and white – this may sound strange but it's how the metering system sees.

If the camera is choosing the exposure it will look at the scene monochromatically and make adjustments to the exposure so that the majority of the frame is middle grey. Most of the time this is an effective way to get a good exposure. However, there are times where you need to the take control from the camera in order to get the images that you want.

We have considered how the meter works, but just because it is on the zero doesn't necessarily mean that the exposure is how we want it to look. If the meter is on the zero then the camera is happy that the average of your frame is middle grey; we will explore some examples of when you're metering system might not give you the result you want.

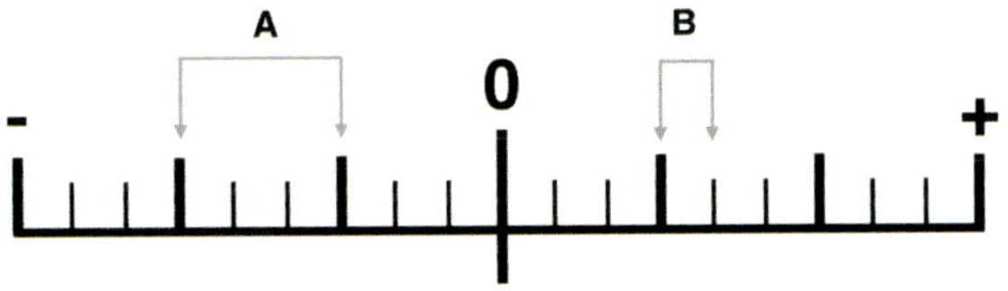

▲ This image illustrates how stops relate to the camera's meter. 'A' shows how one whole stop is indicated on the meter. 'B' shows how a third of stop is shown.

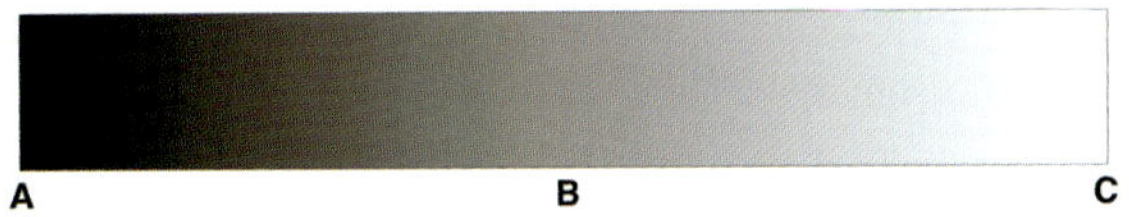

▲ The grey scale. 'A' is black, 'B' is middle grey and 'C' is white. All shades of grey are shown in between.

If the light meter sees a lot of black through the lens, it will want to make everything middle grey, with the effect that everything in the picture will look brighter than real life and therefore not correct to your eye. An example of this kind of situation is taking images of a black car or a dark sky. The subject is black so we will generally want to represent it as it appears. To show the subject in the image how it looks we will need to go against what the camera is trying to do and make it underexpose using any element of the exposure triangle. The meter will look wrong but the image will look right.

If you're metering system sees a lot of white, on the other hand, it will decide to try and get to middle grey by darkening everything down. One example of this is when you are taking pictures in snow. If you point the camera at snow the metering system will see a lot of white and will decide that it is too bright. The camera will then darken the image to get the white down to middle grey. This means that the snow will appear muddy looking and generally darker than it should. To get around this we ignore the meter and can adjust an element in the exposure triangle to make the image brighter. The meter will appear to be over exposing by around EV+1.3 stops (1.3 stops brighter than middle grey), but the snow will appear to be correct because snow is obviously brighter than middle grey.

SHOOTING TO UNDERSTAND THE METER

Change your camera's colour settings to shoot black and white, since this is how the meter sees the world. Set the mode to 'P' mode (program mode); the camera will be choosing your exposure. Take images of whatever is nearest to you and catches your eye. Afterwards, review the image and see how much middle grey you see in the frame. The majority of the image will be mostly middle grey rather than extreme black and white. This means that the meter has done its job well. The only problem is that the shutter speed and aperture may not be anything like what you want it to be. This illustrates that the meter's priority is to change the camera's exposure to achieve middle grey, but it does not have a creative brain. This is why you need to take control of the exposure triangle. Use the meter to help you but don't follow it without understanding what it is doing.

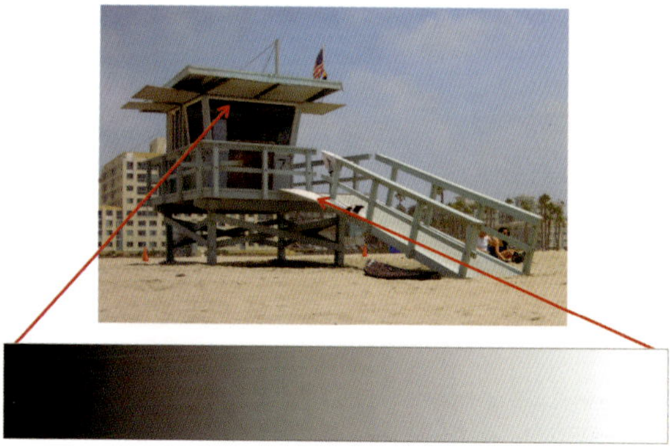

▲ The grey scale directly relates to your images. Here the extreme black and white areas are shown in an example. This can be difficult to see because this image is in colour.

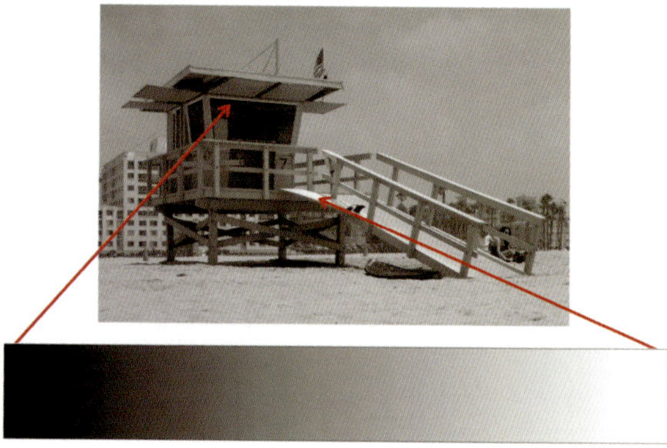

▲ The metering system in the camera sees your image monochromatically; it is often easier to see the relationship between the grey scale and your pictures when the image is also in black and white.

Histograms

Histograms can be a useful representation of what the camera is seeing in terms of exposure with your image-making. You can see this guide on the camera's back screen and on software after shooting. It is there to help you understand what the camera thinks about the exposure in relation to the grey scale. It looks like a little mountain range on a grid and will pop up in conversation every so often with photographers.

So what does it mean? If most of the mountain range is in the middle then the camera can see lots of middle greys, and in theory the exposure of your image is 'correct'. If the mountain range is to the left, the camera is seeing lots of blacks so the image might be underexposed. If the mountain range is to the right, the camera is seeing lots of whites and could be overexposed. Most people strive to get the mountain range as near to the middle as possible, because this is what they perceive as correct. Please do not get too caught up in this mindset and lose sight of your image-making. There are often images that will look good to the eye but the histogram is not 'correct', and this doesn't matter. It's good to be aware of what the histogram tells us, but at the end of the day, if you like how your image looks on the back screen of the camera, that is more important than getting too technical. Essentially if the histogram or mountain range is mostly in the middle it means that most of your image is middle grey in exposure.

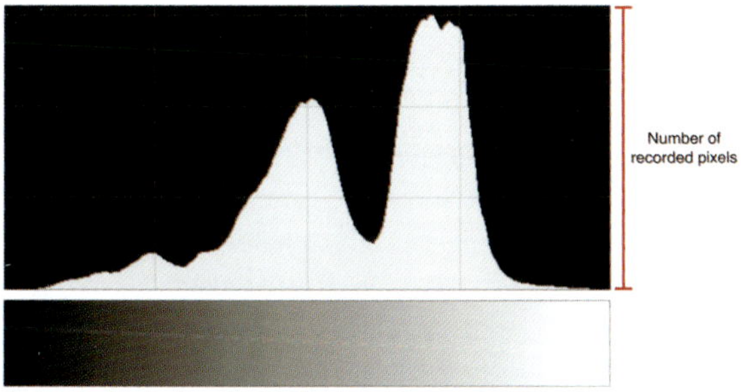

▲ Here the histogram is seen next to the grey scale to show how they relate to each other. A histogram simply shows how many pixels are in each shade of grey. The bottom of the graph represents zero pixels and the higher you go up the mountain the greater the number of pixels that are found in that particular part of the grey scale.

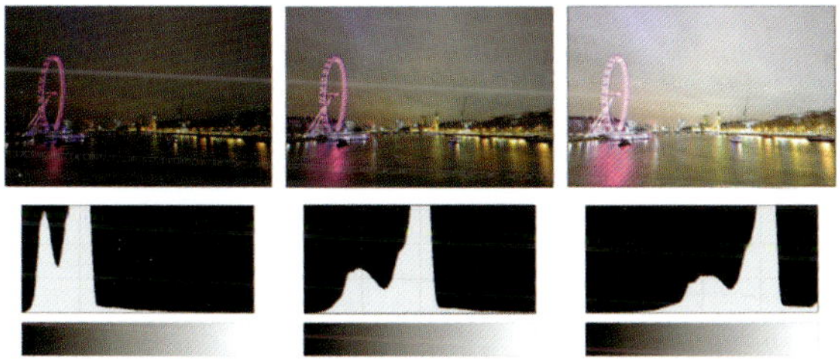

▲ This example shows that if the image is mostly darker than middle grey, the histogram leans to the left. If it is brighter, it leans to the right. If most of the image is middle grey, the histogram will predominantly sit in the middle.

Exposure compensation

The exposure compensation function on most cameras has a square with a plus and a minus on it. This is a way of either over- or underexposing quickly if you need to do so.

If you change its value from 0.0 to +1.0, for example, then it will make the image brighter by one stop. If you go from 0.0 to −1.0 it will make the picture darker by one stop. The big danger of using exposure compensation is that you could set it and forget that you have used it. A day after using it you might cheerfully get the camera out of the bag, take some pictures and the exposure will be totally wrong. Use this tool with caution and don't catch yourself out.

Please note that this function only works when an element in the exposure triangle is being chosen by the camera. If the camera is in manual mode with

▶ The exposure compensation function will have a plus and a minus to indicate that it is a tool to make your exposure darker or brighter.

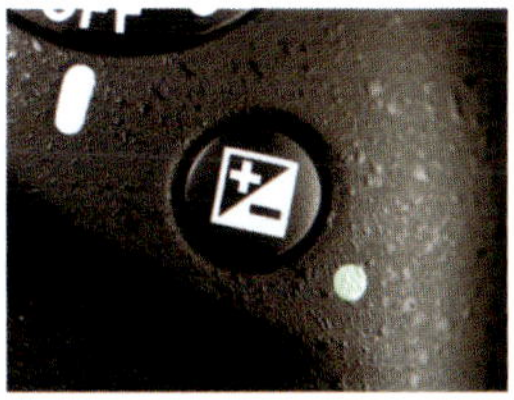

▶ Always check your manual to find the metering patterns on your camera. On some devices it is easy to get this mixed up with the focusing modes.

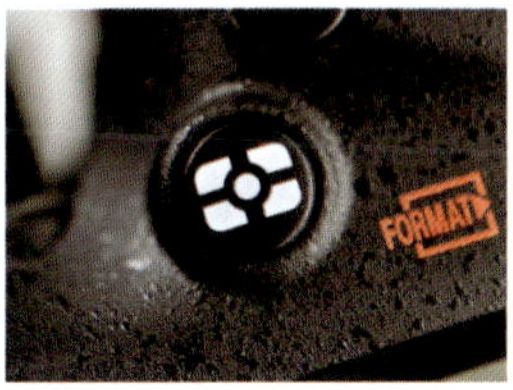

manual ISO it will not make any difference to your imagery. The reason for this is that exposure is only controlled by shutter speed, aperture or ISO. If you use exposure compensation it can only change one of these elements and by being in manual you lock them down.

Metering patterns

Many cameras have at least three metering patterns. The stock setting is to meter for the whole frame and get an average of middle grey. There are other settings that can meter for smaller parts of your image. On most devices these smaller patterns meter for the area that you are also focusing on and will try to make that area middle grey by changing elements in the exposure triangle. It is generally best to stick to the stock setting to give you an average for the whole frame.

One example of the occasional use of smaller metering patterns is when something is backlit. This is a lighting situation where an overall average might not work, so you need to select a specific area which would usually be the primary subject in the frame. Try not to play around with these settings too much; if you want to make your image brighter or darker, use elements of the exposure triangle. This approach will enable you to learn and practise more with the core exposure settings i.e. shutter speed, aperture and ISO.

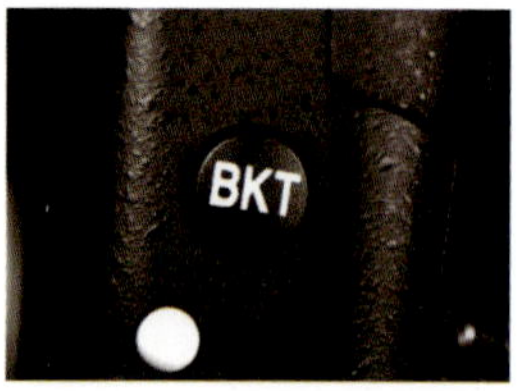

◀ Auto exposure bracketing shows itself in many ways on different brands and models. Check your camera's manual to confirm the location of this function. On the button shown, BKT indicates bracketing.

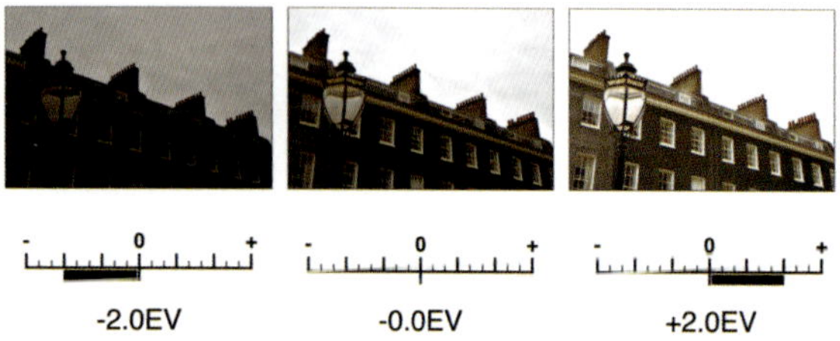

▲ These images are taken at two stops apart using auto exposure bracketing. The camera's meter is seen next to the examples to show how the EV (exposure value) relates to the meter.

BRACKETING IMAGES ON YOUR CAMERA

Find the auto exposure bracketing option on your camera, and with your camera on a tripod, do some sets of bracketed images of a landscape scene. Use the camera on aperture priority mode at *f*/11, so that the camera chooses the initial exposure and the depth of field will be wide. Preferably choose a scene where there are extreme bright and dark areas. A day when there is a lot of direct sunlight will work well. Review the images and see what exposures you prefer. You might prefer it darker because it is more dramatic; it is completely subjective.

BRACKETING AND HDR PHOTOGRAPHY

Auto exposure bracketing

Auto exposure bracketing is a function on the camera that lets us take a number of images at different exposures automatically in sequence.

Sometimes it is a good idea to take a set of images of a subject at different exposures if we are not sure of the correct exposure or if we want to have a set of photographs to choose from. To do this we can use auto exposure bracketing to take three images at different exposures, of a landscape scene for example, giving us a variety of options to choose from.

This approach is especially advantageous when the landscape image has a lot of contrast, such as an image with harsh shadows and direct sunlight. Deciding on one exposure can be tricky, so why not just take a few different ones and choose later? This could prevent you from having to go back and take further images because you didn't get the correct exposure the first time.

When the camera is set to bracket exposures, it will also give you the option to choose the difference in exposure between the separate images. The best exposure difference to start with is 2EV. This means that the set of images that you take will be two stops apart from each other. This approach is not usually used for time-lapse photography, but is a very useful process to be aware of in relation to other areas.

HDR (HIGH DYNAMIC RANGE) PHOTOGRAPHY

You may have noticed that when you capture a single image with your camera it doesn't reflect as much detail as you can see with your own eyes. High dynamic range photography enables us to capture a larger range of detail than we can normally and therefore the result will be closer to what we see in reality.

The best way to capture for HDR photography is to use auto exposure bracketing to get a set of different exposures of the same scene. After you have successfully captured your bracketed images you can then put them together in software to make

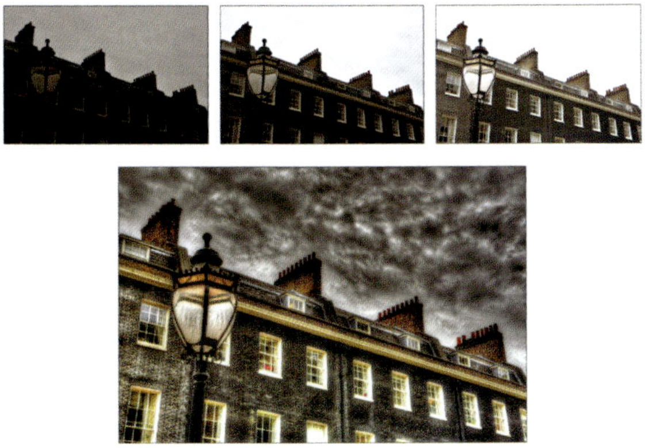

▲ Three images bracketed at two stops apart are combined into software to create an HDR (high dynamic range) image.

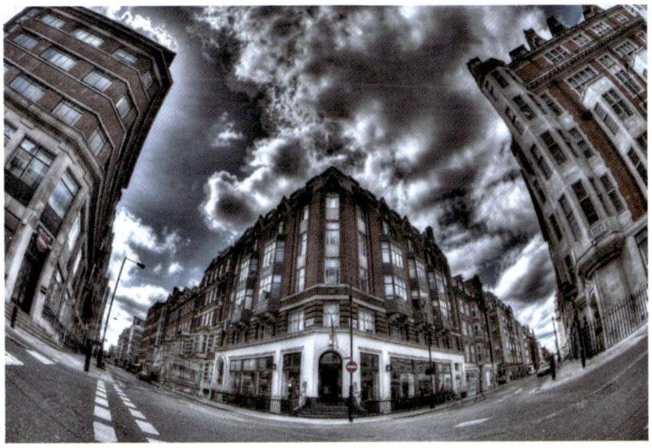

▲ In the time that the separate bracketed images were taken for this HDR image, the clouds moved as the wind blew them. Because the separate images are overlapped in the final HDR file you can see repeating in the clouds. This effect is called 'ghosting' because of the see-through nature of the visual effect.

an HDR image. Most advanced software programs will have this functionality. The software will overlay each image. It will throw away all of the areas that are too dark or bright and leave us with more detail than we would normally see from one photograph. The result is striking because of the sheer amount of detail that it shows.

How to set up your camera for HDR photography

Whilst we are capturing our separate bracketed images for HDR photography we do not want the camera to move. It is best to use a tripod to keep the camera steady whilst shooting. The camera settings that you can use as a starting point are aperture priority, f/11 and ISO 200. The camera will choose the shutter speed based on the amount of light that you have to work with.

To capture the separate images when bracketing it is best to use a remote or trigger so that you are not moving the camera whilst taking the pictures. Be careful of the weather; if the camera is rocking because of wind blowing on the tripod the camera will move between the frames captured, which will make the final result less sharp. Also, make sure the camera does not focus between shots. Focus on your subject, turn the focusing system off and then capture the bracketed images.

Ghosting with HDR

If you are using auto exposure bracketing to capture individual images at different exposures of the same scene, then you will usually be shooting at least three pictures to be combined together to make one. If something is moving whilst you are capturing the separate images, the moving object will be in different places on each photo. When you put the HDR image together this will create some ghostly looking anomalies, which is appropriately called 'ghosting'. Some people like this; others try to avoid it. As long as you are aware of it, then you can decide whether to introduce it into your imagery or not.

Capturing a HDR time-lapse

This is an exciting hybrid of two areas, and there are a lot of HDR time-lapse videos out there. It can be very laborious to achieve because for each frame of the time-lapse video you will need to capture multiple frames using auto exposure bracketing and merge them into an HDR image. It is becoming easier to do this now, however, as cameras are starting to come with in-camera HDR options. With this option you could capture HDR images using the interval timer, then put the individual frames that have been made into HDR images in camera into a time-lapse video on a computer.

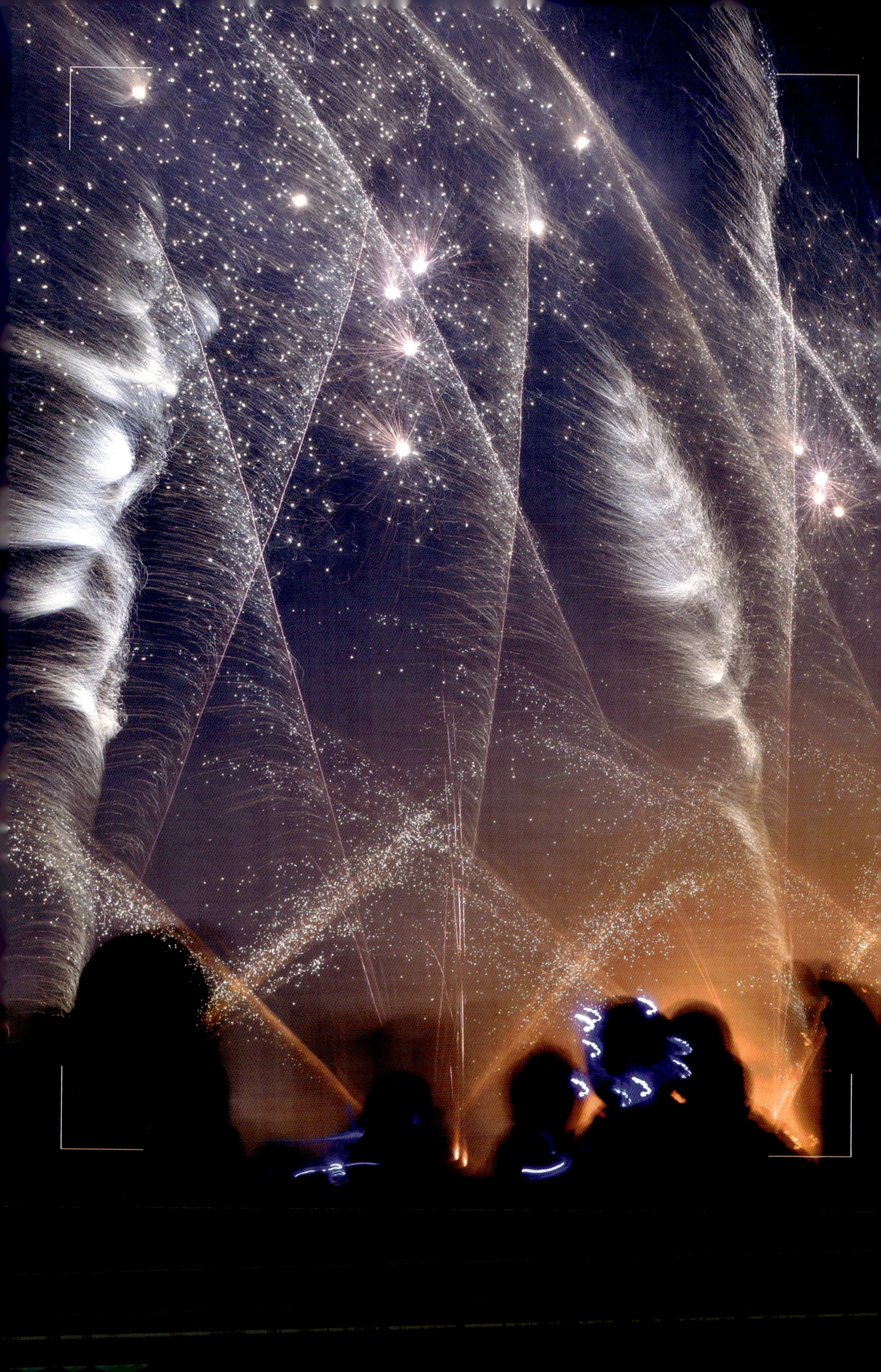

Chapter 5

Setting up your camera for time-lapse photography

In this chapter we will look at setting up your DSLR camera for time-lapse photography, to help you to refine the way you operate the camera before and during capture. There are always many ways to do the same thing and we will look at the different options so that you can choose the one you prefer. Learning about the buttons on your camera will help with confidence, and that is invaluable. We will look at the physicality of using a tripod and focusing options, as well as other tips and tricks that will enable you to execute your capturing process efficiently and effectively.

YOUR FOCUSING SYSTEM

Any focusing system, whatever the device, will always work better in some situations than others and we need to know the reason for this in order to focus successfully in every situation. Focusing systems like to have contrast and detail to grab onto; a building, for example, is perfect because there are generally a lot of lines and detail for the focusing system to work with in order to make your image sharp. If you are trying to focus on something that has no detail, such as a wall that is painted white, you will have problems with acquiring focus. The lens will most likely do something called 'hunting'; this is where the camera is searching for contrast to focus on but can't find it. The lens appears to be whirring in and out of the subject and might actually not focus at all.

The amount of light will also have a major effect on how well your focusing performs. If there is little light, it means that the focusing system cannot 'see' the contrast and detail clearly and therefore may hunt. On a bright day it is much easier to focus because the focusing system can see better. New, advanced DSLR cameras on the market are getting very good at focusing in low light but if you are having problems, experiment with settings.

Focusing for time-lapse photography

Time-lapse photography is generally of moving subjects. Initially you might think that some kind of focus tracking would be needed to follow the movement, but we actually don't want the camera to focus at all, not during capture anyway. Time-lapse and landscape photography are two very closely related areas; both are usually captured using a tripod so the camera will not be moving and, although there will be movement within our frame, a large amount of the scene will usually be stationary.

There is no need to track any moving subjects because we are letting the movement happen in the frame. To make sure the time-lapse is sharp, focus once but effectively – focus before shooting commences, then lock the focusing system down so it does not focus automatically for each shot that is taken during the time-lapse. If the focusing system is left on during capture, it will end up focusing on objects at varying distances from the camera. If this happens, the elements in the lens will move around slightly as the focusing system drives the lens. Due

◀ Fireworks provide the perfect subject for time-lapse photography because there is plenty of colour and movement. Set up your camera on a tripod and make sure that you use slow shutter speeds to capture blur in the moving lights. Camera settings: 3" (three seconds), *f*/14, ISO 400.

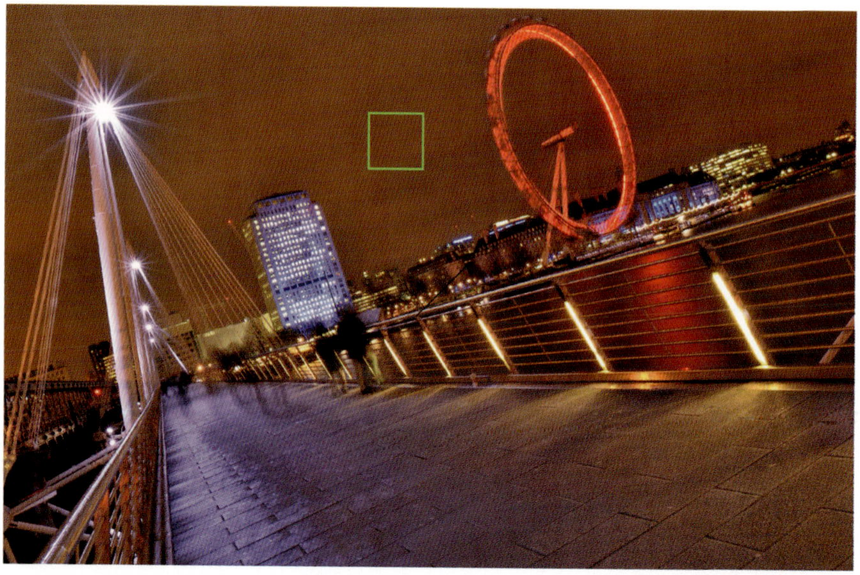

Although this image is in focus, it is being used to illustrate how not to focus. The single focus point represented by a green square is on an area with little detail and therefore the camera would struggle to acquire focus here.

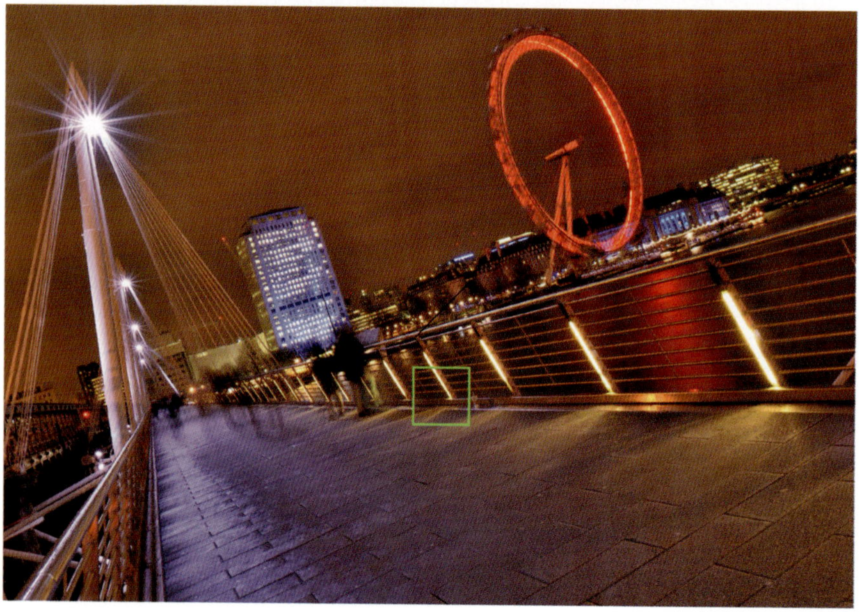

This image shows a much better approach with focusing. The green square is focusing on a section of the image with plenty of contrast and detail. This enables the focusing system to successfully achieve focus and help you maintain sharp imagery.

to the fast playback of the individual frames in a time-lapse, the final result will appear to vibrate.

To rectify this mistake could be laborious and require time spent using software. With the time this will take, you might as well go out and re-shoot the time-lapse video. The key is not to have the problem in the first place. We are now going to explore some great tips, tricks and approaches with focusing.

Pre-focusing your camera

Every time you set the camera up for time-lapse you will need to pre-focus. Follow these steps:

1. Focus the camera on the desired area in your image
2. Take a test shot to check sharpness
3. Lock the focusing system down so it does not work any more
4. Start the time-lapse

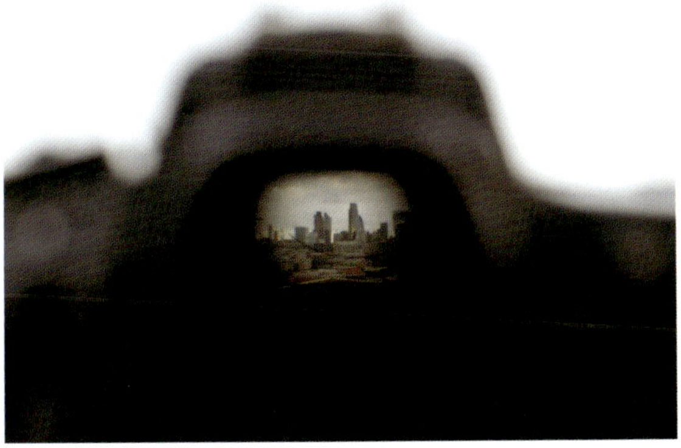

▲ Looking through your camera's viewfinder to focus for time-lapse photography can be a strain on your neck or back if the camera is lower than eye height. It is, however, a very fast and effective way to focus because of the speed of the focusing system.

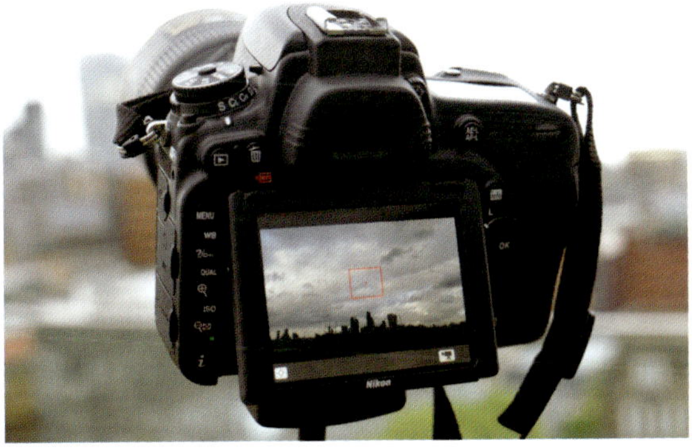

▲ Live-view focusing can be much more convenient to frame your image and focus with. Rather than looking through a small eye piece you see a big clear digital screen. This is much better in low light situations.

There are many different ways to pre-focus, which we will look at now. Read through all of the options but remember that you will probably only need to use one or two and choose the options that are the easiest and simplest for you personally.

Different ways to focus with your camera

With most DSLR cameras we are able to focus quickly and effectively in two ways. One is to look through the viewfinder to focus and the other is to use the camera in live view, using the back screen of the camera. These are actually two separate focusing systems and they both have their own advantages and disadvantages.

Viewfinder focusing

Focusing through the viewfinder is not always practical. After a whole day of bending down to look through the camera's viewfinder your back will start to hurt, which makes this way of focusing only practical if you are using a hand-held camera, or a tripod with the camera at head height. This focusing system is actually the quickest and best for tracking moving subjects, but this is irrelevant for time-lapse.

Live-view focusing

When using live-view focusing, we are able to use the back screen of the camera to view our subject and then focus. We get a live feed from the sensor when live-view is on and this makes it much easier and clearer when focusing, especially in low light situations and on a tripod. The live-view focusing is not as quick as the viewfinder system, but it is generally the most appropriate for time-lapse. On most cameras you should see a little square whilst in live-view. Put this square on the part of the subject that you want sharpest and focus. The square should change colour to confirm focus.

Auto/manual focus button

You can pre-focus for your time-lapse and then switch the button on your lens or camera to manual focus rather than auto. This is usually indicated with a simple switch with A/M. This is not the best way to shoot because you might move the camera by moving the switch and this could reframe your image. You may also forget to turn the switch back to auto focus for the next set-up. Although not ideal, this is a definite way of making sure the camera doesn't focus whilst the time-lapse is running.

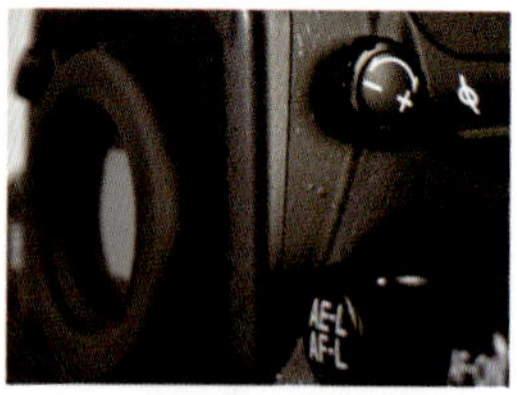

▲ The diopter (top right) enables you to adjust the focusing of the eye piece to adapt to your own eyesight. If you are focusing manually, this ensures your judgement is accurate.

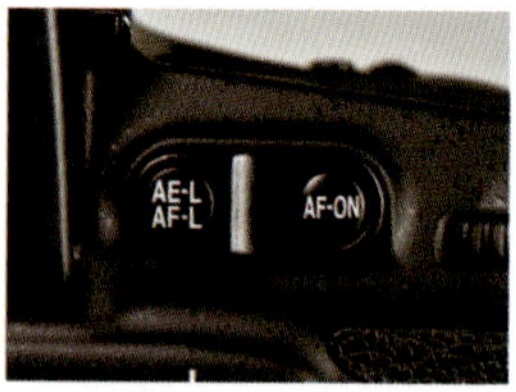

▲ Most DSLR cameras have a button to the right of the viewfinder on the back of the camera. One of these buttons will be used for back button focusing or can be programmed to do so. Your thumb would then be used to activate the focusing system.

Manual focusing

Make sure the camera's focusing system is turned off using the A/M button on the lens or camera before focusing. You can then look through the viewfinder or at the live-view on the back screen to view the scene. Rotate the focusing ring on your lens until the view looks sharpest and you are ready to shoot. At this point, you have already pre-focused because the AF system was turned off to begin with, so you can just start shooting. Be careful if you have a zoom lens, as you might rotate the zoom ring on the lens by accident rather than the focus ring. If you do this, make sure that you check the focus is still sharp, because zooming the lens can put the image out of focus.

Diopter

If you decide to use manual focusing whilst using the eyepiece, the diopter is especially important to know about. The camera's diopter can usually be found right next to the eye piece and can resemble a button or winder found on a watch. This switch will focus the eyepiece in the camera; it has no bearing on how sharp your image looks when shooting with auto-focus. If you are using the eyepiece to do manual focusing and it is not adjusted correctly to your eyesight, your judgement will be wrong because you will be unable to see whether the image is sharp or not before taking an image.

The best way to adjust the diopter to your own eyesight is to put the camera on a tripod and focus on something with plenty of detail that is not moving using the camera's auto focus system to focus. Look through the cameras eyepiece and adjust the diopter until the view looks as sharp as possible to you. Remember, this will now be set to your specifications and if you give the camera to someone else, their eyesight could differ and therefore they might think the camera is not focusing.

Back button focusing

This is a technique that is often talked about, but it is not referred to as 'back button focusing' in the manual so most people struggle to find out what it is. If you set up your camera to focus with your back button only, the front button will no longer focus, but will still take pictures as it did before. So if you want to pre-focus, hold the back button down with your thumb and once the scene is sharp, release the button.

When using the interval timer it triggers the button that you take the images with when you take a picture normally. This means that you can pre-focus the camera and then start the interval timer for the time-lapse capture and it will not focus during capture. This is fantastic for time-lapse and landscape photography and often changes the way many photographers work. It is also very popular for wildlife and sports photography.

Don't focus and then zoom

If you are using a zoom lens it is always best to zoom, compose your image and then focus. Never focus and then zoom in or out before capture. This is important because when you zoom the lens, the pieces of glass inside move around and can put the image out of focus. The extent of re-focusing required does depend on what lens you are using, however, and on how far you zoom it. Don't let this catch you out; remember to zoom then focus.

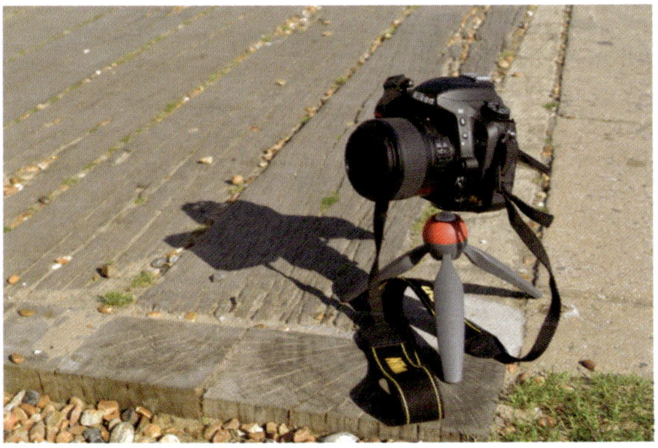

▲ Always be careful of placing your tripod on uneven surfaces. Always check that the camera is not being moved by anyone walking past or loose bits of stone, for example.

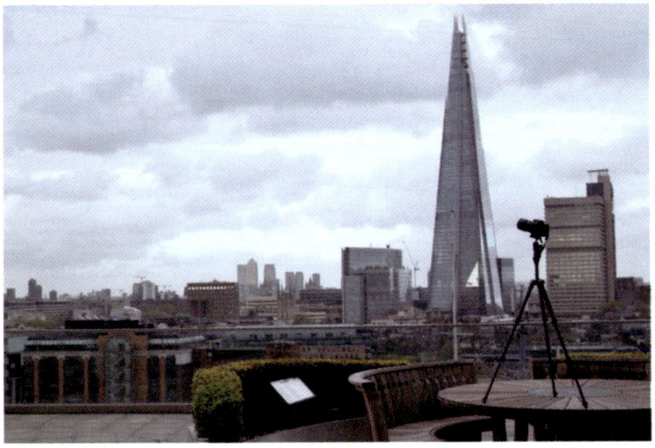

▲ If you want a different point of view of your subject that your tripod cannot provide – if it is too short, for example – look around and improvise. In this example a safety fence was in view of the camera, so additional height was required to capture the time-lapse. A nearby table gave the perfect solution to the problem by providing the height needed.

Setting up your tripod

This part of the process is a means to an end and is not the most glamorous part either, but care and consideration has to be taken. When the tripod is opened up to be used, make sure all adjustments are tight before the camera is mounted and double check the camera is attached to the tripod securely before taking your hands away from it.

Check the ground that the tripod is to be placed upon. If you are setting up on floorboards you may step on a board that a leg of the tripod is resting on and the camera might move during the time-lapse. This can also happen on tiles and soft ground such as sand, mud or loose rocks. You might even need to stand away from the tripod whilst the time-lapse is being captured.

THE SIX STEPS OF TIME-LAPSE

When you are setting up your time-lapse it is constructive if a process is followed; this way you can ensure that nothing important is forgotten at the time of shooting. It is very easy to overlook something when on location; we find ourselves in unfamiliar surroundings and we can be distracted by what is around us. Below is a process that you might find useful. You can always change it and make it your own, but it's a good starting point.

1. Light: Look at the amount of light and balance up the exposure triangle to get the desired exposure. Look at the colour of the light and make white balance changes.
2. Purpose: Think again about what your goal is. What are you trying to communicate and how can you achieve it effectively?
3. Frame: Make sure you look at all four corners of the frame. Check that you have composed the image in the same aspect ratio that you are using for delivery.
4. Movement: In terms of the movement in the frame that you have chosen, look at how it is paced and what interval will suit the general speed. Do you want to show time moving quickly or slowly?
5. Focus: Always focus after you have finished composing the image. It is never a good idea to focus and then move the camera because you could lose sharpness. Once you have focused, make sure that the camera will not be focusing for the duration of the time-lapse capture.
6. Start: Press start, sit back, and have a mojito!

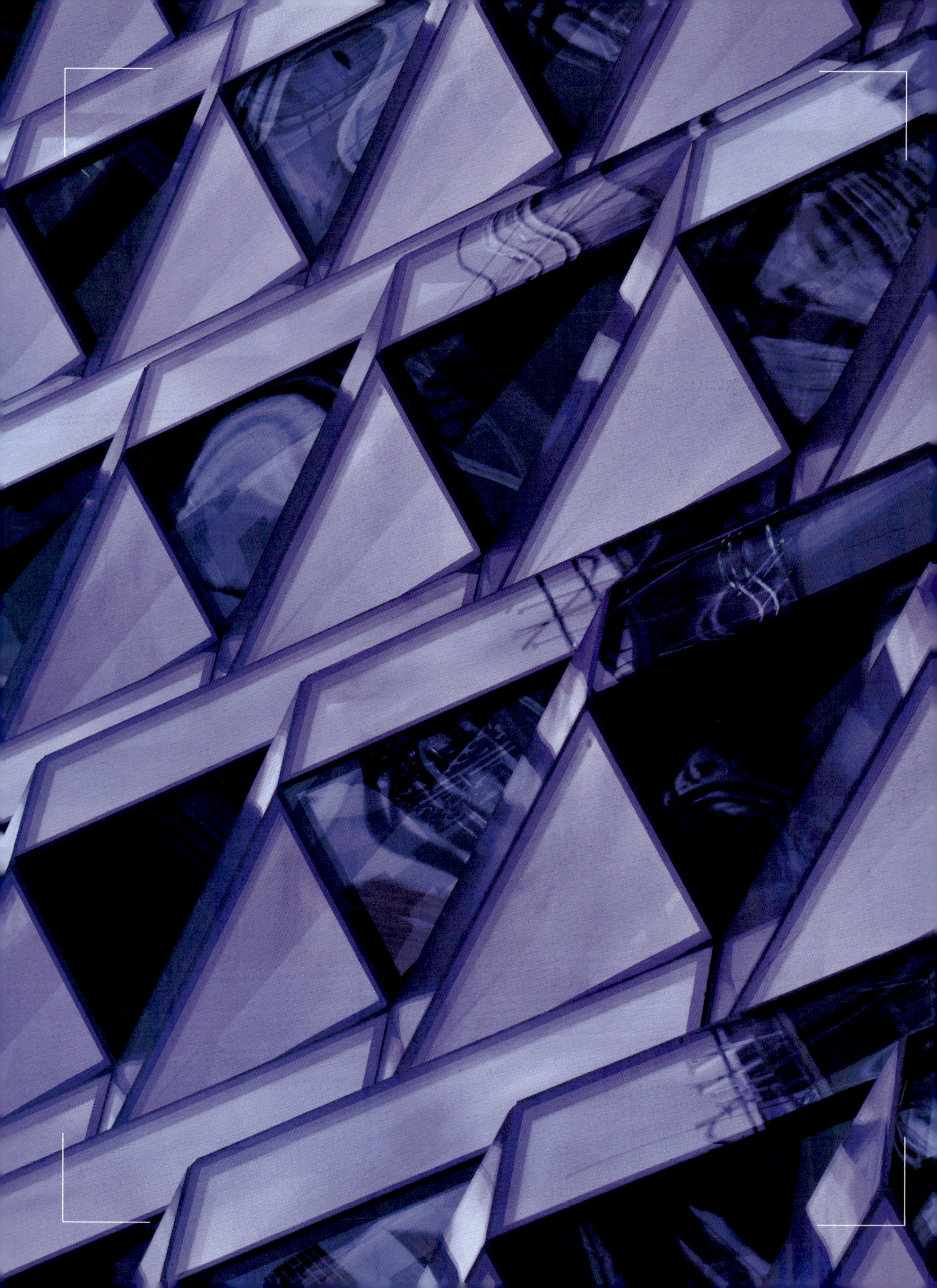

Chapter 6

Colour and composition

In this section we will explore how to control the aesthetics of time-lapse videos. Colour and composition are areas that enable you to create an individual look or style, but more importantly to experiment. We will look at how to manage the colour of light sources that you might be using and also how to approach composition, with some great ideas to apply when shooting.

VISUALIZING YOUR IMAGE

When you are looking around preparing to shoot, it helps to be able to visualize your time-lapse video before it is captured. This is something that will come naturally with time. To visualize your imagery you look first at light to assess the lighting situation and then imagine how you would like to frame your subject with the lens that you have. Having this foresight will help you decide if what you are doing will make the final cut; will it be good enough to show off? This process will help you produce better work, making the editing process much less time consuming. You will eventually get to a stage were you could be capturing 20 percent of what you were producing before, but you have much better content.

This will also help with technical aspects such as battery life and card storage; also, when you look back at your work you will see how much progress you have made with your photography. This chapter explores aspects that will help you visualize your image in an informed manner.

Colour

White balance

It is impossible to talk about the colour of light without discussing the importance of 'white balance', which is essentially the colour of light. In image-making we can control the overall colour cast, to adjust for different colours of light, using the white balance settings.

To find an example you don't have to look far. At home you may have lights in the kitchen or living room that are orange, or white. If you hold a white piece of paper under the light source you can see the colour of the light it produces; this is the white balance.

Most people are blissfully unaware of this because our eyes do a very good job of adapting to different lighting situations. When using an advanced camera, we need to train our eyes to see the white balance so that we can evaluate our surroundings and control the colour of the light we are working with, if necessary.

Camera options for white balance

On the next page is a list of the white balance options that are most common in advanced digital cameras. Each option is designed to balance different lighting situations, such as sunny or cloudy, for example. On these cameras you can change settings in the menu, but some newer models enable you to

◀ Different approaches with colour can easily enhance your imagery. These glass windows are transformed by the result of experimenting with colour settings. Camera settings: 1/800s, *f*/8, ISO 400.

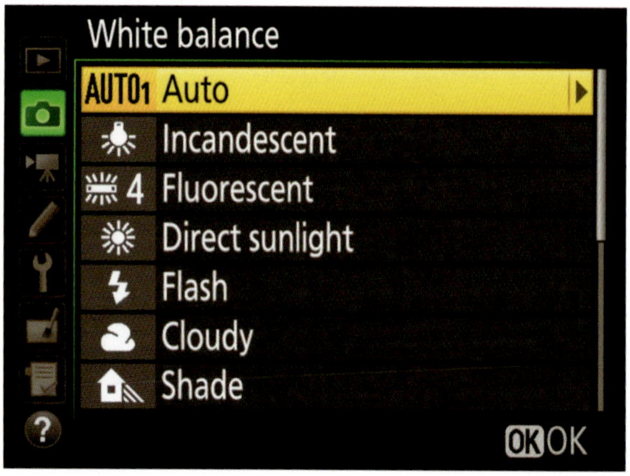

▲ The white balance settings in your camera menu should look something like this. Some devices have these assigned to a shortcut button as well.

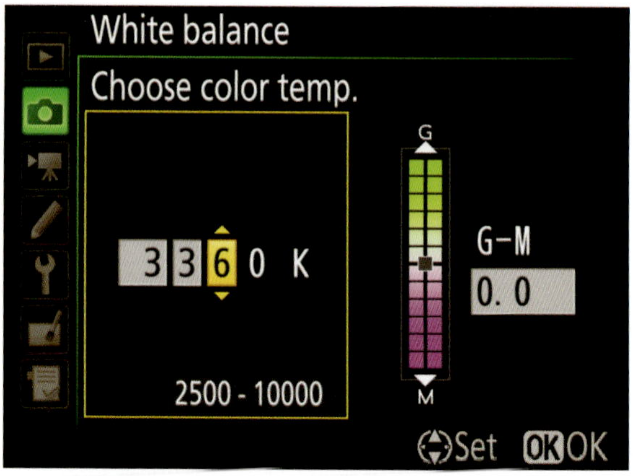

▲ Advanced control of white balance is available in most DSLR cameras. Kelvin changes your white balance settings with much smaller increments between colour changes. All other settings, such as incandescent or flash, will have a Kelvin rating or value.

change between settings whilst in live view, enabling you to see the colour of the image before you take the picture.

- Auto
- Incandescent
- Fluorescent
- Direct sunlight
- Shade
- Cloudy
- Flash
- Kelvin
- Preset white balance

Most of these options are self-explanatory in respect of the lighting situations they are meant for; however, there are a couple at the bottom of the list that are not so obvious. Firstly 'Kelvin': the Kelvin Scale is a numbering system that measures colour temperature, and you will find a long list of values to choose from, such as 3000K (the K stands for Kelvin). These values cover every white balance option available and are useful in practical terms: if you change between the Kelvin numbers click by click you can fine tune the white balance settings in a way that cannot be done with other options, such as 'cloudy' and 'shade'.

'Preset white balance' is a mode that enables the

USING A REFERENCE FOR WHITE BALANCE

Find any light source, man-made or natural, such as a lamp or window. Hold a white piece of paper near the light and observe what colour the paper goes. It could be orange, blue or green, amongst others. Go into the camera's menu, locate the white balance settings and take a set of pictures of the white reference, each with a different white balance setting.

Keep the white piece of paper next to the light source because this is our reference point in the image. When reviewing the final set of images you will see that the piece of paper changes colour gradually between each shot. The image where the paper looks whitest is the correct colour balance for that light source. You might prefer a warmer look, however; essentially it is up to you how your imagery looks and controlling white balance will give you more creative flexibility.

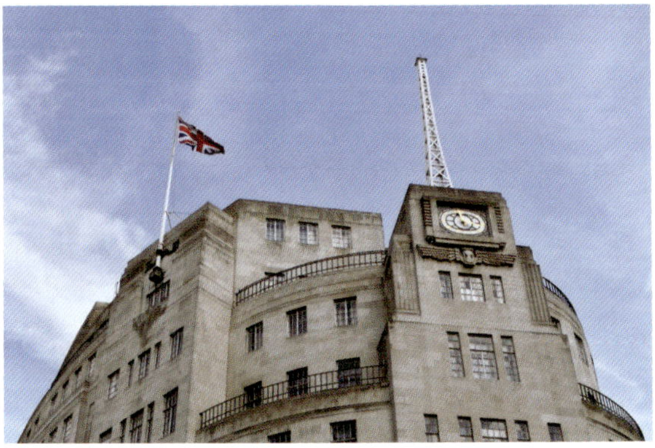

▲ In most situations auto white balance will give you a neutral image. Usually auto will represent the scene as it looks in reality.

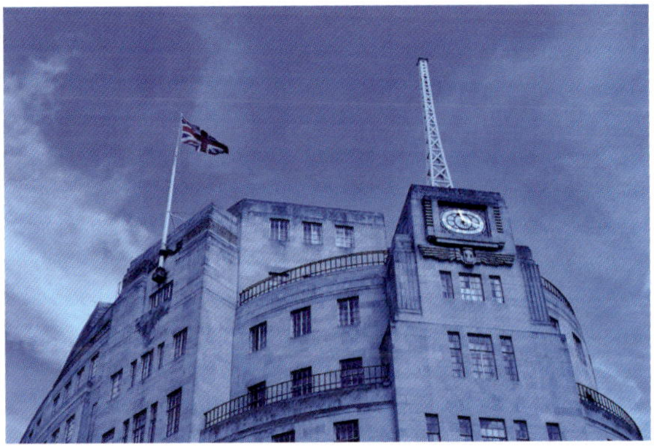

▲ This frame shows what incandescent white balance will do to daylight. The wrong setting is often used to get interesting colours for creative reasons.

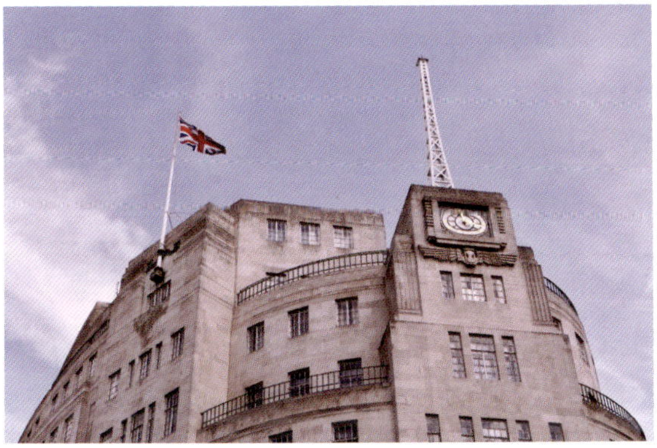

▲ A fluorescent white balance produces strange colours when used with daylight but will give a white neutral light with fluorescent lighting.

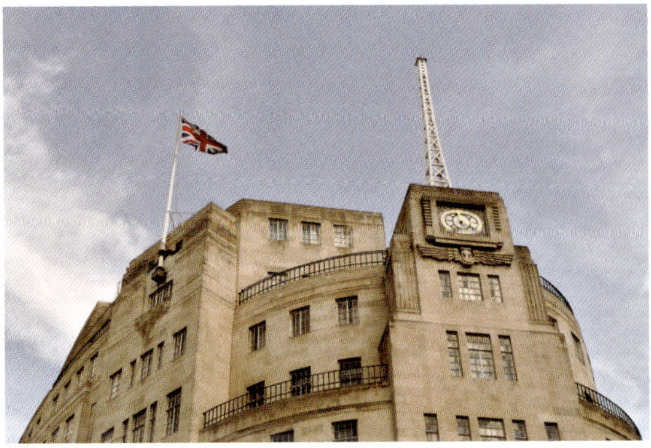

▲ Shady white balance is often used in direct sunlight because it makes the image slightly more orange in colour, which changes the feel of the image. This picture looks much warmer than when the camera is set to auto.

camera to choose a white balance that will neutralize the colour of any given light source. Using a white reference point in your subject, you can take a reading and let the camera get the correct white balance for you. Look in the manual of your camera for how to set this up because this is a quick and easy way to achieve the correct balance.

The correct white balance

When we want to achieve the correct white balance, it means that we are taking the colour of the light source and neutralizing it with the camera's settings. An example of this is the colour you get from office lighting. Sometimes this can be blue or orange, and to correct it we would change the white balance

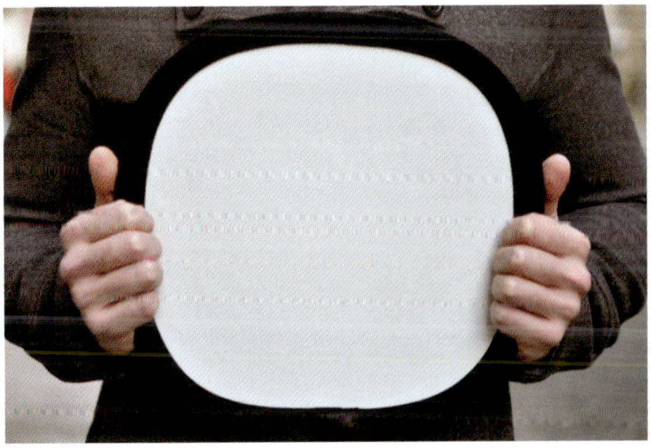

▲ A white balance decision can be easier to make during capture and/or after shooting if you have a white reference to check the white balance against. This kind of white reference can be bought in shops or online, but equally a white piece of paper can be used. Be careful though, as paper can be off-white and this will affect the reading from the reference point.

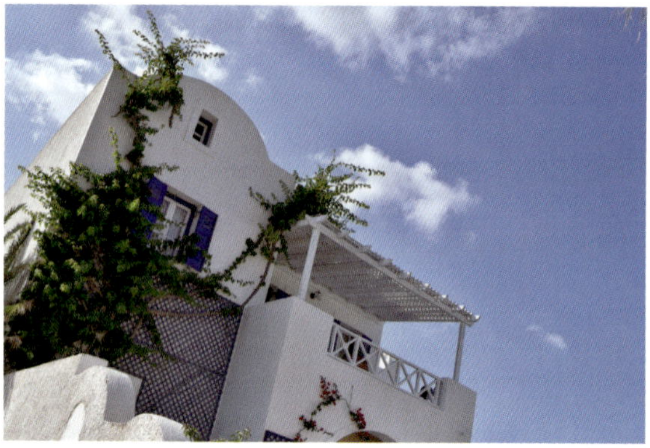

▲ The 'correct' white balance can look very stark and flat sometimes, but it can help to represent colours in a realistic manner.

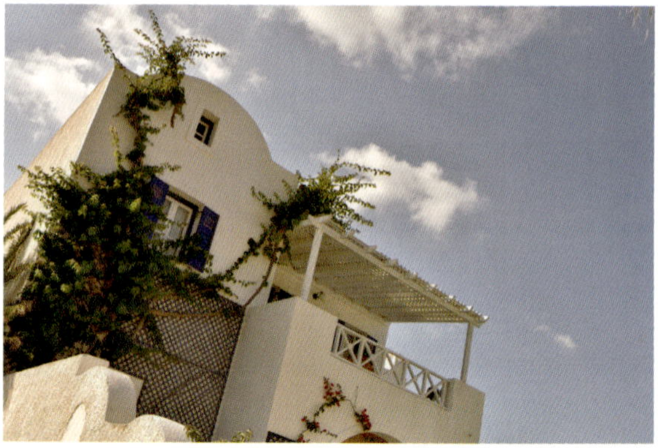

▲ A creative choice of white balance can often be more aesthetically pleasing for the viewer.

setting in the camera to make it look like a white light source in the imagery. It can be useful to have a white reference, such as a white piece of paper – then you can change the settings until the paper goes white. However, if we correct the colour of a light source it can look flat and clinical, so getting the 'correct' white balance sometimes kills the mood of the image.

Remember, you can only adjust white balance for one light source at a time. Therefore it can be very tricky to balance an image when many different light sources are present. On most modern cameras the auto setting for white balance will get a very good overall look in this type of situation and if you need to change the colour afterwards it is easy to do so if shot using the RAW file option. It can be difficult to correct colour after shooting with JPEG files as they are limiting from an editing perspective.

With respect to time-lapse it is best to keep the white balance on a fixed setting for the duration of capture. Sometimes if the camera is on auto white balance during capture, it can change the colour between images dramatically, which can detract from the final result. Do experiment with settings, however, as the effect you achieve does depend on how the light is changing and the subject matter. Different settings will work well for different subject matters in order to get varying moods with the use of colour.

Creative use of white balance

It can also be very rewarding to approach white balance creatively and just choose the setting that gives you images you like the look of. This approach is often used with film-making as well as photography. You can create a blue white balance, which is technically incorrect, but the image will communicate with colour and create a cold feeling. If you want to convey a welcoming or comforting feeling with your imagery you could choose a white balance setting that would make the scene look orange, thus achieving a warm white balance.

The creative use of colour will give your imagery visual diversity and you might even find yourself relying less on software; getting it right in camera saves time when editing. Don't feel that you have to follow any rules with white balance: just choose the look that you think works best with your situation.

The colour of natural light

The colour of natural light can change depending on time and location. If we have direct sunlight during the day we usually have a neutral or white colour. In the morning and evening, however, the light can give us a huge palette of colours, depending on the weather: orange, red, and even purple; it is very unpredictable.

Many photographers talk about the 'golden hours'; these are when the sun rises and also when

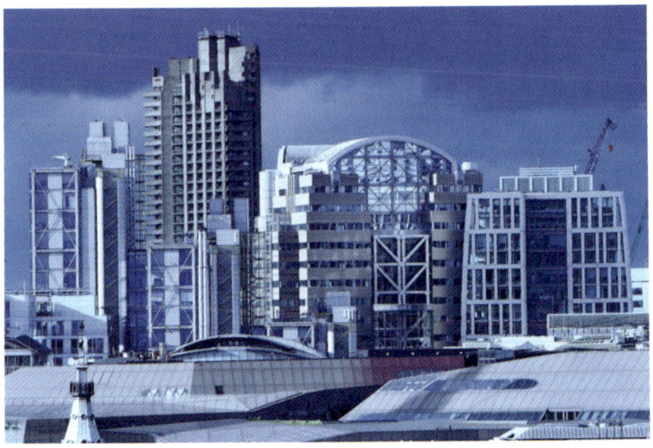

▲ A really blue white balance has been chosen to make the image feel cold. This is not the correct setting but creatively, very interesting.

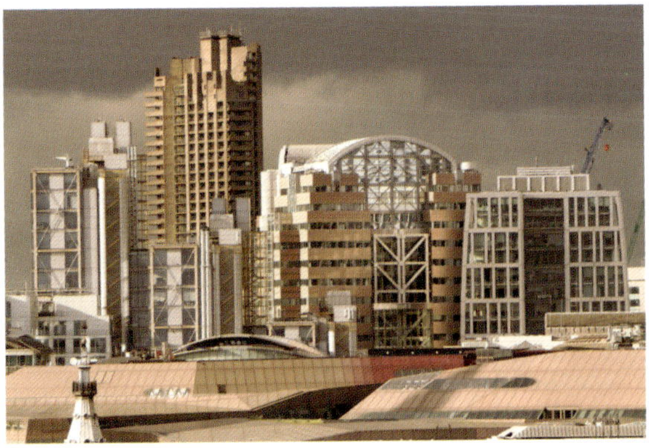

▲ Even though this image was taken in the middle of the day when the light had little colour, it looks as though it was taken at sunset because of the creative use of white balance.

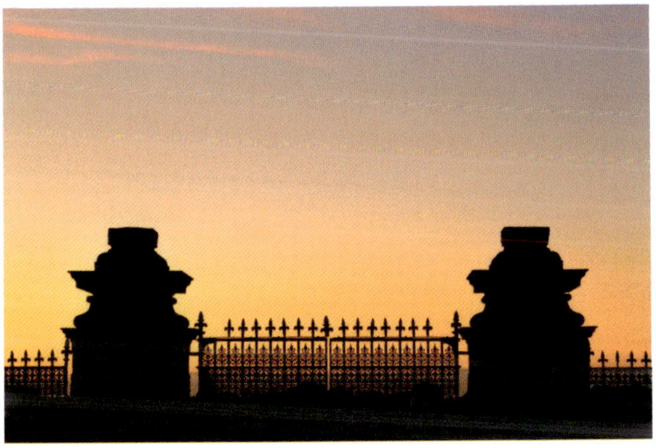

▲ The 'golden hour' is a time of day when the sun is rising or going down and is a fantastic time of day for time-lapse photography. Camera settings: 1/640s, *f*/6.3, ISO 5000.

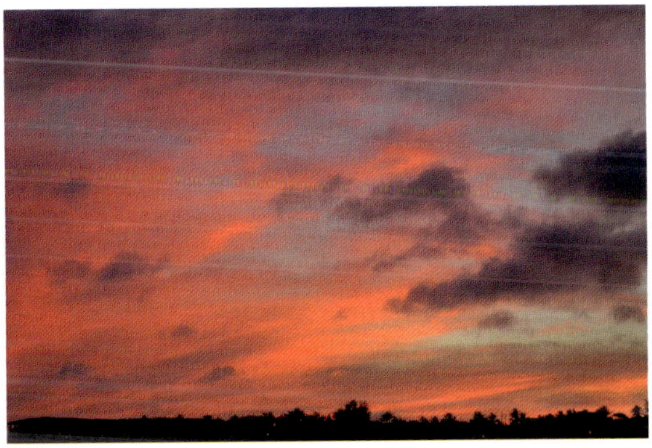

▲ When clouds are present during the golden hour it helps to achieve a range of different colours and shapes that are perfect for a time-lapse. This, paired with the movement the clouds provide, opens up some exciting opportunities. Camera settings: 1/60s, *f*/5.3, ISO 800.

it sets. Due to the sun being so low, the direction of the light is quite different from what we get during the main part of the day, therefore resulting in long, dramatic shadows. It is called the golden hour because we usually get warm golden coloured light to work with. We have to remember, however, that this is all very weather-dependent, with some days looking flat and underwhelming and others looking dramatic and inspiring.

The colour of man-made light

Man-made light can change depending on the type of technology used to create it. Some bulbs can be very orange, blue or green, for example. When image-making in a city or town there are always lots of different light sources that will have different colour characteristics. It is best not to attempt to get the correct white balance in this situation because you can only balance for one light source at time. Instead choose a white balance setting that simply gives you the overall balance you prefer. Experiment with white balance settings and take creative control over the colour of your imagery.

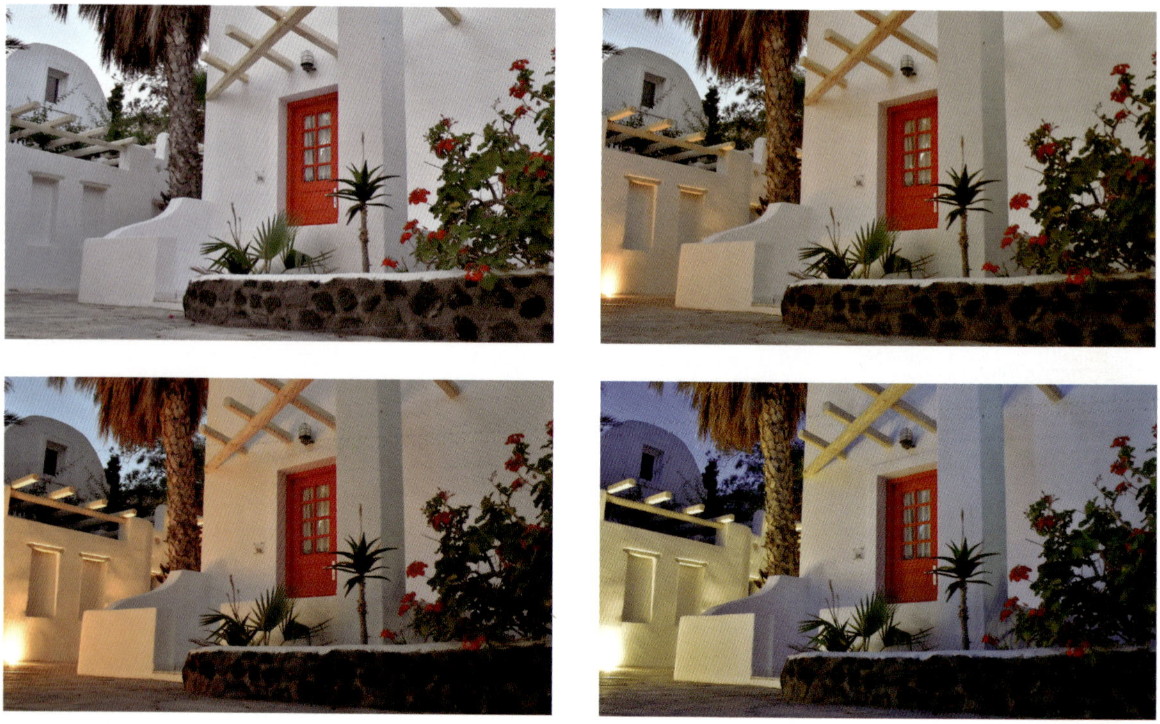

▲ This time-lapse shows how the colour of man-made and natural light can change during sunset. With this example the camera was set to auto white balance, so it did change over time and looks very natural. Experiment with a fixed or an auto white balance setting with your time-lapse photography when the colour is changing to see what you can achieve creatively. Camera settings: 1/100s, *f*/11, ISO 1400.

Other colour controls in your camera

There are powerful settings in your camera's menu, which change how the colour and contrast of your images look. Manufacturers call them 'picture controls' or 'picture modes' amongst other names. These settings are an easy way for the user to access settings like contrast, brightness, saturation and hue. Ultimately these modes make up the look of the picture or video that you are capturing. On many cameras you can go into these modes and customize them so that you can get what you want out of the camera if the stock settings don't offer the look you are trying to achieve. Don't feel tied down to your camera's settings; customize them and make your own.

Often if people are shooting video they will go for a flat profile with low contrast and saturation because this makes it easier to play around with the files on editing software after shooting. There are some considerations with file formats that might influence your decision in what you choose. If you are shooting RAW photographs then these colour modes can be changed afterwards. If you are shooting JPEG photographs, time-lapse videos in camera or regular video however, the colour modes cannot be as easily changed after capture.

COMPOSITION

When we hold the camera up to our eye we essentially have a frame to place around the world in front of us. This frame gives us a tremendous amount of storytelling power; by controlling where we place the frame in a scene we can change how the story

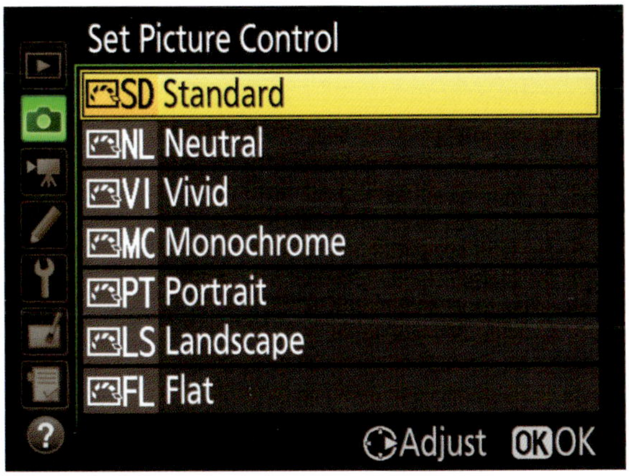

▲ Most cameras enable you to have some control over the colour modes.

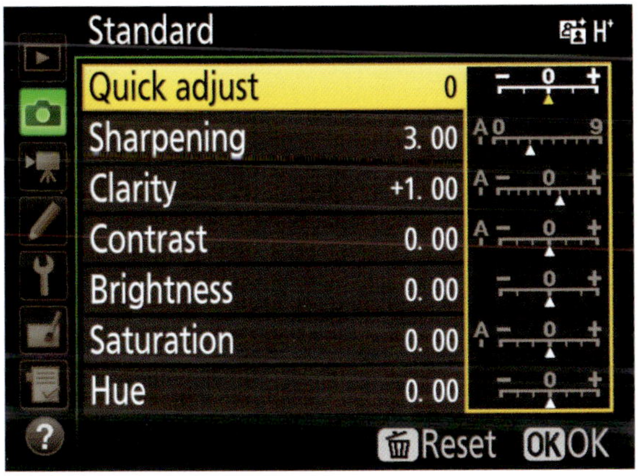

▲ When you have the choice of colour modes you tend to have more advanced control, as shown in the example image. By using these menus you are able to customize the colour and look of your images.

is told through our image. Once you have learned how to use your frame compositionally, your image-making takes a huge leap forward. When taking a still photograph the first thing to consider is whether to choose portrait or landscape orientation. The shape that you use to surround the subject could dictate the compositional tool or tools that can be applied.

With time-lapse or video, however, you will always be shooting landscape format because the delivery is always to the orientation of video. Try to resist the temptation to move the camera into

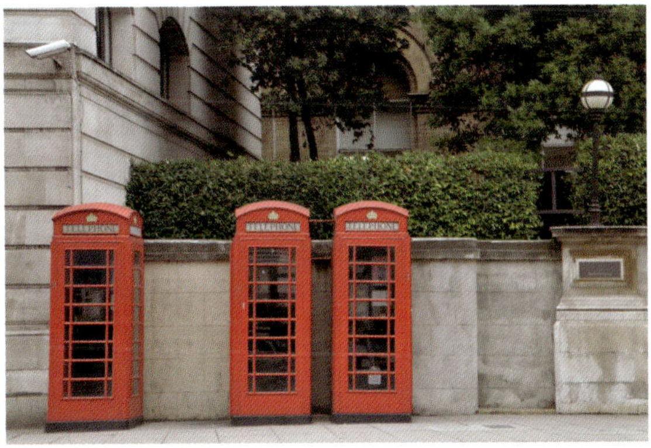

▲ This image has very low contrast and saturation and therefore looks very flat and muted. Camera settings: 1/60s, ƒ/8, ISO 100.

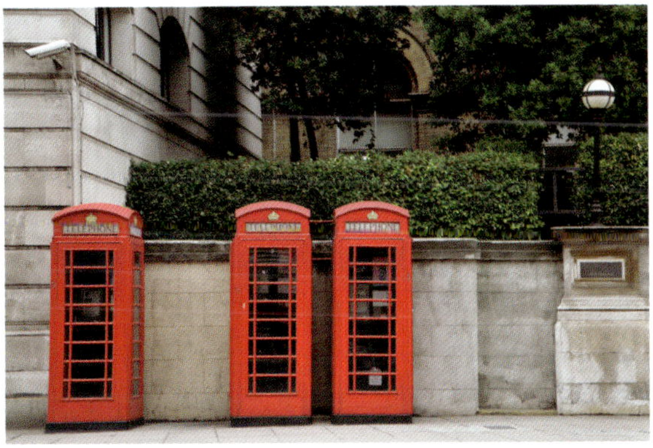

▲ This image has high contrast and saturation settings. The reds in the phone boxes stand out really vividly because of the saturated colour.

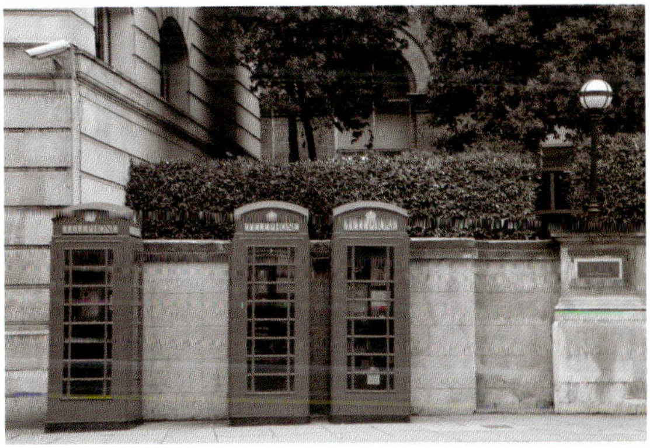

▲ The use of monochrome is particularly interesting.

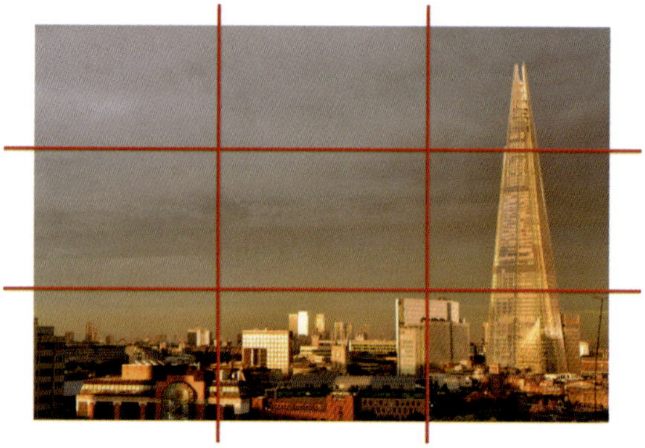

▲ The rule of thirds is shown here with the grid over the top of the image. You can choose to apply this any way you wish or not at all. It is a popular rule for composition and, even if you were previously unaware of it, you might find that you are using it already.

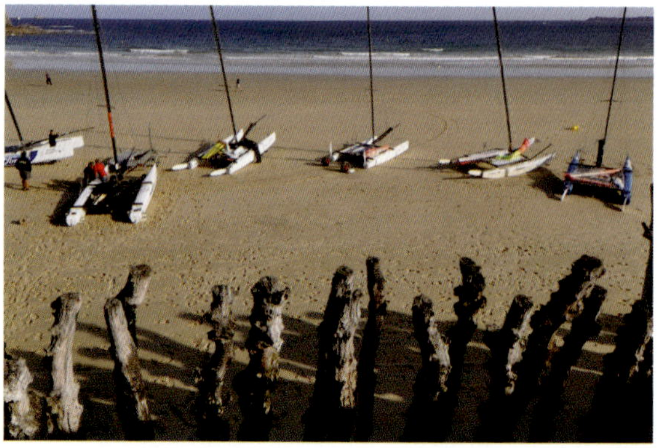

▲ The horizon at the top of this image frames the scene. In this time-lapse video the shadows creep across the beach as the sun moves, creating a strong visual. Camera settings: 1/400s, ƒ/10, ISO 200.

portrait when shooting time-lapse as the frame will simply be the wrong way up for the delivery format. The one exception is if you are using the interval timer to trigger the camera and you will only be using still photographs from the capture. The size of the frame on your subject can be controlled by zooming the lens in and out or walking forwards and backwards. This can also change how you compose the image.

Your box of compositional tools

Every photographer needs a metaphorical box of compositional tools – one that is full of ideas, which we will explore. Let's compare a photographer to a plumber: a plumber will go to different jobs every day and each time a different set of tools will be used to solve problems and repair something. As a time-lapse photographer, treat every shoot as a set of problems or something that you need to fix.

Each and every time you arrive at location, look at problems that you could potentially have. By reaching into your toolbox full of compositional ideas, you will be able to solve problems and fix the issues in order to create a visually exciting image. Like the plumber, every job is different and therefore the tools required to solve any problems are as well.

Rule of thirds

This basic but effective compositional tool is one of the best known and is a perfect place to start with composition. To use this rule, imagine a grid over your subject which is divided up in to thirds horizontally and vertically. You then move any point of interest to fit into the grid in some way. If you ever find yourself unsure of how to frame or balance up the picture, rule of thirds is a safe bet to get a well balanced composition. Just because this is called a rule, please don't feel that you have to follow it as such. It is only one compositional tool among many.

Horizon at the top

Putting the horizon right at the top of the image will accentuate the foreground and will make for an interesting composition, if the subject matter permits. This can actually go against the rule of thirds, but don't hesitate to break any rules if it enhances the image. If your foreground is more interesting than the background, this technique will help enhance the interest in the frame and clearly lead the viewer's eye to the foreground.

Horizon to the bottom

Moving your horizon to the bottom of the frame is

When the horizon is at the bottom it is possible to illustrate epic landscape scenes, especially when there is interest in the sky. Camera settings: 1/250s, ƒ/8, ISO 100.

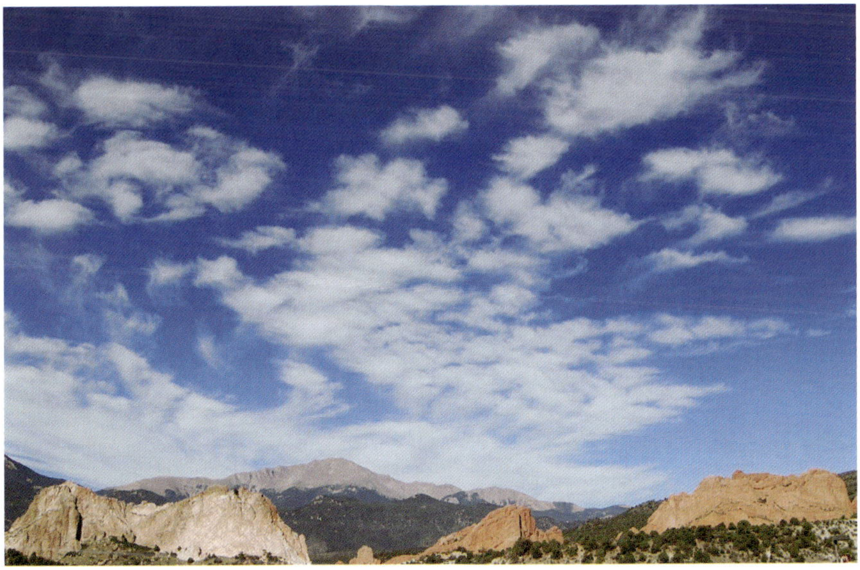

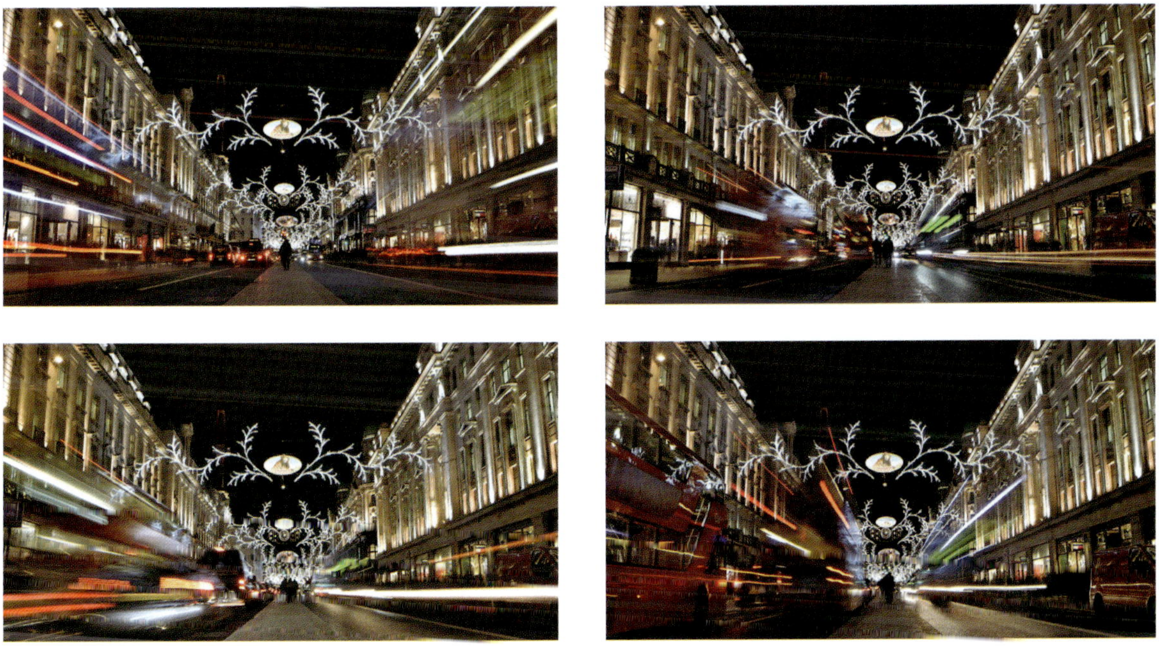

This sequence of images is taken from a time-lapse video that uses leading lines as the main compositional tool. The shutter speed is set to three seconds so that the traffic has motion blur. Camera settings: 3s, ƒ/9, ISO 100

a great idea, especially if your foreground is quite uninspiring but the sky is breathtaking. Be careful with this approach though, as it's easy to accidentally cut the ground out completely; this would result in your image having no sense of context or scale to the sky. Always keep a small amount of foreground, even if it is a sliver.

Leading lines

Leading lines do exactly what they say on the tin: they are lines that lead you into an image. The great thing here is that lines can be found anywhere, in fact they are probably in a large number of your

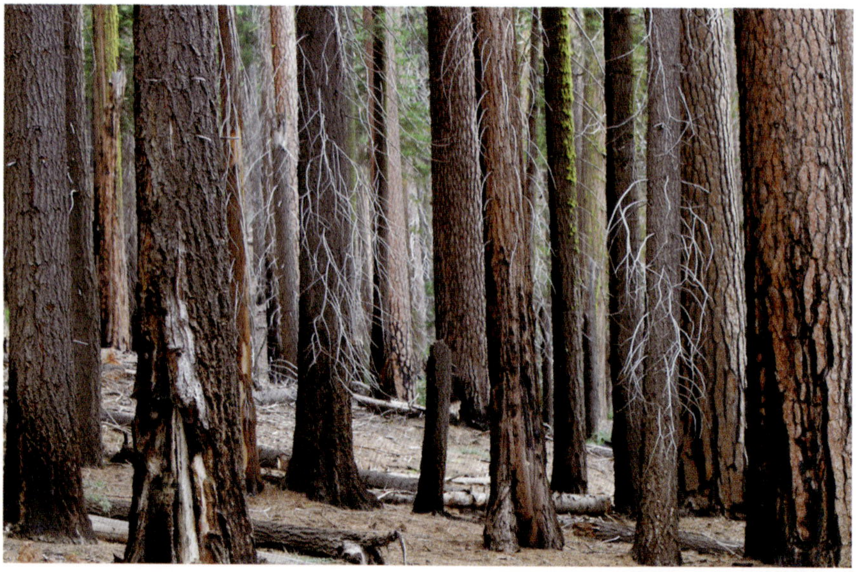

Strong verticals can be quite a statement in photography. Look for lines and shapes before detail. Camera settings: 1/125s, ƒ/4.5, ISO 400.

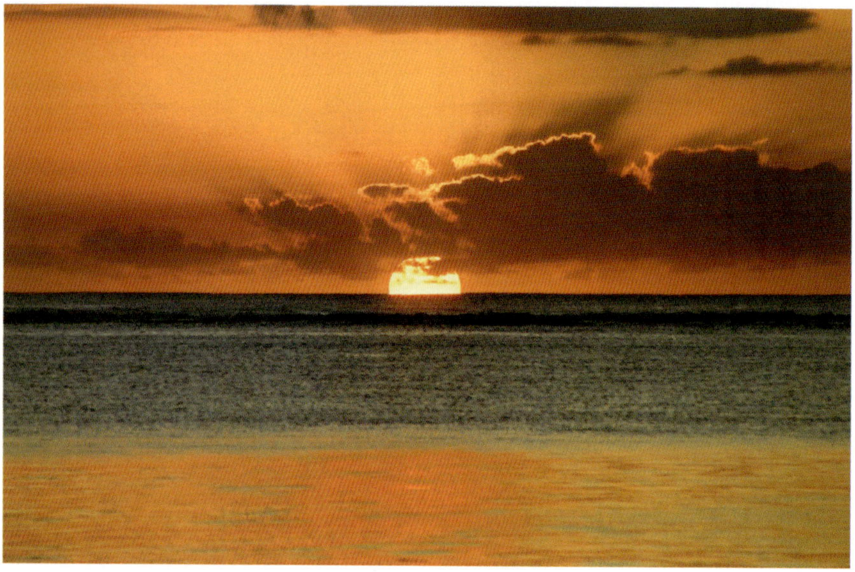

Horizontals are used a lot with landscape and time-lapse photography. The water in the lower half of this frame shows at least four lines that help make the image striking. Camera settings: 1/60s, ƒ/8, ISO 800.

images already. This compositional tool will enable you to create a bold and striking image in most cases. If you want the viewer to look at a particular place within the image then you may be able to use leading lines to lead the eye to a certain point. The lines themselves can actually be the main feature and, more often than not, will help create a stunning image.

Verticals and horizontals

A strong compositional line in an image can go in any direction so don't be shy to use them. Move the camera around like a steering wheel on a car to make them go in different directions. A vertical or horizontal line can be placed anywhere in your image. Most of us probably use horizontals anyway with time-lapse or landscape photography, but explore verticals too, as they can help to break up a busy image and provide compositional structure.

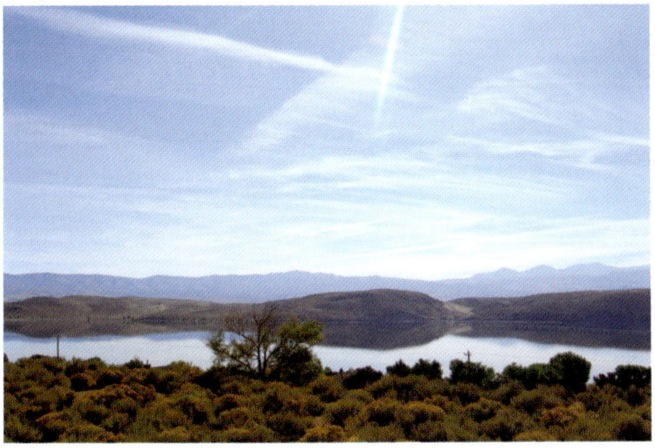

▲ In this image we have different layers, which are divided by the horizontal lines. Always remember clouds and water tend to work well for time-lapse. Camera settings: 1/320s, ƒ/9, ISO 100.

Diagonals

The use of diagonal lines is a bit of a statement in an image and can be a fantastic compositional tool. You could use existing diagonal lines or you could tilt the camera to achieve them. If you choose to tilt the camera then remember all objects and other lines within the image will move. Leading the diagonal line into the corners of your image can make for a striking picture where otherwise there might not have been.

Reflections

Always keep an eye out for reflections that you can use within your time-lapse photography. Movement will always work well in your videos, but reflection of movement is a really exciting area to explore. Look at glass and metal surfaces; see what happens when different light reflects and refracts. A surface that is not perfectly flat will bend the light and make subject matter look distorted, and this can have an interesting visual effect.

Shapes

An invaluable way to see the world in order to compose your images is to look for the shapes that you have to work with. Consider shapes before you see any other detail and think about how these shapes might fit together. You may see rectangles, squares,

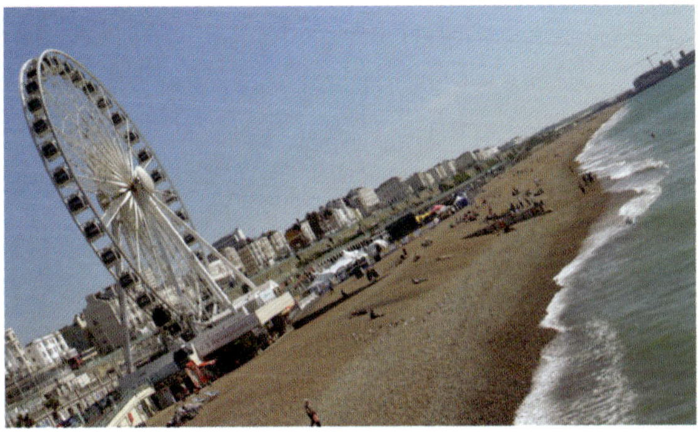

▲ Diagonal lines are a statement in many cases. It is popular to have diagonals going from corner to corner in the image. This example is from a time-lapse video – it works very well because of the amount of movement in the frame.

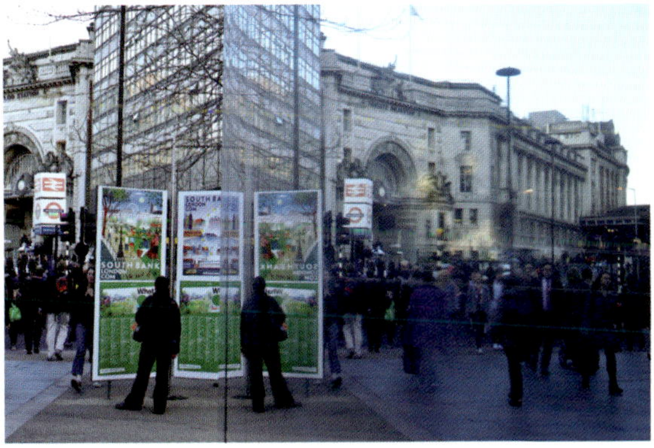

▲ When using reflections in your imagery, try experimenting with the type of reflective surface you use. Different surfaces reflect light in various ways. Camera settings: 1/320s, ƒ/7.1, ISO 1100.

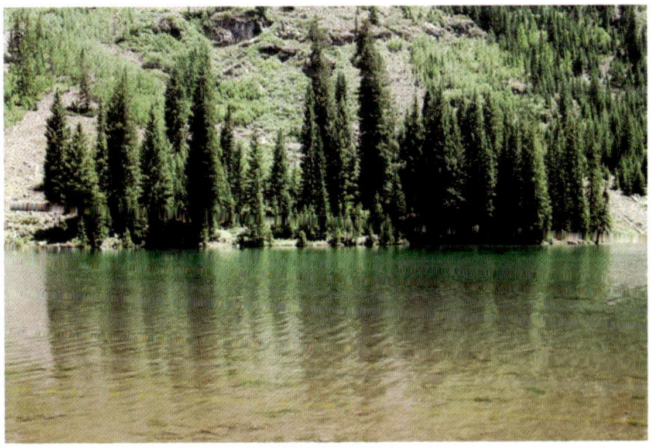

▲ Reflections in water always work well. The texture of the water will change and therefore give diversity in how reflections appear. Camera settings 1/60s, ƒ/3.5, ISO 800.

FINDING SHAPES IN YOUR IMAGES

Print some of your favourite images you have taken on A4 paper with your home printer. The quality of the prints does not have to be high so don't worry about using photographic paper or even printing in colour. Take a thick permanent marker pen and draw along all of the strong lines and shapes on your images. This makes you look at your imagery in a different way and this simple exercise could help to advance your compositional skills quickly.

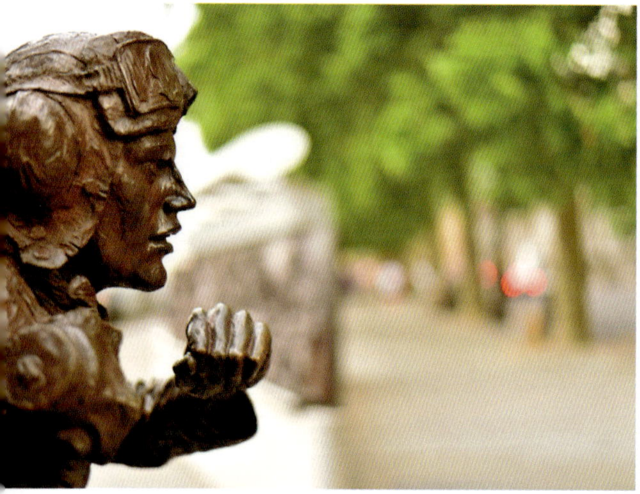

▲ Depth of field can be used to simplify a scene. Here the background has been put out of focus, making it less cluttered. Camera settings: 1/400s, *f*/1.8, ISO 400.

triangles or circles. Try this exercise to help you see shapes: squint your eyes so that definition will be reduced, but you see the outlines of shapes more easily. This will help you to compose your images based on the shapes within the frame.

Simplify

When you simplify an image you communicate to the viewer the subject matter simply and directly. One way to simplify is to fill the frame with your subject. To do this you can zoom in further with a zoom lens or move closer to the subject. In this way you get rid of the background which could otherwise detract from the subject matter you are trying to portray.

Another way to simplify the image is to use a shallow depth of field and put the background out of focus altogether. Use the smallest aperture value available; settings such as *f*/2.8, *f*/1.8, or *f*/4 will do this easily if the subject is close to the camera. If part of the image is out of focus then the sharp section will be the obvious point of focus, making the image easy to read for the viewer. Simplicity can also be achieved by moving a subject until it is in front of a plain background.

Negative space

This compositional tool is a powerful way of grabbing the viewer's eye and is also very contemporary. Negative space is essentially an area with no notable detail or points of interest. This tool can be used to frame an image and to divert the viewer's eye to an area that you want them to take note of. The negative space can also be the feature in itself and help to communicate a clear message in the frame.

Centralizing

This idea is very simple and just requires your main subject to be directly in the middle of the frame. Centralizing the dominant subject is a big statement so choose the subject well. If you choose this option remember to move yourself around and see how the background and foreground can complement each other. Sometimes moving a few meters can completely transform the image, so walk around and see where the best shooting angle will be.

Scale

Photographers and film-makers have played with scale in their imagery for many years. We have a great deal of power as image-makers to accentuate size and scale to make the image 'feel' a certain

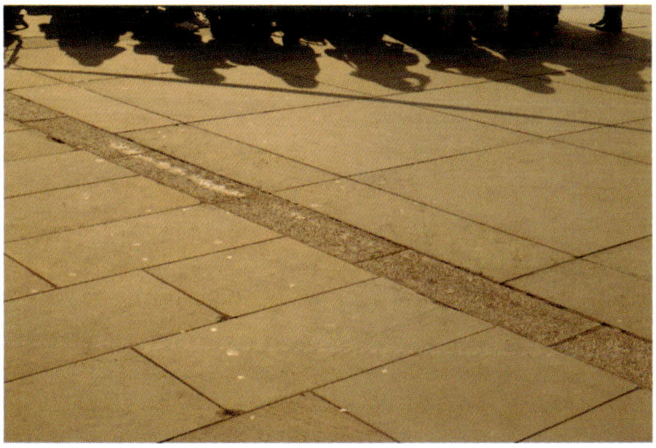

▲ Negative space is where there is a section of the image that is effectively featureless. This is quite contemporary in style and well worth experimenting with. Camera settings: 1/60s, ƒ/11, ISO 200.

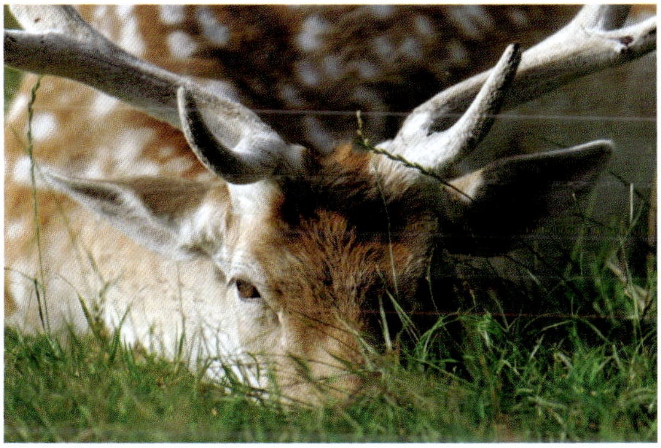

▲ This image is strong because of the central placement of the face of the animal. If you put your subject in the middle of the frame this is called centralising and can make your frame bold and instant for the viewer. Camera settings: 1/800s, ƒ/4, ISO 200.

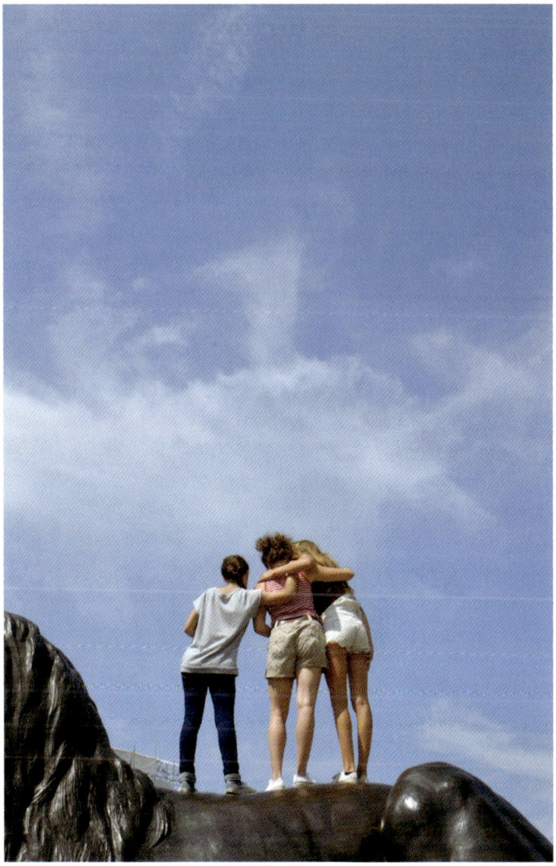

▲ By using a large area of sky the people in the image are being dwarfed by the enormity of it. This then plays on the idea of scale. Camera settings: 1/60s, ƒ/16, ISO 200.

way. Why not challenge the eye and make the viewer question what they are seeing? Scale can be played with by using distance, different lenses and shooting angles.

Creating depth

To create a sense of depth in your imagery, use the distance between objects to help keep a three-dimensional look within a landscape scene. If you find a clear foreground and background, you can move yourself around; play with focal length and depth of field. If you want to be able to feel the depth of a landscape scene use wide-angle lenses – around ƒ/11 or ƒ/8 – to get a large depth of field.

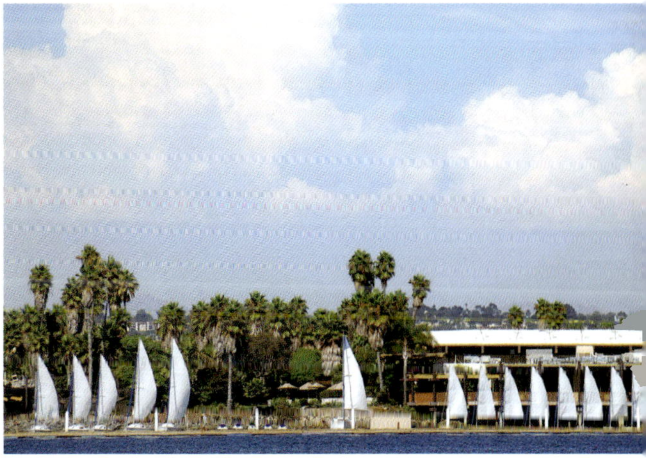

▲ Using the sky to make man-made objects look small is a great approach with time-lapse. These boats almost look like models because of the way that the frame is composed. Camera settings: 1/1600s, ƒ/5, ISO 200.

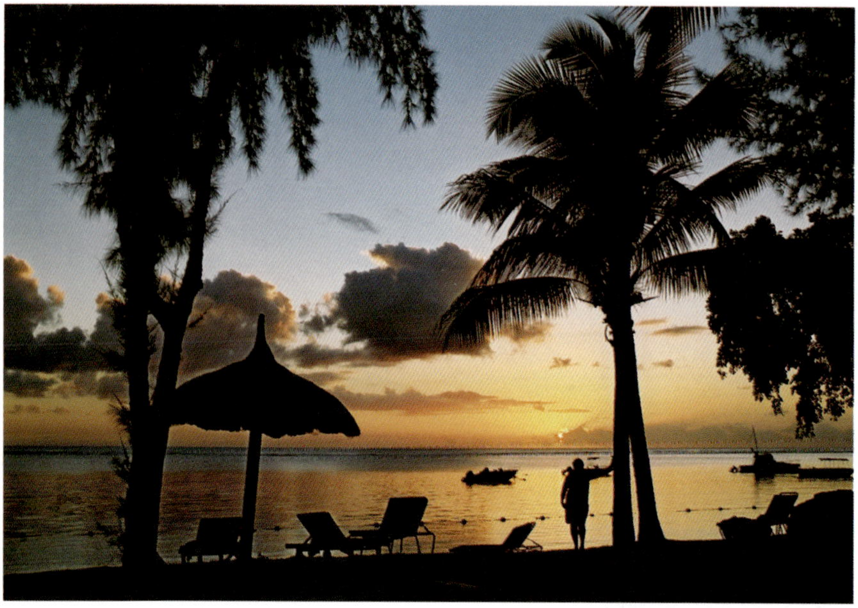

This image shows a subject in context of the surroundings to help tell the story. But the image also has depth; the layers of the image are very far apart. Both of these ideas are very successful when applied to time-lapse videos. Camera settings: 1/60s, ƒ/5.6, ISO 2000.

Context

Giving a subject context in your imagery will help with storytelling, as well as visual composition. Sometimes we can lose context with our imagery by concentrating too much on how something looks and forgetting how it communicates a story or message. When telephoto lenses are being used we have to be particularly careful; sometimes we zoom in too much and lose the area surrounding a subject. This can take away from the impact of the storytelling.

Try zooming out a little and see how it affects the image. You will be surprised with how much more you are able to say with more context. With time-lapse keep an eye out for where movement is coming from and where it is going to. This will ensure the entirety of the story is told through the movement.

Out of focus

Generally we strive to create the sharpest imagery that we are able to achieve, but try putting things completely out of focus deliberately. The look you will get when doing this is called 'bokeh'. This term also describes the out-of-focus area in an image when using a shallow depth of field. If you put the whole image out of focus, however, you can get some really interesting shapes and textures. When movement is added to this it will help to increase visual diversity within your time-lapse videos.

Breaking the rules

Photography is about fun and experimentation so once you have learned the compositional rules and explored them fully, start breaking them. You have to be destructive to be constructive; make your own rules and then follow them. Sometimes the most eye-catching images are the ones that break every compositional tool that you know. Common ideas and 'rules' are only made up in the first place by experimentation, so be a pioneer and don't accept that everything has already been done.

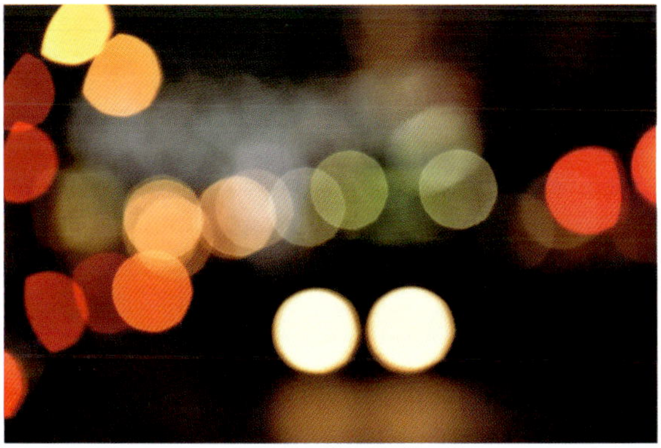

▲ This image of a busy street with traffic is deliberately out of focus (bokeh). The orbs of light are the shape of the aperture in the lens. Camera settings: 1/80s, ƒ/4, ISO 800.

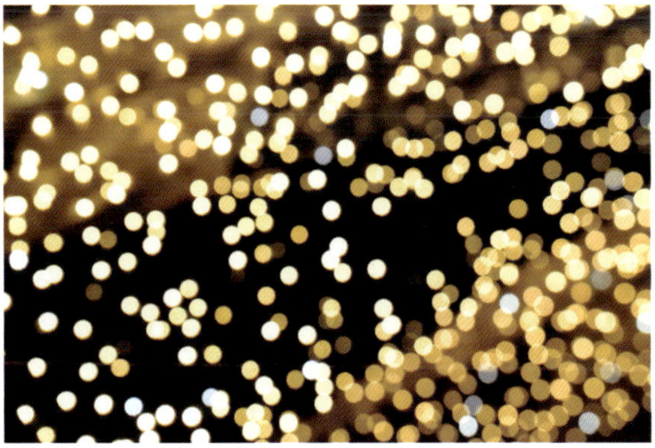

▲ A different look that also uses bokeh as the main feature. This looks great when it is moving in a time-lapse video. Camera settings: 1/250s, ƒ/9, ISO 400.

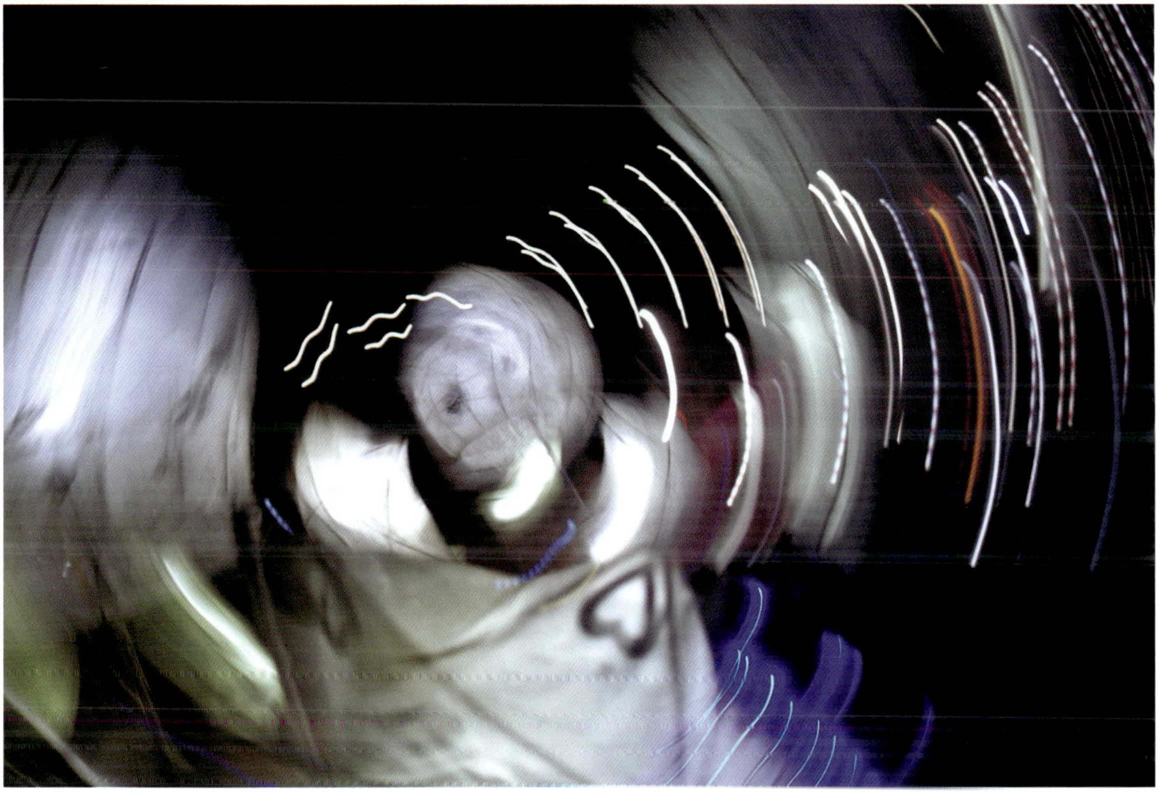

▲ This image does not apply any of the compositional rules but has interesting colours and textures. Always break rules if it makes the image interesting. Camera settings: 1/5s, ƒ/1.8, ISO 100.

Making your own rules

If you find something that you like compositionally that is not listed here or elsewhere, don't feel that it is not a valid idea to use. Please have the confidence to follow your gut feeling about how you like your images to look compositionally. Remember, every rule that you make up means you might be closer to finding your own 'look', which differentiates your imagery from that of other photographers.

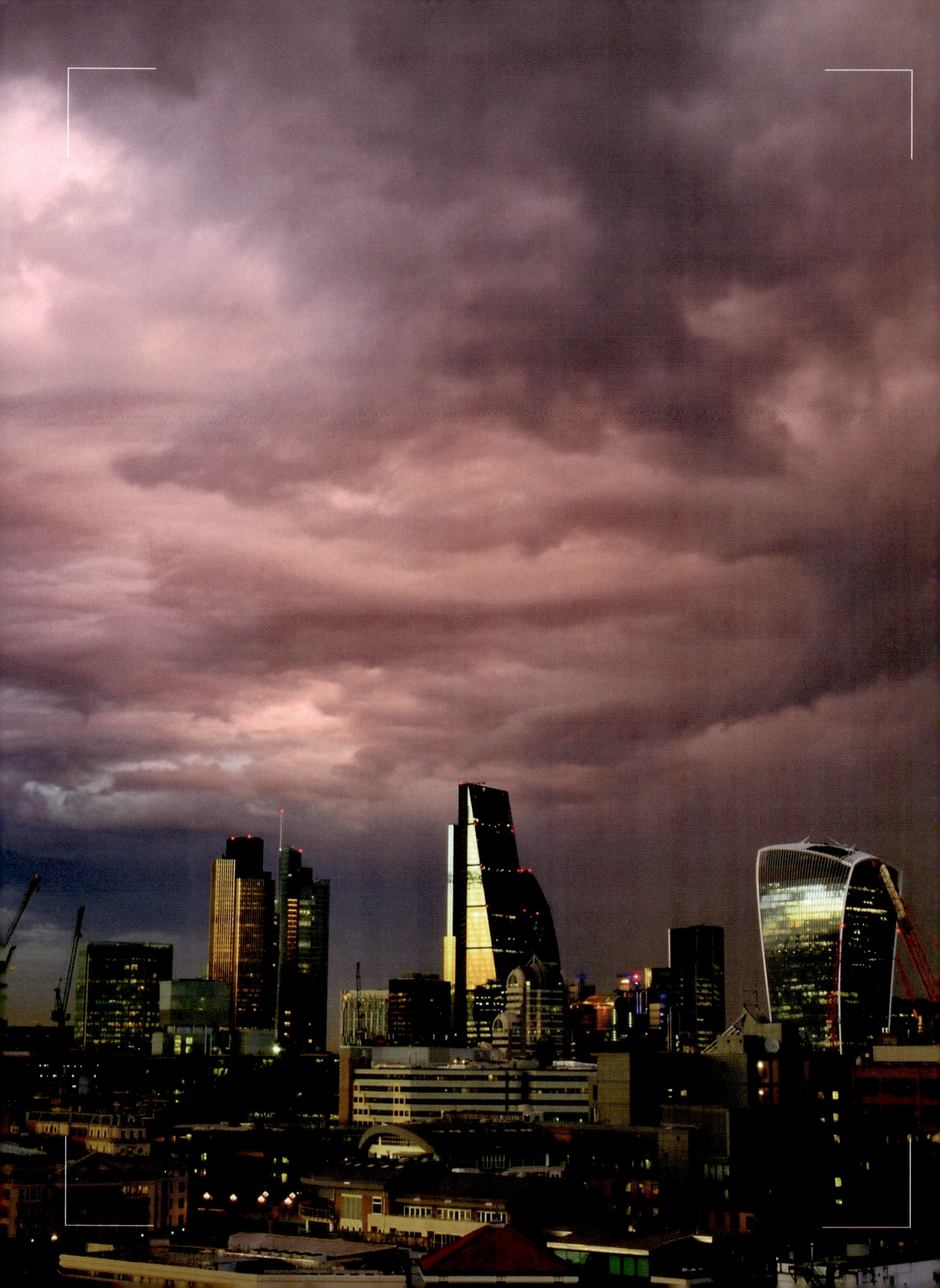

Chapter 7

Planning and shooting time-lapse videos

In this chapter will look at how we can successfully plan and shoot our time-lapse videos. We will look at sequences of stills that have been taken from time-lapse videos to provide examples of settings that can be utilized, the thought processes behind them, and other tips and tricks. Use these examples to see what kind of imagery you like and to build on your technical skills.

First we will consider our approach when working on different projects. Formalizing your work structure and project management can be an effective way to make sure you use your time efficiently and will help you to achieve more in a short space of time.

USING A PROJECT STRUCTURE

Any image-maker will generally work on different areas at the same time and this can be difficult to keep track of. Try to organize items into categories; each area of interest will then become a project. Projects mostly consist of a number of pieces of work that share a theme, idea or technical relationship. Having one or more projects to build upon will help you sustain and increase your learning momentum, whilst maintaining structure to your work.

After trying different time-lapse videos you might start to see trends in subject matter and realize that certain aspects appeal to you. A project structure will help you progress; when the direction is clear, you will arrive at your destination sooner than you might have thought.

Repetition within a project

Repetition is one of the best ways to learn and therefore repeating a time-lapse shoot will be hugely advantageous to you. Choose one particular location that you find inspiring, then keep going back to repeat what you did before, but build and add to the body of work every time you return. Repeating a time-lapse shoot will show that even though the location is the same, the light will be different on each visit.

Try going back at different times of day to repeat the same time-lapse; you will see a huge difference in shadows, colour, the amount of light, and atmospheric conditions depending on the weather. This repetition will give you important creative and technical practice and help you to create outstanding work more easily.

Going deeper into a project

After the realization that a particular subject interests you, go a bit deeper. Do some research about the kind of subjects you are shooting. Information is becoming easier to get hold of; you can research the Internet and libraries to look at other photographers' work in order to learn from them. Make sure that you find your own angle on any subject you endeavour to record. It is a good exercise to emulate the work of others, but you need to make your own path.

Once you have started learning more about the subject that you are working on then you might

◀ This image was taken as part of a time-lapse video and has since been used as a stand-alone image. This image would not have been captured unless the camera had been shooting with its interval timer. Camera settings: 1/1.6s, f/10, ISO 100.

also find a different tangent to follow. This could be an area related to what you are working on and can actually complement the work that you have already done. One project can quickly become a collection of small projects and these small pools of work will give you a variety of subjects that you can choose to work on at any time. Working this way ensures that you won't be scratching your head wondering what to do next.

For example, you might be creating time-lapse videos of an area near a river. After research you might find that there is a boating club next door and they take boats out every Sunday afternoon at 3pm. You then know exactly when to go along with your camera to get relevant interest and movement. Without researching your areas of interest, you could lose out on this kind of insight.

Keeping track of different projects

It is easy to lose track of what you are doing and actually mislay work as a result of doing too many unrelated projects at once without any organization. Why not start to project manage? It might sound like a corporate approach, but to 'project manage' simply means to organize what you are doing in a structured way.

You could do this by keeping a diary of what you have done and where you plan to go next. Use what works best for you. Some people use a calendar; some people use charts. It could be a digital calendar on your phone or a physical booklet that you make notes in. If you are able to come back to a project, pick up from where you left off and be aware of what to do next, then you are in control and will not lose work.

Working without projects

For most people it will make sense to work to a project guide or structure – it does help with direction and purpose – but this way of working may not suit everyone. All the ideas in this book should be taken as suggestions; you might choose to use them yourself, but you might not. If you feel that working to projects does not suit you then just simply take your own route. Some people find creativity in chaos; you might prefer not to work to a structure and be more instinctive.

LOCATION

Light and location

More often than not a key ingredient for great time-lapse videos is a fantastic location. If you arrive somewhere and it already looks amazing then you are half-way there. Whatever the location, remember that photography is about light. If you pair a great location with amazing light then you will reap the benefits. Movement in your time-lapse is of course important as well, so combine movement with light and make stunning imagery.

Discovering different locations

Start with locations that you know and have already photographed, but go back and shoot with different light at various times of day. Once you have exhausted all of the locations that you are aware of, move on to the unknown.

Do some research and find out where other photographers shoot in your area; this could provide a good source of information, although the best places may be where other photographers have not yet discovered, so try to find your own shooting locations off the beaten track. This can be done by looking at maps online to get a bird's eye view of an area that you find interesting or are curious of. With most online maps you can view from street level as well, so have a look around from the comfort of your own living room and see if there is anything that might work well in a time-lapse video.

Keep a record of your locations by printing off maps, make notes on the maps and mark out the area where you have made a time-lapse. Record the time of day, the direction that the camera was pointed and the camera settings used. Build a project around a certain area that you find inspiring. Revisit and keep striving to create a better time-lapse video every time you go back. Move onto different locations as often as possible, but make sure that you record where you have been.

Initial visit to your location

You can survey where you will be capturing a time-lapse to see what shooting angles might work for the effect you are trying to achieve. Remember to take your camera with you, even if you only intend to have a quick look around, because you never know what will happen with the light and the weather.

If you are visiting for the first time to explore an area, do some test stills or time-lapse videos to take home and review. This way you can go back to the location again with a clear idea based on what you learned from the first visit. Be honest with yourself and only repeat what works best. Always remember to keep notes on where you went and how to get there.

GPS (Global Positioning System)

GPS data pinpoints your location anywhere in the world. Many cameras and phones have the ability to record this data and tag it to an image that is created at that location. Your DSLR will most likely be able to accept a GPS device or have this functionality built in already. Either way you can tag GPS data to your images and you will always know exactly where they were created. This will make life easier when revisiting locations because you can program the GPS coordinates into a phone or sat nav and let the device guide you there.

EXAMPLES OF TIME-LAPSE VIDEOS

The next section looks at different examples of time-lapse videos. We will deconstruct them by looking at camera settings and any specific considerations made when shooting them. Sequences of still photographs taken from the time-lapse videos are presented so that movement and composition can be viewed and understood. This will give you the information you need to recreate them or to use them as inspiration. Even if there is subject matter that is not shown here, there will be a time-lapse with the set-up and considerations that will work for almost any shoot.

TRAIN STATION

Any subject that has plenty of movement works well with time-lapse photography. Train stations, especially when busy, illustrate this well. Before you start the shoot, have a good look around your chosen location, preferably during rush hour. Take time to observe the motion of trains and people; look at the direction and flow of movement. Observe patterns in the behaviour of people and timing of barriers and trains, which will help you when framing the image, placing the tripod and deciding on the storytelling

Get a copy of the train times or use a website or app on your phone to work out when certain trains are due and from which direction. You can be very efficient with the time you spend on location because if the trains are running on time, the movement can be quite predictable. Be aware of safety when you are using a tripod in a busy area like a train station, especially if you are near crowds or train tracks.

The train lines and buildings in a station can be used as a compositional feature in the image and can help create eye-catching imagery. Try to combine compositional ideas with movement. You could, for example, use movement within a crowd as a leading line or moving trains to fit the 'rule of thirds' idea.

Look up the weather forecast and, if appropriate, what time the sun rises or sets. All of this information will help you plan the shoot and give you more control over what you are doing. Remember, it's always good to revisit the same location another day when the light is different to contribute visual diversity to a final edited video.

This example

This example was shot from the platform of a busy station during rush hour. Prior to the day of the shoot the train station was investigated to find a suitable location and angle for the camera to get a good viewpoint for movement and to create an eye-catching visual. The train times on the chosen platform were researched and noted so that the time-lapse could be set up at the right moment.

Having been to the location, it was clear that there was not enough room for a full-sized tripod in the busy station, so another solution was needed. The DSLR was therefore mounted on a mini tripod and perched on a bench in the station to give the camera some height.

The idea was to capture the train arriving, dropping off the people and then moving on. It's a simple idea and could be used as part of a bigger time-lapse video, but also stands alone in its own right. The decision was made to use slow shutter speeds to get motion blur. This way you do not see the people – just the blur and lines they create. The train also completely blurs when it is moving and this helps to communicate speed.

Equipment

The equipment used was a mini tripod (perched on a bench) with a full frame DSLR camera and a 20mm prime lens. All of this equipment fitted easily into a standard backpack which made it easy to carry to the location. A full sized tripod was not used because it would have been a hazard to commuters.

Mode

The camera was in aperture priority mode, so that the depth of field would not change during capture.

Aperture

The aperture was set to $f/8$, and this in combination with a wide-angle lens gave a wide depth of field, ensuring that sharpness was retained throughout the image.

Sensitivity

The sensitivity was set to ISO 100 to ensure that the image was clean and free of noise. A low sensitivity in low light will drive the camera to choose a slow shutter speed to let more light into the camera, because it cannot change the aperture or ISO. In this example this worked in our favour: a slow shutter speed created deliberate motion blur in the images.

Shutter speed

The shutter speed that the camera chose was 1/2.5th of a second. Based on the ISO and aperture value chosen the camera decided this was sufficient to get a good exposure with the light it had at that time. The camera will only ever choose the appropriate shutter speed to let enough light in; it cannot predict what you are trying to do creatively. If the shutter speed that was chosen by the camera was not giving enough motion blur, then manual mode would have been the next port of call and the shutter speed would have been set manually, as well as the aperture and ISO.

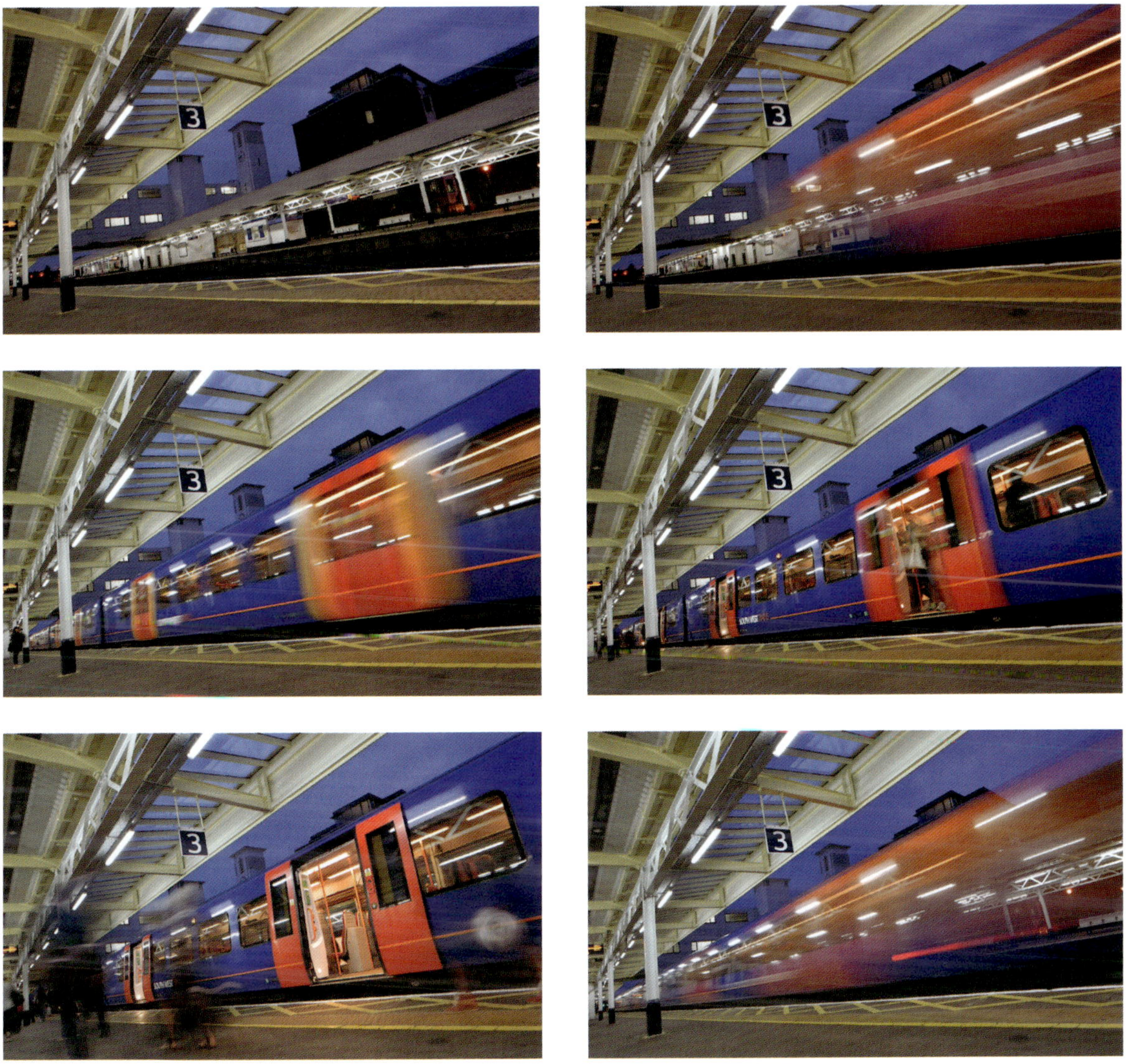

▲ This time-lapse video was taken from a bench at a train station. A slow shutter speed was used so that movement was accentuated.

Time-lapse settings

This example was captured using interval-timer shooting mode in the camera at one frame per second and the camera was shooting for around five minutes. The separate JPEG images were then made into a time-lapse video in video editing software.

Other considerations

The camera was pre-focused on the station roof to the left of the frame because the focusing system works well with high contrast and the roof is also around the same distance from the camera as the train is when it comes to a standstill. Once the focus was sharp then the focusing system was turned off. This ensured that the focusing system did not try to focus for each separate frame taken whilst shooting the time-lapse.

The white balance was set on auto – not ideal for a subject with so many light sources – but even so, the camera did a great job.

The shutter speed was left to the camera because if the exposure changed slightly as the train entered the frame then the camera could adjust the shutter speed to even out the exposure between frames. A slight change would not make an obvious difference in the motion blur, but in another situation this might not work as well, since motion blur will look different as the shutter speed changes.

Compositionally the strong lines on the platform and roof of the station were used as leading lines. The camera was tilted to the left slightly in order to enhance the impact of these features.

CHANGING LIGHT WITH LANDSCAPES

Using vast landscapes with interesting features will always help provide a great foreground when the weather and the light are changing in the scene. If your image looks great as a still photograph then you have a head start on creating great content.

City landscapes provide an inspiring subject to work with because of the shapes and reflective surfaces that can be found. If you are able to find a high vantage point then you can look down on the city and capture the movement of people, traffic, clouds and changing natural light as well as changing man-made light.

Before going to shoot this kind of time-lapse video, make sure that you have checked the direction of the wind and found out what time the sun rises or sets; think about how long you will need to be there to capture the changes. Be careful of wind moving the tripod and working with heavy equipment when high up on a building or ledge.

This example

This example was shot from the top of a tall building near the Thames in the middle of London. Because of the height, you are able to see across to tall office blocks. The weather was looking really bad when arriving at the building, and it got worse when starting to shoot, but that same weather eventually provided some amazing colours and cloud formations for capturing stills and time-lapse videos. Essentially, luck was a big factor but choosing the correct settings and capturing the light successfully was critical to making the best of the situation.

Equipment

A heavy duty tripod was used to reduce the chances of movement from wind. A DSLR with a 16–35mm lens was chosen because this was the first visit and exact framing was not known so if elements did not work compositionally, the zoom on the lens could be changed.

Mode

Manual mode was chosen with this time-lapse, the main reason being that it was getting dark very quickly and the creative decision was made to let the time-lapse get darker as the light dropped. If the camera had been in aperture priority then it would have adjusted and therefore not faded to black right at the end.

Aperture

An aperture value of $f/10$ was used to get a large depth of field to make sure everything was sharp. The lens was zoomed to 24mm and with this combination of focal length and aperture, the depth of field is more than sufficient to make everything sharp.

Sensitivity

The camera's sensitivity was set to ISO 200. A low value was chosen to ensure that there was minimal noise in the image, which means that the clarity and sharpness were retained. If you get digital noise with clouds in the frame, the noise can look quite obvious to the viewer, so care has to be taken with this kind of subject matter.

▶ As natural and man-made light changed over time, this time-lapse captured the transition from day to night. Bad weather provided some inspiring imagery.

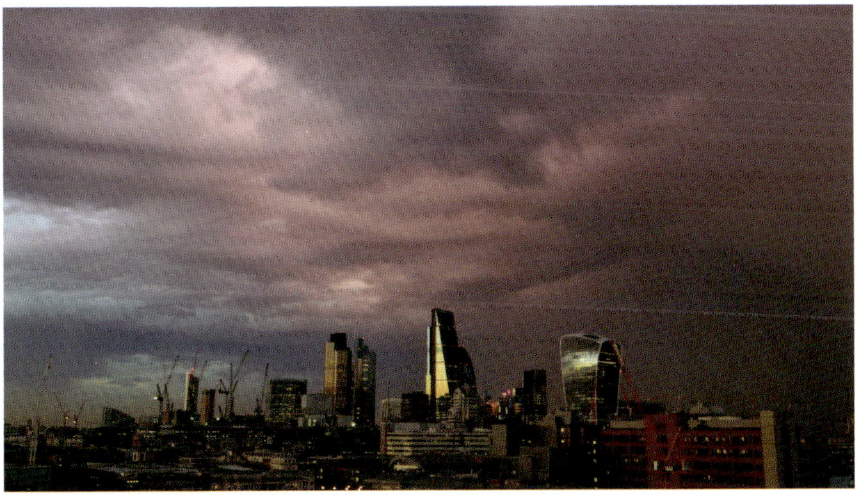

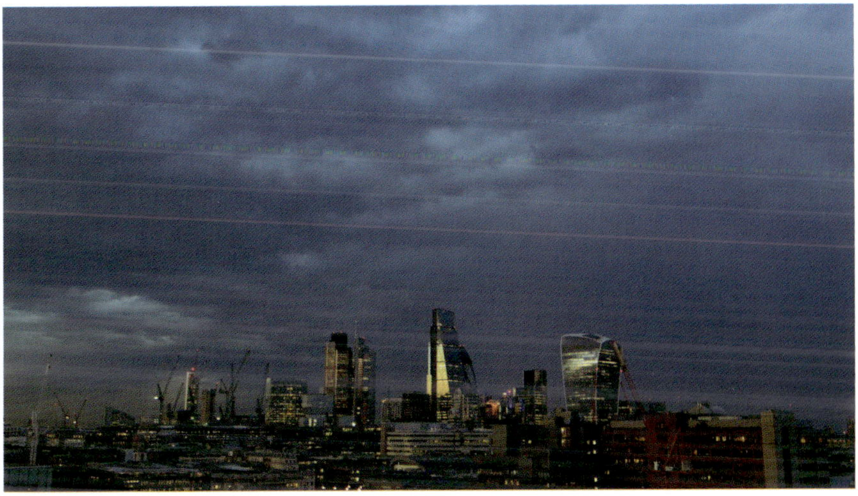

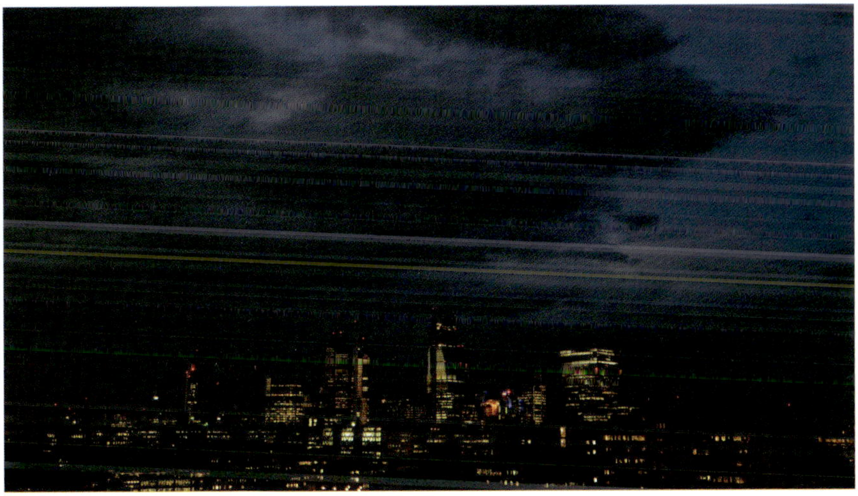

Shutter speed

The shutter speed throughout was 1/1.6 seconds and was the last setting that was made on the camera. The priority with this time-lapse was not to get motion blur but to get an appropriate exposure. In this case, the shutter speed was chosen for exposure reasons and not creative reasons.

Time-lapse settings

This example was captured using the time-lapse photography mode. The interval was set to take an image every three seconds. This was chosen so that the playback would be fairly quick because the clouds were moving slowly in this scene. If the interval was set to take one frame per second, the final video would show the clouds moving more slowly.

Other considerations

At the beginning of the day images were taken from this viewpoint but the light was uninspiring and the weather flat. Later on in the evening the light started to turn purple and blue, as shown at the beginning of this time-lapse. The way that the cloud and colour of the natural light came together was only there for about five minutes and then it was gone. The light dropped quickly and the lights in the buildings went on to add some man-made lighting towards the end.

FROM THE DASHBOARD

Any road with traffic will provide all kinds of different movement that will work well for time-lapse photography. Larger motorways tend to have more vehicles and illuminated signs, which will ultimately give you more to work with. Different times of day will give very different types of movement and light. This provides diversity for your image-making. Any light on a car, van or truck will become your friend as these lights will create some fantastic effects if a slow shutter speed is used, like in this example.

Set up a small tripod with a camera on the dashboard, making sure it is not obstructing your view of the road. You have to be very careful of safety here: you don't want the camera to fall off onto your steering wheel for example. After the camera is secured, plan a journey that will take you along some busy roads that have a lot of lights. It is very tempting to start pressing the camera's buttons and having a look at the back screen at what you have done whilst driving. Resist this urge and keep your eye on the road. Time-lapse videos are important, but your safety is essential.

This example

This example was taken from inside a car from the dashboard on a drive along a busy motorway. A slow shutter speed was used to create lots of motion blur as the car moves the camera along with it. The idea with this time-lapse was to get as much motion blur as possible to create an eye-catching result with plenty of colour and movement. In the final result nothing is sharp and the direction of the motion always leads you into the centre of the frame. This creates a mesmerizing effect that would not be possible without time-lapse photography.

Equipment

A DSLR camera mounted on a pocket tripod was taped to the dashboard so that it was secure. A 35mm prime lens was used; if a zoom lens had been used, the shake and movement of the car might have moved the zoom in and out gradually during capture. A prime lens is fixed and cannot zoom, therefore negating this problem. Also, this lens is quite light in weight and the camera was less likely to fall over without a heavy lens attached.

Mode

The camera was in aperture priority mode so that the depth of field would not change but the camera would make sure the exposure was balanced well automatically.

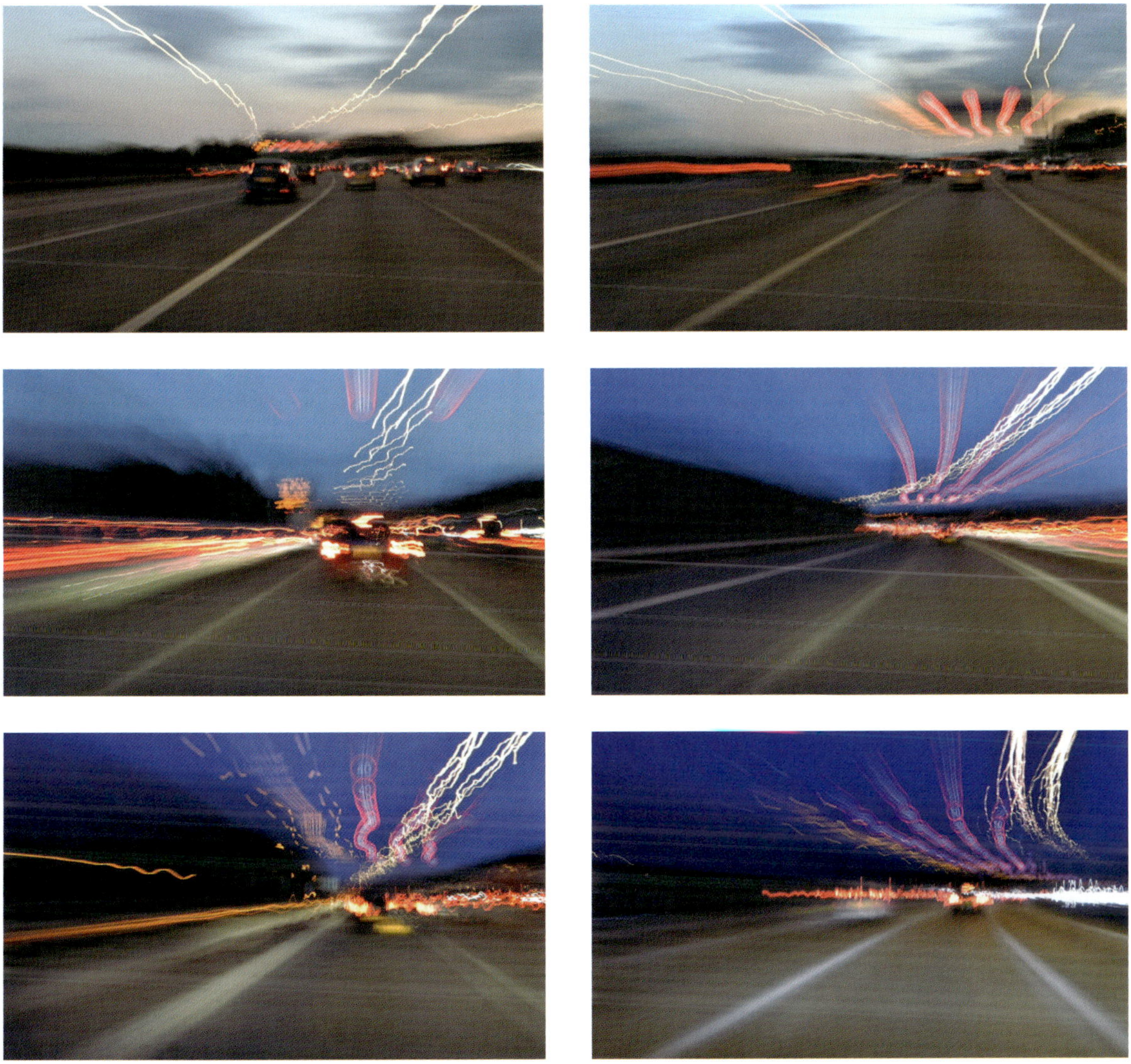

▲ This time-lapse was shot from the dashboard of a moving car. The vivid streaks of colour and blur were created by the use of a slow shutter speed. Strong leading lines with the blur caused by the movement of the car and the surroundings created eye-catching imagery.

Aperture

An aperture of *f*/16 was set in order to ensure the depth of field was wide. *f*/16 is a very small aperture opening which reduces the amount of light falling into the camera. This was chosen to ensure the shutter speed that was chosen by the camera was very slow in order to achieve motion blur.

Sensitivity

ISO 100 was set to keep the digital noise to a minimum and to enable the camera to choose a slow shutter speed.

Shutter speed

Because the ISO is set to a low sensitivity and the aperture is set to reduce the amount of light, this enables the camera to choose a very slow shutter speed in a low light situation. During capture the shutter speed changed from around 2" (two seconds) to 30" (thirty seconds).

Time-lapse settings

This example was captured using time-lapse photography mode. The interval was set to take an image every second. Because the camera's software is so advanced, it simply adjusted to take an image as frequently as it could. For example, when the shutter speed was down to 30" (thirty seconds), it would adjust accordingly to capture one shot every thirty seconds, even though the interval was set to one per second. Check that your camera does this before relying on it; if it doesn't you have to take care when the shutter speed is changing and choose an appropriate interval to match the longest shutter speed that might be used.

Other considerations

Always think about safety when shooting this kind of time-lapse video. A small DSLR camera was used so the driver's view out of the window was not obstructed. Very strong industrial tape was used to attach the camera and pocket tripod to the dashboard and the camera was completely ignored during the journey. If you plan to do a time-lapse such as this one, it might be worth getting someone else to drive and as the passenger you will then have your hands free to control the camera or check the settings.

ADVERSE WEATHER

When the weather is adverse we don't usually decide to go out and take pictures. We don't want to get wet or risk our expensive equipment getting damaged – not to mention the cold temperatures and potentially ruining a favourite pair of shoes. This weather itself, however, can be absolutely amazing for time-lapse photography. Don't miss out on the storms and rain: you could get some spectacular content that other people would not because they didn't want to venture outside.

Obviously if it is raining, try to find a ledge or roof to stand under. You might even want to bring a small tent with you. Bring some hot cocoa and let your camera capture some amazing content whilst you curl up and keep warm. Even though it may be a bit more effort working in difficult weather it can be very rewarding. When the weather is 'bad' there can be some impressive changes in cloud formation because of the movement of the wind and temperature. Often atmospheric conditions will give you some eye-catching colours that will look fantastic in your time-lapse video.

This example

This time-lapse was captured on a day when there was changeable weather; it was rainy and cold. The camera and tripod were set up in the direction of where thunder could be heard and by chance during the time-lapse a rainbow and lightning were both captured. The building on the right-hand side of the frame was used to create some interest when there was nothing notable happening with the weather. The lightning was only discovered after capture and this proves that sometimes you have to go with instinct, set up your camera and hope for the best. It is more likely that you will capture something exciting if you have your camera shooting rather than sitting in your camera bag.

Equipment

A full frame DSLR camera was used, mounted on a full-sized heavy tripod to reduce any movement made by the wind blowing against the camera. A 16–35mm *f*/4 lens was used so that any change in framing would be easy, given that the tripod was heavy and not easy to move. An umbrella was held over the camera and a raincoat was worn by the photographer. No camera equipment was hurt in the making of this time-lapse.

This time-lapse captured a rainbow and a flash of lighting as well as the fading light during sunset, all in one video. Always try to capture as much as possible in your videos to give the viewer plenty to see.

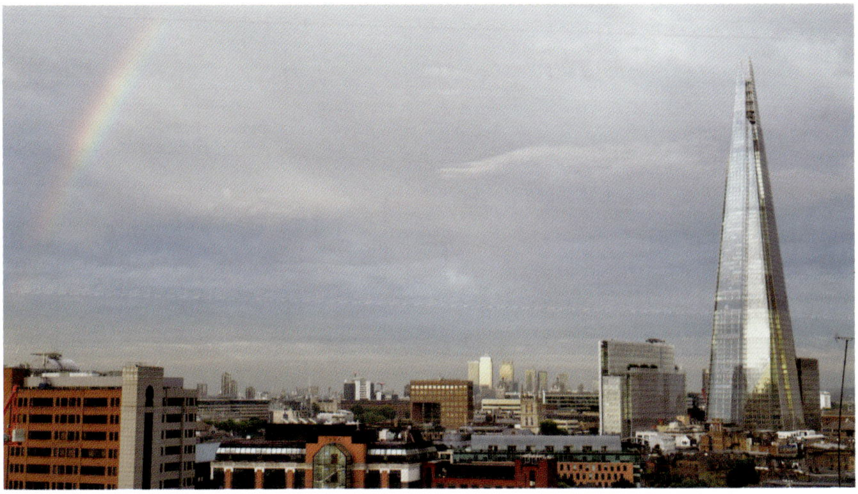

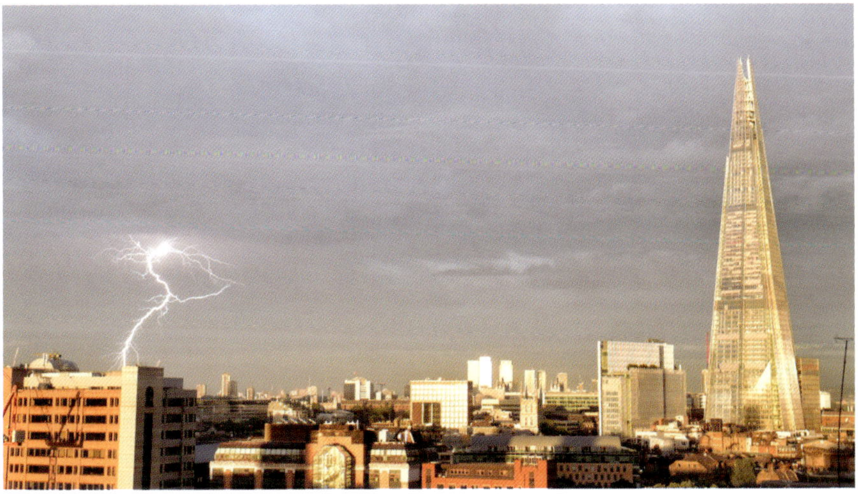

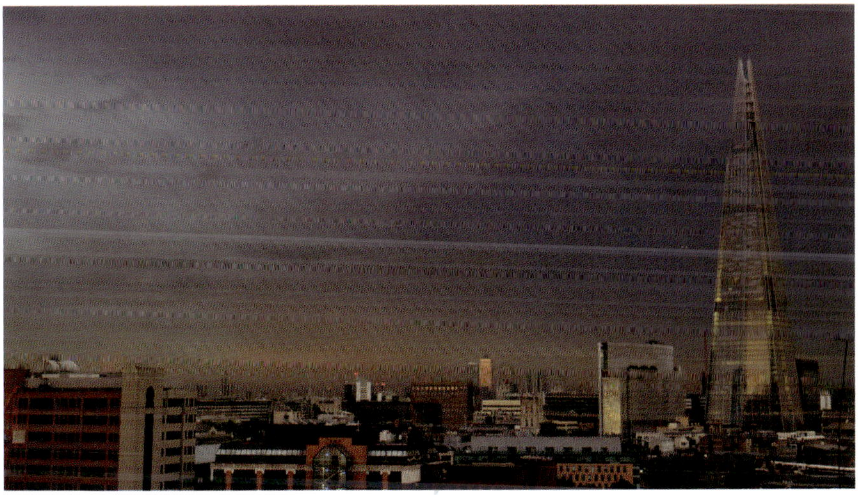

Camera mode

Manual mode was chosen on the camera to lock down all of the settings. Aperture priority was tested but did not reach the desired exposure because the camera was trying to brighten the scene up too much. It was decided that when it got darker it would be better for the image to also get darker along with falling light.

Aperture

To get a wide depth of field the aperture was set to *f*/10. A wide-angle lens was being used so an adequate depth of field could be achieved to keep the buildings and clouds sharp. Such an extensive scene will always need a very large depth of field if sharpness is required.

Sensitivity

An ISO of 400 was set because with the camera model being used this ISO would give no digital noise. A slightly higher sensitivity than would otherwise be used was useful to help balance up the triangle in order to get the exposure that was required with the light available.

Shutter speed

It was not critical in this case to get any motion blur in the images so 1/80th of a second was used to balance out the exposure. Shutter speed was not being used for any creative reason, so it was chosen to balance the exposure of the image after aperture and ISO was set.

Time-lapse settings

The interval timer was set to take one image per second. The camera was set to capture RAW images in case a large photographic print was required from a lightning bolt being captured. The RAW files were batch converted to JPEG files and then made into a Full HD video in editing software. The frequency of capture was high because the weather was unpredictable and it was unknown exactly what would happen. A more frequent interval increases the chances of capturing changing conditions and in this case that approach worked well.

Other considerations

In this example, the camera was pre-focused using back button focus. This means that during capture the camera did not focus for each frame, creating unwanted movement in the lens. If you are specifically trying to capture lightning it will be better to use a slower shutter speed than used in this example, as the longer the shutter is open for, the more chance you have of getting the lightning in the frame. Ideally this should have been the approach at the time but a lesson was learned here by the photographer; if you can learn a little from each shoot or piece of work that you capture, you will progress very quickly.

WALKING WITH THE CAMERA

Time-lapse videos do not always have to be captured on a tripod. Experiment freely with different ways of making your videos: pick the camera up and walk along with it whilst the interval timer is running; perhaps try putting the camera on a moving object, such as an escalator.

If you want to try walking with the camera there are a few things to consider. Don't walk too fast because the final video might go by too quickly, depending on the interval chosen. Put the camera strap around your neck to steady the movement of the camera, and keep your eyes in front of you when walking. As you walk, hold the camera as steady as possible, trying not to press any buttons on the camera unless you mean to do so. Remember, time-lapse is all about movement so experiment with moving the camera itself.

This example

This example was captured whilst walking down a busy road in the middle of a city. Although it can be difficult to walk along a busy street, more people and traffic provide interest and movement for the time-lapse video, which will help visually. This example was shot using a slow shutter speed to create severe motion blur. The final result does not show detail – simply blurry shapes and colours.

Because the camera has been held quite steadily all the way though, the blur mostly goes into the centre of the image and this creates leading lines from almost every corner. The subject matter is still fairly clear in the final video even though it is blurred. (It is very easy to blur everything out of recognition when hand-holding a camera like this, so care needs to be taken to hold the camera steady.)

Equipment

A DSLR camera and the strap that comes with it were used in this time-lapse. The strap was worn around the neck of the photographer to steady the camera whilst walking.

Mode

Manual mode was used so that the exposure would not fluctuate a great deal during the capture. There is over- and underexposure in the stills, but the overall look of the final video is consistent, which makes it easy to watch. If the video gets brighter and darker quickly then it can easily put the viewer off.

Aperture

An aperture of *f*/22 was used to make sure a slow shutter speed was obtainable. It was a bright day and therefore a small aperture helped to ensure there was minimal overexposure in the images.

Sensitivity

The camera sensitivity was set to ISO 100 so that a slow shutter speed could be used.

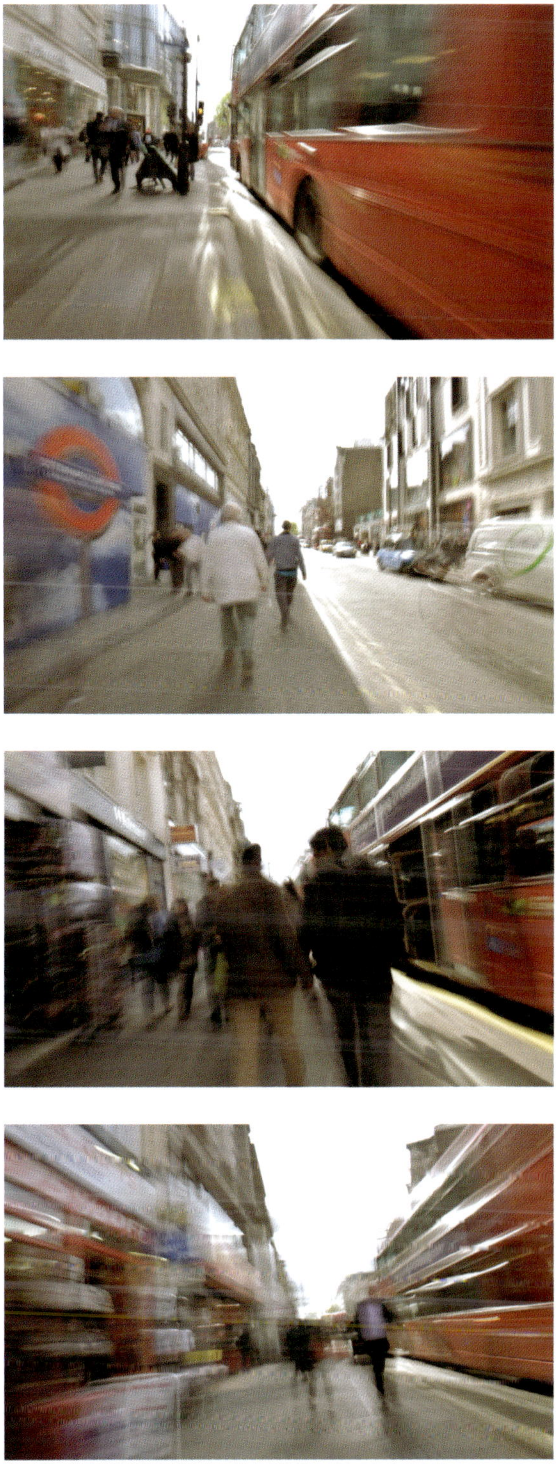

▲ Walking with the camera as it captures time-lapse with the interval timer has created imagery that is almost abstract and a final video that is eye-catching.

Shutter speed

A slow shutter speed of 4" (four seconds) was used to get motion blur. In this case the camera was moving and therefore nothing is sharp, but the final video delivers a punchy eye-catching look with the movement and pacing achieved.

Time-lapse settings

The camera was set to capture in time-lapse photography mode so that the final video could be reviewed immediately after shooting. The interval was set to capture one frame every four seconds to match the shutter speed of the camera.

Other considerations

This time-lapse was created simply to experiment with settings and subject matter. This was captured walking down a very busy road in a city. In this situation, having a camera around your neck walking along is quite common so you do not look out of place. Also the sound of the city drowns out the clicking of the camera, so no-one notices that the camera is actually shooting.

LOW LIGHT CITY SCENE

Movement can be either the make or break for any time-lapse video. There is no better place to find movement than in a big city with plenty of traffic. This type of motion gives us some fantastic opportunities for our work, especially at night when all the lights come on. It is best to plan a route across a small part of a city to make sure you can get the best out of your shoot.

Plan your start and end point and think about where on the way might be good to stop for a drink so that you are comfortable. Security is important to think about when you are in a city: consider covering up the brands on your camera strap and camera bag. When using a tripod keep an eye out for walkways and roads because you do not want people tripping over it. Remember to take a test image or short time-lapse to see if the results are coming out the way you want before starting the main time-lapse clip.

This example

In this example it was clear that there were two different directions of movement in the traffic which complemented each other. This location was visited in advance to shoot still photographs and that is when the movement was noticed. It does make sense to review work that you have made in the past and think about how your still images would work as a time-lapse video. The blur shown in the image is from cars and buses as they travel in straight and curved lines, and this gives different directions of movement in the final video.

Equipment

A full frame DSLR camera on a tripod at waist level was used to capture this time-lapse. The camera had a 24mm *f*/1.8 prime lens attached because with previous visits to this location it was noted that a zoom lens was set to 24mm anyway. Using a prime lens means that you do not have to carry as much weight around. If you have planned your composition then prime lenses are a great solution, but if it's your first visit to a location then a zoom may be more appropriate.

Camera mode

Aperture priority was used on the camera in order to make sure the depth of field didn't change during capture. If this had not achieved what was desired in terms of exposure, manual mode would have been used.

Aperture

The aperture was set to *f*/14 for this example. This decision was made to give a large depth of field and also to let less light into the camera with the small aperture. This enables us to choose a very

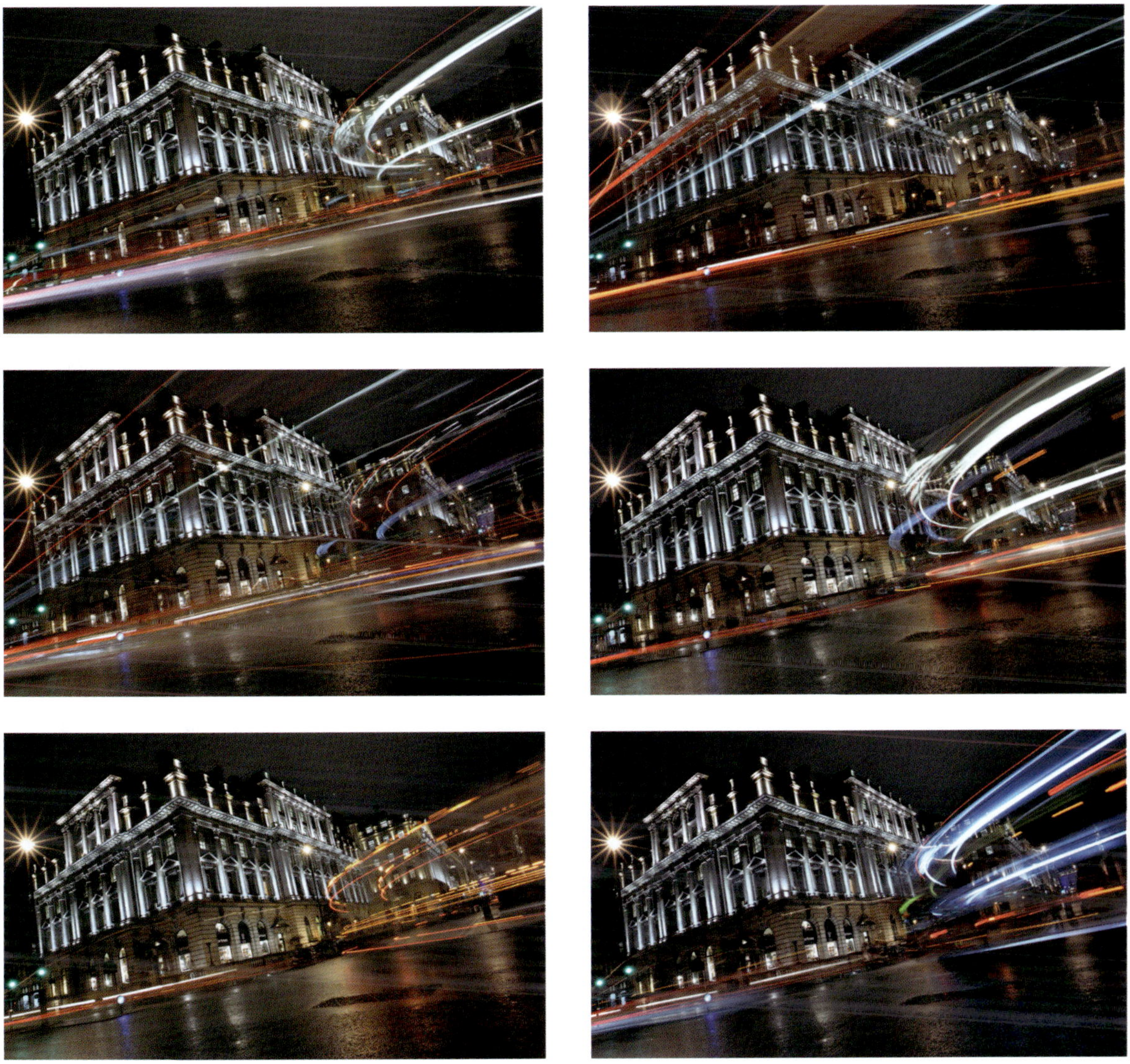

▲ This video was captured on a small tripod on the corner of a busy city street. By using a slow shutter speed traffic trails have been achieved.

slow shutter speed, which was the main priority with this video.

Sensitivity

A sensitivity of ISO 100 was selected on the camera to make sure the images were clean and free of noise. The low sensitivity that the camera was set to enables a slow shutter speed to be used.

Shutter speed

After setting the ISO and aperture values the camera chose a shutter speed of 3" (three seconds) which was long enough to get good traffic trails based on how fast the traffic was going in this scene. If the camera had not chosen a slow enough shutter speed then manual mode would have been selected to take full control and the exposure triangle would have been balanced differently.

Time-lapse settings

The camera was set to capture using time-lapse mode. This means that the final video is viewable immediately after shooting and the look and pacing of the end result can be checked before moving on. The interval was set to take a picture every three seconds to match the shutter speed that was chosen by the camera.

Other considerations

This location had been visited and used for still photographs many times. Because some inspiring images had been taken previously, the decision was made to go back and shoot a time-lapse – this scene would not have been unearthed unless it had been used on a stills shoot previously. The same imagery as before was repeated but this time for a time-lapse video rather than a single still image. Compositionally the camera was tilted to the left to enhance the leading lines of the traffic and buildings.

LOOKING UP

One thing that many of us don't do often is look up. Looking up can provide some exciting imagery, whether you are shooting stills, video or time-lapse. When you look up you change the perspective of the subject you are looking at and also include the sky in the image. As we know, clouds work very well in time-lapse photography and if we use a building against the clouds then the difference in movement will work well. Time-lapse videos of clouds on their own can make fantastic visuals, but it helps to have something else in the frame to give context. You can also create a good sense of depth in your images if you look up and use buildings, trees, or even people.

This example

This example is shot on a cloudy day during the summer, looking up at a contemporary glass building. The time-lapse was made more for the cloud movement than the building itself. The building has, however, got some interesting shapes and reflective surfaces that work well when the clouds move over it.

Equipment

A full frame DSLR camera was used on a full-sized tripod. The lens used was a 16–35mm *f*/4 zoom. Because the camera was very close to the building a 19mm focal length was used to fill the frame with the top of the building.

Mode

Manual mode was used when shooting this example. The reason for this is that when the clouds move across the sky the exposure could change significantly. The camera would have automatically changed its exposure and the final video would potentially have flicker because the images would get brighter and darker quickly in the playback. When the camera is locked down in manual mode the exposure will not change and the end result will look consistent.

Aperture

The aperture chosen was *f*/8. This ensured an adequate depth of field so that the clouds and the buildings were both sharp.

Sensitivity

The sensitivity of the camera was set to 100 ISO. This means that there will be no noise in the image. There is also a lot of light, so a lower sensitivity was appropriate.

Shutter speed

A shutter speed of 1/250th of a second was used in this example. Usually a slower shutter speed would be used to get the blur of the clouds moving but in this case the cloud movement looked very good with a fast shutter speed. If the visuals had not been pleasing then the shutter speed would have been changed.

Time-lapse settings

This example was created using the time-lapse mode to create a final video in camera. It was appropriate to review the clip immediately because if it had not worked then another clip with different settings would have been created.

Other considerations

After arriving at a location high up on a building, it was decided to look around before getting the camera out of the bag. Often we do not think about looking up, but in this case the photographer did. This shot would have been completely missed without looking around before setting up the camera. Always ensure that you investigate your surroundings before you start shooting.

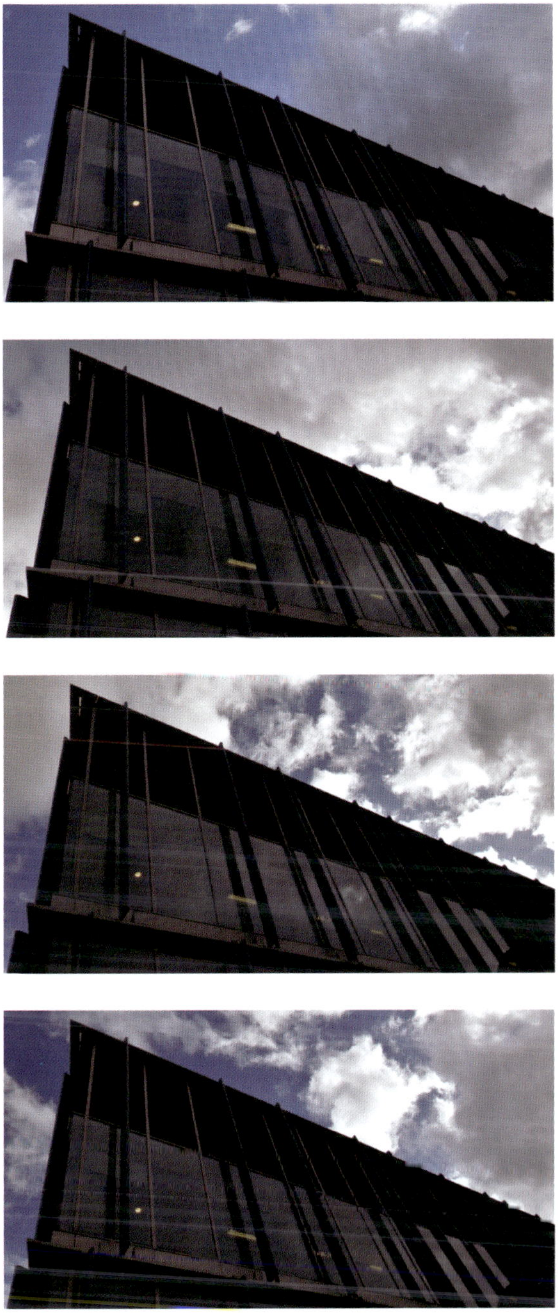

▲ Looking up enables you to view a comparison in movement between stationary objects such as this building and floating clouds. The reflections in the glass also add to the final effect of this time-lapse video.

AT THE FAIRGROUND

When it's dark and all that is left is man-made lighting it is possible to use very slow shutter speeds and get lots of motion blur. Movement and man-made lighting can together create very strong and colourful imagery. Finding a good shooting position is the first step. Finding an appropriate shutter speed to capture the blur is the next. This deliberate blur in the images cannot be seen with the naked eye so you will need to use your imagination and assess the direction and speed of the movement. This will help you put all of the elements together to achieve a fantastic low light time-lapse video.

This example

This example is of a merry-go-round. The camera is facing upwards and has been set up close to the ground in order to accentuate the circular shape of the ride. This time-lapse is shot late at night in winter to make sure that there is no ambient light. This way the colours of the man-made lights give a punchy image with vivid colour.

Mode

The camera is set to aperture priority to ensure that the depth of field does not change. The light in this subject does not change greatly, so the shutter speed will not change either; therefore we do not have to worry about any slight changes in motion blur. In fact, if the shutter speed were to change slightly it could look quite interesting.

Aperture

An aperture of *f*/10 was used to get a wide depth of field. With a wide-angle lens at 24mm (as used in this example) this aperture is sufficient to achieve a large depth of field.

Sensitivity

A sensitivity of 100 ISO was used to make sure that no digital noise was seen in the image. This low sensitivity was also chosen to ensure that the shutter speed would be slow enough to get motion blur.

Shutter speed

Based on the aperture and ISO settings, the camera chose a shutter speed of ⅓ of a second. This was just about perfect for the movement and rotational speed of the merry-go-round. If the camera had not selected this kind of shutter speed, manual mode would have been used instead in order to control it.

Time-lapse settings

The camera was being used in time-lapse photography mode so the final video could be viewed straight away after capture. The interval was set to match the shutter speed and therefore set to trigger the camera once every two seconds.

Other considerations

Fairgrounds are very popular locations for photographers to capture low light imagery like this. The same merry-go-round was used a year before this shoot and those images can be seen elsewhere in the book. Always revisit locations and see how your imagery can vary and change, depending on the light and other variable factors.

This merry-go-round was captured with a slow shutter speed to communicate the movement in the rotational spinning of the ride. This has created an exciting time-lapse video.

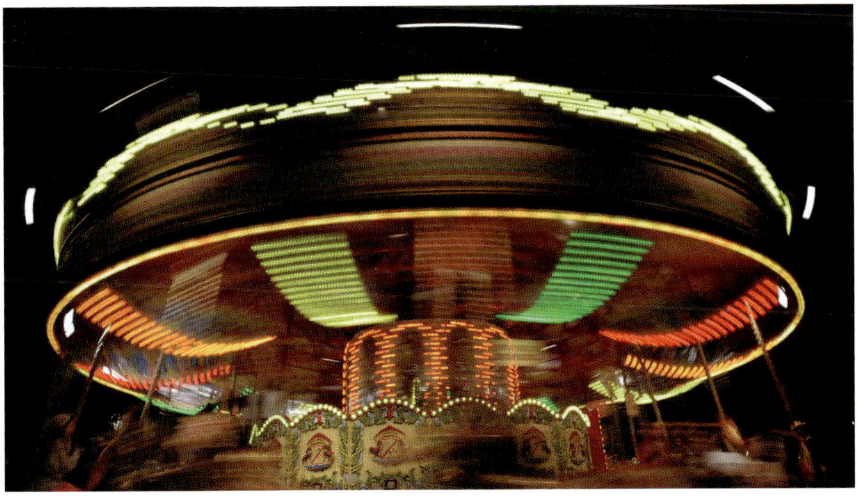

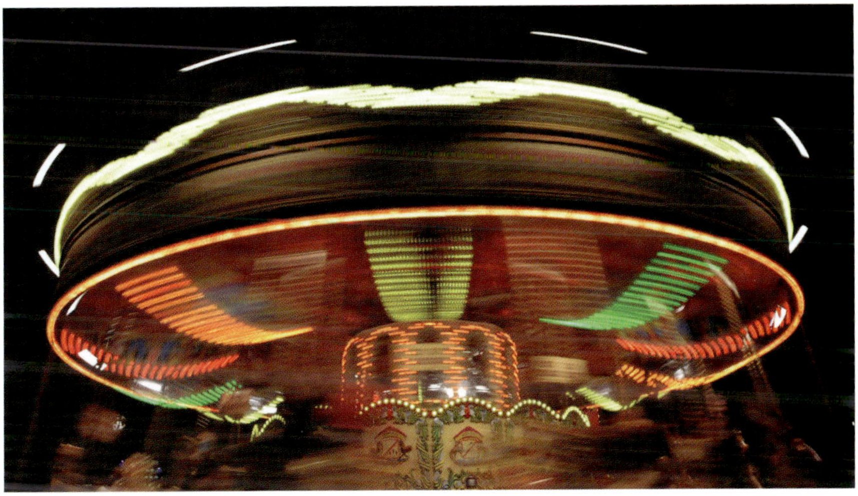

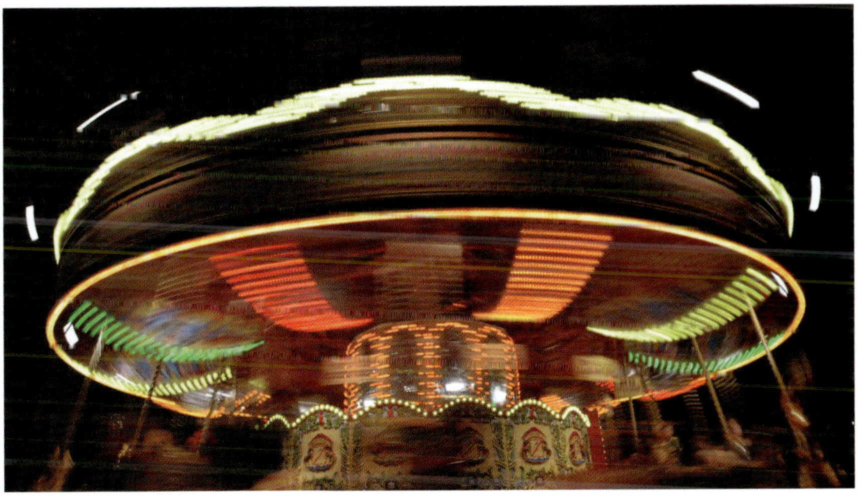

A SUNNY DAY

Hard direct sunlight and clouds can give some interesting opportunities for time-lapse photography. When you have clouds in the shot like this, it is helpful to think about which way the wind is blowing – perhaps create a short test time-lapse to find out the direction of the clouds. Sometimes the movement is obvious because you can see it with your own eyes. Try to position the camera in a way that uses movement to assist the composition of the image. When it is sunny and cloudy we get pools of hard light falling through onto the scene. In the final time-lapse video you will see these pools of hard light moving quickly over the scenery. This is visually exciting and shows you movement that you would not otherwise be able to see.

This example

This time-lapse was shot from a tall building in London during a fairly bright, warm day. There were plenty of clouds in the sky and it was quite windy. The bright sunlight was shining through holes in the clouds and pools of hard light were moving over the city landscape. This vantage point is used in other examples in this book and demonstrates that revisiting the same location can be very rewarding.

Equipment

A full frame DSLR camera was used for this time-lapse video. It was mounted on a full-sized tripod and had a 16–35mm lens attached, and the lens was zoomed in to 35mm for the shoot. The wind was quite strong so the tripod was being weighed down by a heavy backpack hung from a hook under the tripod. This reduced the amount of movement in the camera made by the wind.

Mode

The camera was set to aperture priority to make sure the depth of field was constant throughout the video. If the camera did not give a good result in terms of exposure then the back-up plan would have been manual mode.

Aperture

The aperture that was used was *f*/8 to make sure a large depth of field was achieved to capture all of the detail in the image such as the buildings and clouds.

Sensitivity

A low sensitivity of ISO 100 was used because it was a very bright day. If a high ISO had been used in the image then the time-lapse would have been overexposed.

Shutter speed

A relatively fast shutter speed of 1/125th had been chosen by the camera to let less light in so that the image was not overexposed. Motion blur was not a priority with this example so that was appropriate. If motion blur had been desired then the camera would have been put into manual mode and the balance of the exposure triangle would have been adjusted.

Time-lapse settings

The camera was set up in time-lapse mode so that the final video would be ready on the card when the camera had finished shooting. An interval of one second was used because the clouds were moving quite quickly. If the clouds had been moving slowly then an interval of around three to five seconds would have been tested.

Other considerations

When we have clouds with harsh sunlight shining through it can make any location look interesting with different pools of light moving over the subject becoming a feature in itself. Be careful on sunny days because it is easy to get overexposure because of the large quantity of light.

Always revisit locations on a different day with different light. This location was used previously when it was stormy but on this occasion it was sunny and cloudy. The sky is full of fluffy clouds which gives fantastic time-lapse movement.

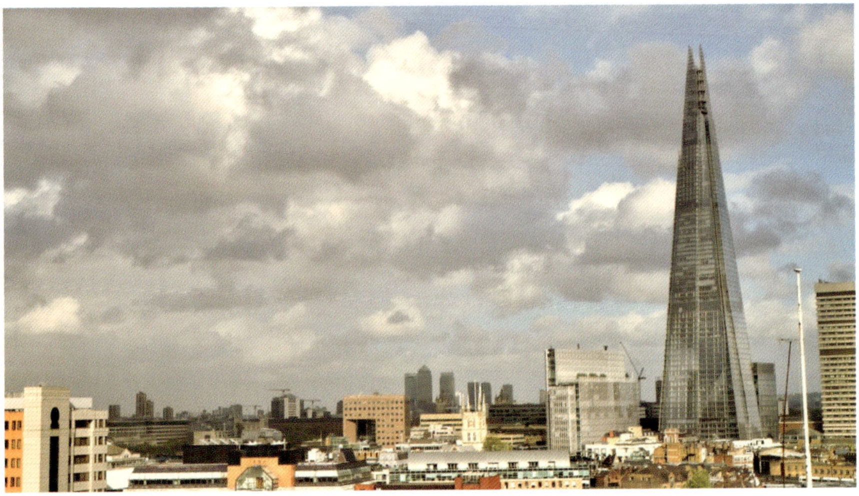

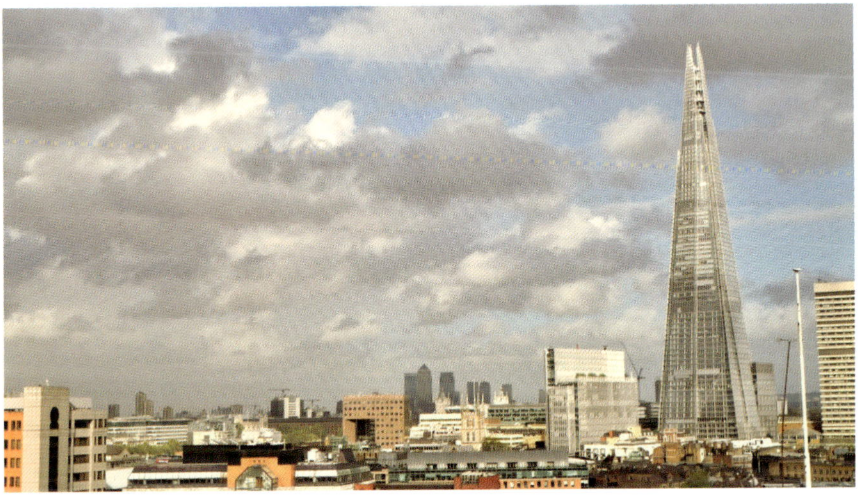

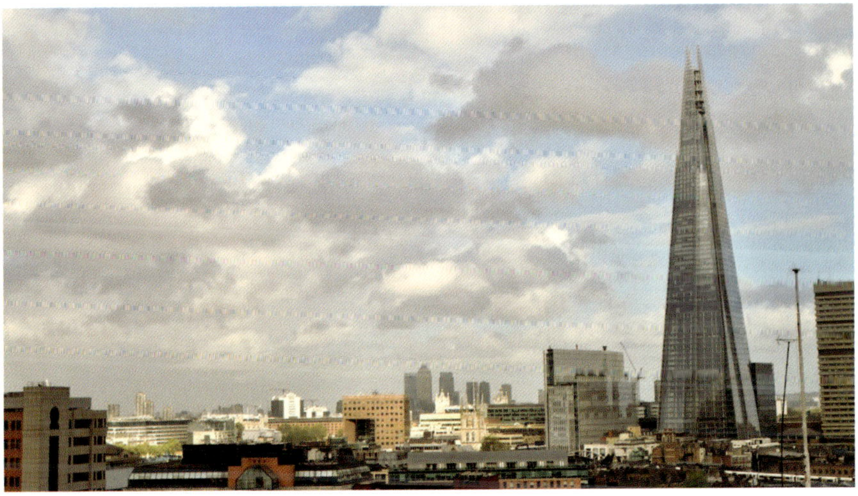

Chapter 8

Film-making and editing for time-lapse videos

Making time-lapse videos and film-making are very closely related and share many of the same processes and approaches. When you put together a time-lapse you are making a small movie because, just like a movie, there are considerations such as camera angles, depth of field and storytelling, to name a few. If a film-making approach is taken to your time-lapse photography, generally the final result will benefit in many ways. If you have not tried film-making before, then this chapter will help you explore a new and exciting area that can be expanded on at any stage.

A big part of film-making is in the initial concept and how it is executed, but any movie is really 'made' in the editing room. Editing your time-lapse videos is just like editing a movie and requires the same software. We will explore film-making terminology as well as ideas with editing that can be applied to both time-lapse and video-making. After exploring time-lapse photography you will be well on the way to becoming a film-maker.

FILM-MAKING FOR TIME-LAPSE PHOTOGRAPHY

In this section we look at film-making ideas and terminology that is useful within time-lapse photography. Whatever you are creating, whether it be video, stills or time-lapse, it is important to have a clear idea of what you are communicating. This ensures that your message is portrayed clearly, whilst delivering visually exciting imagery at the same time. To portray a message clearly we need to know the ways in which it can be communicated.

There are two ways that we can approach our time-lapse video: we can use one camera angle of the subject for the duration of the capture, or we can shoot from different angles and edit them together afterwards. The advantage of the multi-angle approach is that we are able to use different lenses and we don't need to stand in the same place capturing the time-lapse for so long. Shooting different angles to edit together to make one video will keep the viewer interested and enable you to expand your creativity. It really does depend on the subject matter though – the style of the video needs to be appropriate for the content.

When you begin to learn about shooting time-lapse videos, a single camera angle will be a good starting point. Aim to advance on to multiple-angle shoots because it will potentially give a more professional look. If you are able to use multiple camera angles you will gain valuable experience as a film-maker.

One camera angle in your time-lapse

If you have a single camera angle in your time-lapse video then you will need to consider how strong that one angle is; does it offer stimulating enough content to keep the viewer interested? We need to make sure it is compelling compositionally, but also that the movement in the frame is engaging enough. If you have a camera angle that shows moving traffic

◀ Visually with time-lapse we aim to give the viewer lots of movement to watch. However, this example shows that it can be equally effective and beautiful to just have a small element of movement in the video. Here we have clouds moving along the top of the frame and over time, the yellow and blue colours change in the sky.

within an airport, with aeroplanes landing and taking off and a sunrise all in the same frame, then that will look fantastic as a single shot because there is so much going on in the frame. However, if there are only subtle changes in light or movement, to keep the viewer interested you will benefit from shooting multiple angles and editing them all together, so that the video shows the different angles in sequence.

Multiple camera angles for time-lapse photography

Creating a time-lapse video that has multiple camera angles will, in most cases, be more visually exciting for the viewer. Try to keep the viewer guessing and tell more of the story as you go along; this way you will keep their attention for the duration of the video clip.

Most people are used to watching television and online media; this desensitizes your viewer to good video content. Essentially we have a lot to live up to as image-makers. There is some exceptional work out there, so make sure you aim to stand out from the crowd. Adopting a film-making approach will be one of the most effective steps you can take with time-lapse photography.

TERMINOLOGY OF FILM-MAKING

Here we will look at some of the terminology used in the film-making world to communicate different camera angles, shots and movements. Each item on the list will then be explained in the context of shooting time-lapse videos. If you ever find yourself speaking with another film-maker then this language will enable you to communicate easily with them. Once you have explored each item you will be able to start making shot lists for your time-lapse video.

Camera shots

Establishing shot
Long shot
Full shot
Half shot
Close-up
Extreme close-up

Camera angles

High angle
Low angle
Eye level
Tilted angle
Overshot
Undershot
Point of view

Camera movements

Panning
Tilting
Dolly shot
Jib shot
Zoom
Tracking shot

For most time-lapse photographers the shots and angles list will be more useful than the camera movements. Making movements whilst shooting a time-lapse video can require specialist equipment that is expensive; if you are keen to try out these kinds of shots, equipment can be hired for occasional use.

We will have a look at each item listed here and apply it to shooting a time-lapse video. Remember, you can mix and match from each of the three lists above. For example, you can have a panning shot that is also a long shot, or a tracking shot that is also an overshot. The images used in these examples are not from a time-lapse video, but are created to illustrate the terminology using a simple subject.

Camera shots

Establishing shot

This is one of the most important shots to have in your video because this gives us all the information we need to follow the story. This shot is generally filmed with a wide-angle lens and is normally at or near the beginning of the video. We can establish aspects such as time of day, location, subject matter and character.

If you are filming a time-lapse video and you do not plan to do multiple camera angles, it is usually preferable to approach the one angle you will be showing as an establishing shot. This kind of shot is occasionally found at the end of the video as the climax: sometimes film-makers show small details of the story to keep the suspense throughout the film and then at the end they will show an establishing shot to finally give the whole story away. Whatever approach you take, it is more than likely that this shot will become familiar to you.

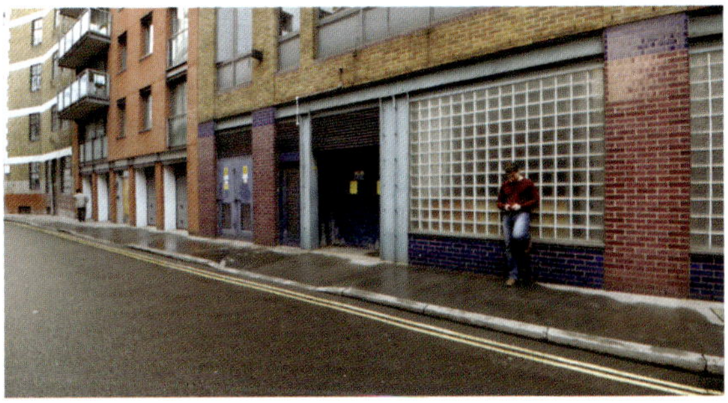

▲ The establishing shot is a useful start for a story when making a video. For this type of shot a wide-angle lens is usually used. Many time-lapse photographers use this shot frequently without realizing it.

Long shot

The long shot is almost always taken using a wide-angle lens to capture a large scene with lots of depth, normally with the main subject placed in the foreground or middle. The approach that is taken with this kind of shot is very similar to landscape photography because an aperture of around *f*/11 is often used to create a big depth of field so that everything is clear for the viewer to explore visually.

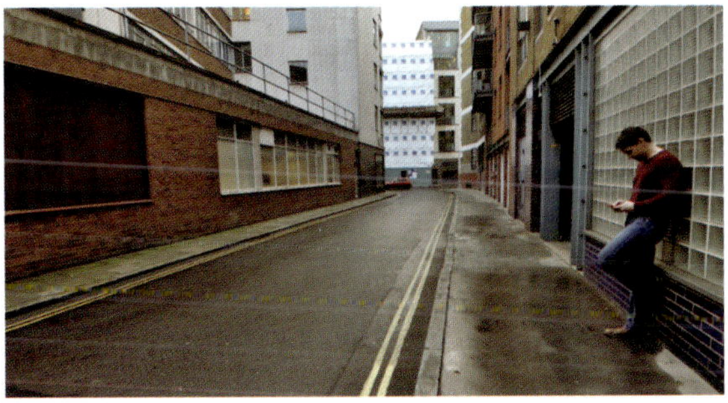

▲ The long shot can be very similar to the establishing shot. Generally it is similar to a landscape shot, but used for your time-lapse movie.

Full shot

This camera shot is of a full person, head to toe. If your time-lapse has people in it then you can decide how much of them are in the frame. Keep an eye on movement though. It could be that people are going up an escalator at a train station and therefore moving out of the frame as they move. When using people as part of the movement in your video, this will help you think about how to frame and compose.

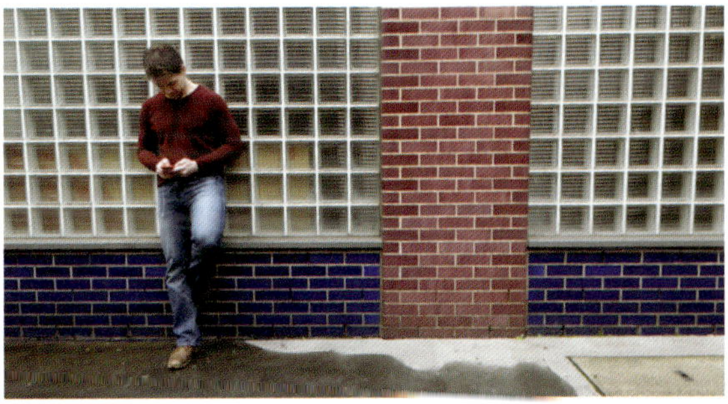

▲ A full shot can be used if you are recording a time-lapse of any scene with people in. This kind of composition will generally be head to toe. You can have a full shot of a single person or of a crowd.

Half shot

A half shot is used when you fill the frame with half of a person, usually the upper half. You can for example do a time-lapse video of two people sitting at a table speaking to each other and if the bottom of the frame is waist level and the top of the

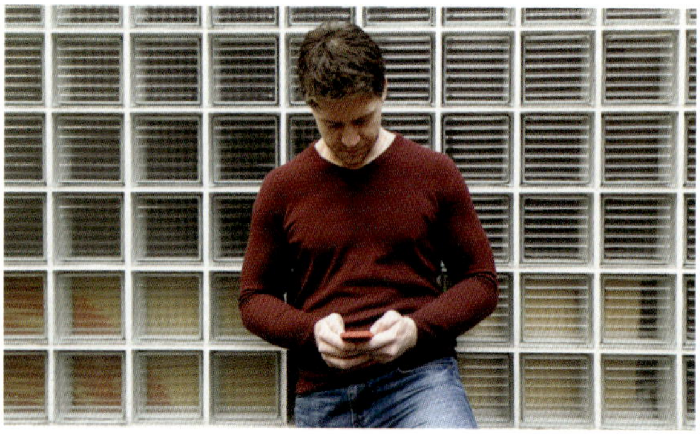

▲ A half shot is usually framed from the waist to the head of a subject.

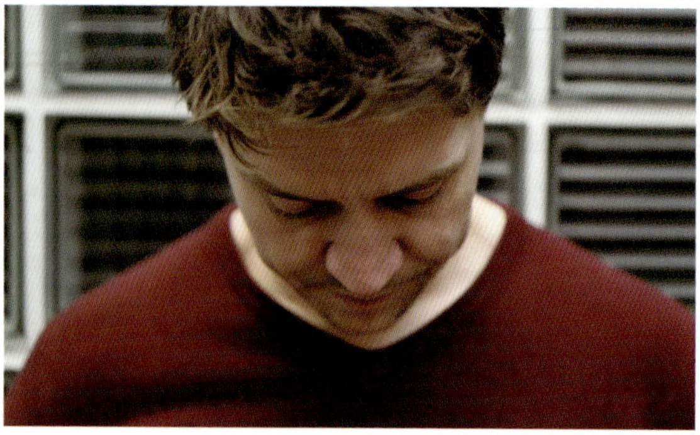

▲ A close-up shot is taken in order to see details of the subject more closely.

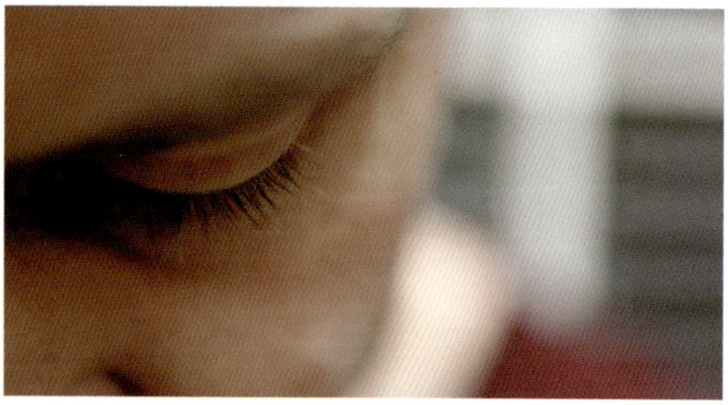

▲ An extreme close-up enables you to capture the small details of your subject. Generally a macro lens is used for this type of shot.

frame is just over the top of the head, that would be a half shot.

Close-up

A close-up shot is used to show medium-sized detail within a scene. If you are making a time-lapse of a taxi driver at work you could make a close up shot of their hand on the steering wheel. If you want to capture smaller details then you go into an extreme close-up.

Extreme close-up

Often shot with a macro lens, an extreme close up will fill the frame with small details from your subject. This kind of shot is used when making time-lapse videos of small nature and wildlife subjects, such as ants or a flower growing. In any situation showing small details which will assist your storytelling, aim to get really close. This helps with achieving visual diversity as well as keeping the viewer's eyes busy.

Camera angles

This section is concerned with how the shot is framed. This could affect decisions such as what lens you use and where the camera is when it is shooting. Most of these angles can be translated back to stills shooting as well and, in fact, a lot of it might sound familiar to stills photographers.

High angle

High angle is where the camera is high up, looking down on your subject. A time-lapse shot from a high angle can show a large amount of moving detail and help us get a sense of scale and distance between objects. If you are shooting anything with a lot of people or traffic, this angle will help you see more of what is going on. If you shoot a busy scene from street level, for example, you will see much less movement, but from higher up everything is more visible. Using this kind of angle will always make a scene impressive, but of course you need to find somewhere high up to shoot from. Look for a hill or a building with a good view.

Low angle

A low angle shot is when the camera is low down on the ground. This will work well when you are capturing movement close to the ground, such as a time-lapse of a flower. This approach will change how the scale of an object looks in your frame.

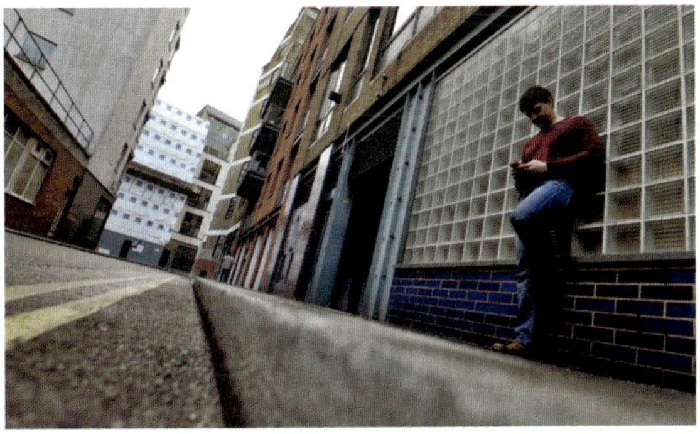

▲ In time-lapse photography a low angle shot can be a great camera angle to utilize. Subject matter can often look more interesting or impressive because of the perspective from ground level up. Often a wide-angle lens is used for this shot.

Eye level

Taken from eye level this shot is the most obvious that can be taken and, depending on what you want from your imagery, it could prove to be very unexciting. Sometimes, however we do need an obvious shot to establish how something looks if you were standing there.

Tilted angle

The tilted angle, often referred to as a 'Dutch angle', is a shot where the camera is tilted to the side, either to the right or the left. This can be a strong compositional tool, but is best used sparingly because it can make the viewer feel uneasy or sick. There is always a slight risk when shooting at an angle as there is no way that you can put this kind of shot the right way up afterwards, unless a wide-angle focal length is used to give room to crop. Shooting at an angle is a great way to add visual diversity to your time-lapse videos.

▲ This approach is more of a wild card. If we are able to add an angled shot we can break away from what the viewer is used to seeing and do something different.

Overshot

An overshot is generally where the camera is high up and looking down. This can be looking over the side of a building, vehicle or wall, for example. If the view point is from high up, the subject can feel small and far away, depending on the lens that is used. If you are capturing a large crowd in a city, an overshot enables you to get all of the scene in the frame.

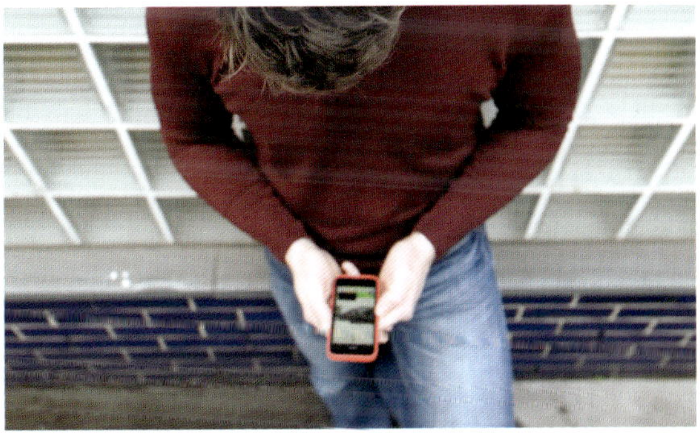

▲ An overshot is usually captured from a high tripod or crane. This is where the camera is looking over the subject. If you were doing a time-lapse over the side of a tall building, you might want to experiment with this kind of shot.

Undershot

This type of shot is from low down and the camera will be looking up. This is a great type of shot when you want to make something look taller or more impressive than it actually is. Be careful with an undershot, however, because if someone is in the way for a frame then they will obstruct the view.

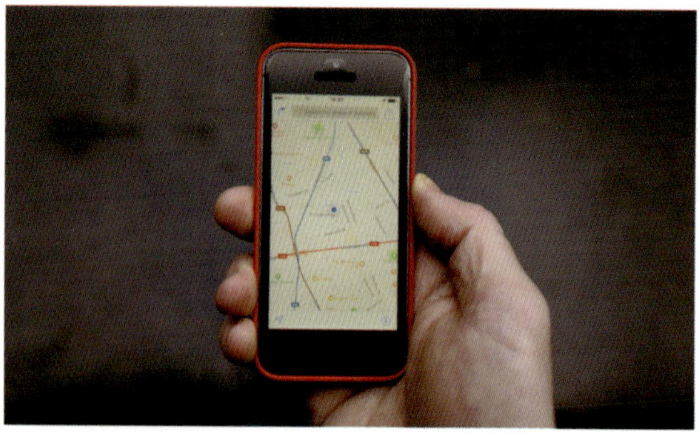

▲ The point of view shot is not often used for time-lapse photography but is quite common in regular film-making. That does not mean you should not use it, though – depending on your content, it might be relevant to use this type of camera angle.

Point of view

This shot does what it says on the tin. If you are making a time-lapse of a person and you want to show their point of view, you would shoot a POV (point of view) shot from where they are positioned in order to help tell their story.

Camera movements

Movement is the biggest difference between stills and video, but for time-lapse photography you will probably not be moving the camera itself while the time-lapse is being captured. The reason for this is that the equipment required is very expensive, and although it is getting cheaper these devices are generally not practical to carry around. We will, however, look at the types of movements that can be used in time-lapse videos or for shooting regular video.

There are of course instances when you will move the camera when capturing time-lapse videos. Hyperlapse actually enables you to capture time-lapse videos where the camera is moving without using any expensive equipment and, as demonstrated in the 'walking with the camera' example (Chapter 7), you can walk along whilst shooting if this will deliver the creative effect you are looking for. Also, remember that just because something is not designed to move specifically for time-lapse photography, it does not mean it cannot be used. See for example, the time-lapse captured from the dashboard of a car (Chapter 7), which shows that any moving object can be used to move the camera – boats, aeroplanes, fairground rides, to name a few. Use your imagination and find ways to move the camera itself as well as movement in your subject.

Panning

This technique is often used for shooting still photographs as well as video and is the same movement either way. A panning shot simply emulates the movement that you will make when looking left to right or vice versa. A sports photographer will do this when they are shooting a racing car on a track, for example.

This is a simple shot to achieve for regular video but if you were shooting a panning shot for time-lapse you would need a motorized tripod of some kind that would pan the camera slowly whilst the camera is capturing stills. Panning movement can be achieved more easily in your time-lapse videos with editing software, without moving the camera during capture. You effectively zoom into the video in post-production and move left and right across the final time-lapse. If you wish to do this in software, make sure that you shoot your video with a wider focal length and with the highest resolution to give room for movement.

Tilting

A tilting shot would emulate the motion that you make with your head if you look up and down. For video this would be relatively easy to achieve on a good tripod with a fluid head. For time-lapse it would again require specialist equipment. Tilting can also be achieved after shooting the time-lapse in video editing software. Make sure you leave room for the tilting movement if you plan to do this because you will crop into the image in order to move around the frame.

Dolly shot

A 'dolly' or 'slider shot' is filmed on what looks like a small railway track. The camera is moved along the track either left and right or forwards and backwards. The end result is a very smooth movement in whatever direction is desired. To get this shot for time-lapse, you will need a motorized slider. This moves the camera along the track very slowly whilst the camera captures the time-lapse. If you are capturing time-lapse with slow shutter speeds to get motion blur in traffic, for example, you will need a motorized slider that is capable of stopping for each and every frame that is captured whilst ultimately moving in any given direction. The other option for this kind of shot is to try a hyperlapse video and walk with the camera.

Jib shot

A jib is basically a small crane that has the camera on the end of it and is controlled by a person standing at the back end of it. This kind of movement is generally not used for time-lapse photography because the rig needed would be very specialist. These kind of rigs do exist but most people's budgets will not stretch this far; it is nevertheless a great shot to be able to identify within film making.

Zoom

A zoom shot can be achieved by zooming the lens either in or out, whilst the time-lapse is being shot. You can zoom into the time-lapse video in video editing software after shooting. This is much easier to achieve than physically zooming the lens during capture and is much safer because zooming the lens in and out might mean that you lose focus.

Tracking shot

A tracking shot is basically a shot that follows something. This is made using a steady cam for video but for time-lapse this would probably be made using a slider, like in a dolly shot. This kind of shot is also used in hyperlapse photography quite often and will create a very engaging video clip.

MAKE A SHOT LIST WHILST WATCHING A MOVIE

Now we have explored the terminology behind film-making, it is time to apply the knowledge to something that has already been filmed by someone else. Watch part of a film or TV series that you thought was visually exciting and make a shot list from it. This will help reinforce the language of film-making and will help you think about how it can be applied to your own time-lapse video. An example of a shot list could be:

1. Establishing/jib shot
2. Full shot
3. Close-up
4. Long shot/on slider
5. Tracking shot

Once you have done this, create a shot list for your next time-lapse shoot. This will give you clear structure and direction and will also help you think about what lenses and shooting positions to use.

EDITING VIDEO

Editing video is something that most stills photographers postpone for as long as possible, but using video editing software is often much easier than stills editing software. If you approach this subject methodically and patiently you will quickly reap the benefits. Being able to edit video is a very useful skill to have when doing time-lapse photography because you will not only be able to complete your videos by putting music and credits to them, but there are additional benefits. For anyone who is looking to make money out of image-making, being able to edit and produce a finished product makes you more independent as an image-maker. Advertising. for example, is much more about digital television screens than posters now. Generally speaking, most companies are looking for both video and stills, whereas previously they might have wanted just stills.

Thinking about the final video

There are certain elements that, if considered, will help to establish direction in your video-making. This will enable you to shoot for the edit where possible. This means that you can shoot less but have more usable content for the final product. The following areas will help you when approaching a project, right from the planning stage through to editing.

Length

How long do you want your video to be? It might be worth watching other videos online that are similar to what you want to achieve. This will not necessarily give you the final answer, but it will give you an idea of what works and what doesn't. More importantly, you will get an idea of what you like in terms of the final video. You might like a long, steadily paced video that you can lose yourself in, which could be seven minutes long; you might prefer something more short and snappy, closer to two minutes in length. Be honest with yourself: if you are watching a video, how long is it until you turn it off and start looking at something else. A final length of one to two minutes tends to be a good target if you are unsure.

Once you have finished the edit, show it to people you know and see when they start to pay less attention or start to fidget; if they start to lose interest then that's where it should finish. Being brutally honest like this might seem harsh but will ultimately drive you to producing better content every time you edit.

Tone/feel

The tone and feel is often set by the subject matter, so this could well be a given before you edit. If you are doing a time-lapse video to contribute to a larger movie, then that will quickly establish the tone and feel for you. For a fast-paced movie, for example, the time-lapse should also feel fast and quick. Always think about context and how the time-lapse feels in its communication. If you have a time-lapse with slow moving clouds then a mellow piece of music and slow paced edit will suit that; respond creatively to what you see.

There are lots of components that can come together to influence the tone and feel of your final video. Some of these elements are; music, colour, pacing, length, subject matter and camera angles. Once you have edited the video show it to someone and ask them what they think about it. How do they feel when they watch it?

Controlling the look of your content

There are many tools in stills and video editing software that are there to help you control how it looks. The tools listed below will generally be found in all imaging software and are fundamental to the look and feel of the image. These tools are also used to rescue imagery in case the settings were wrong in camera at the time of capture. This list only covers some of the tools available in any given software package. It might seem like a short list, but if you do not tackle these basic tools and get a good feel for what they do to your image, you could end up wasting time editing in an unnecessarily complicated manner.

Contrast

This tool is available in any imaging software and can make your image more punchy or eye-catching to look at. If contrast is increased, the darker areas

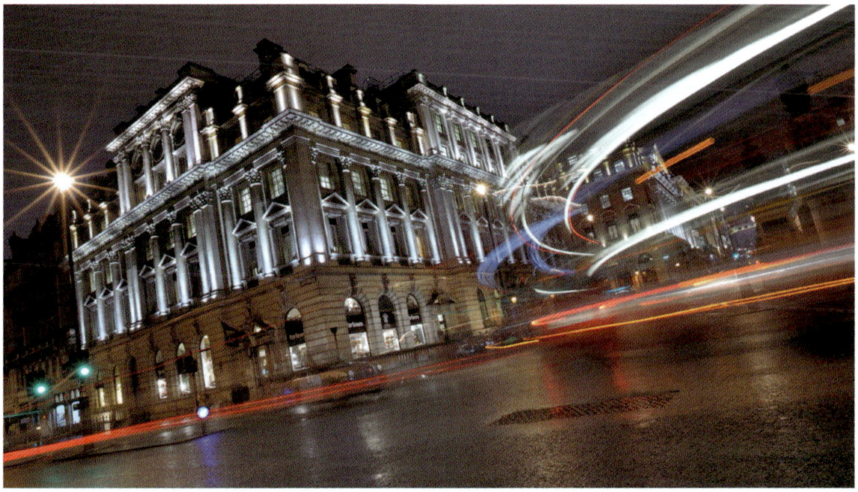

This image has the contrast turned down very low. Although this can enable you to see more detail, it can also make an image look very flat.

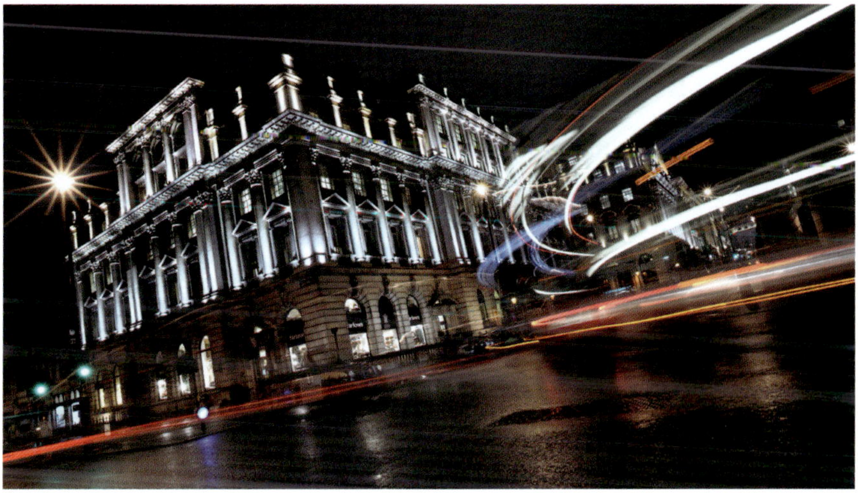

In this frame the contrast is turned up very high. This produces a punchy image but you lose a lot of detail in dark and bright areas.

get darker and white areas brighter. If we reduce it we can make an image look very flat because it decreases the extreme changes between dark and bright areas. We need to be very careful with contrast changes.

Most people like to increase the contrast in their images because it makes the image punchy, but by increasing the contrast too much we can lose detail in the dark and bright areas. It can be much better to actually lower or leave the contrast as it is in order to retain detail, but increase the colour saturation to get an eye-catching image.

Brightness

Brightness appears to increase the exposure of an image, which sometimes helps to increase detail in the dark areas. If you increase it too far, however, you will lose detail in bright areas, so there can be a trade-off. Use brightness to add a little lift and make the image slightly more cheerful looking, but use with caution.

Saturation

Saturation is your way of being able to increase or decrease the overall amount of colour in your image. If you increase saturation a touch, you can make your image quite eye catching with vivid

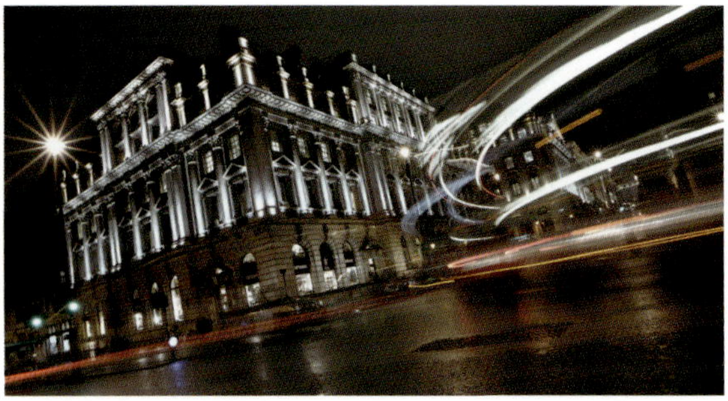

▲ This image has the saturation turned almost all the way down to illustrate a muted colour. Sometimes a muted colour works very well, depending on the subject matter.

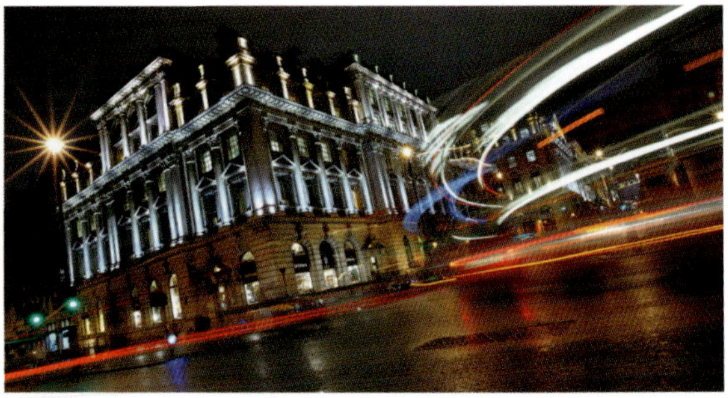

▲ In this frame the saturation is turned up very high to show the difference. A high saturation is very popular because of the vivid punchy colours.

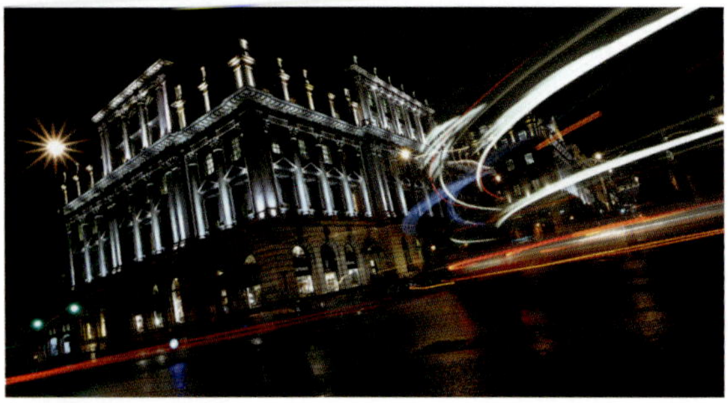

▲ This image illustrates the frame as captured in camera and has no shadow protection applied.

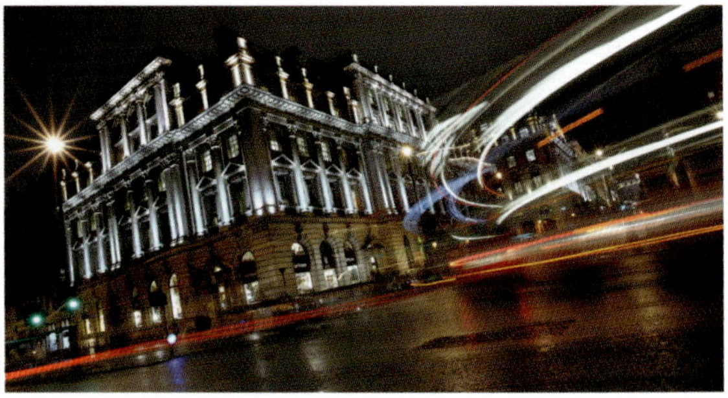

▲ This image shows the same frame with shadow protection heavily applied. This lifts the dark areas and means more detail can be seen without making any changes to the bright areas, which avoids possible or further overexposure in highlights.

colours that will stand out more to the viewer. If you go too far with turning your saturation up then you will lose detail and colour will take over; you can get blobs of unwanted colours if the level is too high. If saturation is turned down completely then your image will be black and white. A popular look is to give the image a muted colour. This means the saturation is turned down slightly so the image is almost a black-and-white image.

Shadow protection

This comes in different forms and is called different things depending on the software, but the idea behind it is invaluable. If you turn shadow protection up, it means that the darker areas are made brighter but nothing else is. Often we try to restore detail by playing with contrast, but this makes changes to the entire image. Shadow protection changes only the dark areas. If you want more detail in the shadows then this is one of the best tools available.

Highlight protection

Like shadow protection this can come in different forms and makes changes to just the bright areas in the image. If you find that you have bright sections in the sky on your time-lapse that are losing detail in the clouds, turn this setting up and your highlights could well be rescued.

AUDIO

When we watch television we often don't think about how the audio is recorded or recognize how important it is. The audio can really make or break any video: if the audio is badly recorded or the backing track is not appropriate then it will be blindingly obvious. If the audio is of high quality and fits with the visuals then we don't actually notice it whilst we are watching.

Good audio will add a sense of validity to your final piece and can completely transform the mood and feeling of the final product. If your final video has no audio you are missing out on a great opportunity with your storytelling. If you play a video to most people they will be expecting audio without even knowing it because we are used to audio backing when watching television. This section explores different ways of capturing and using audio for your time-lapse video so that you can enhance your work. Don't worry if you have never recorded audio before, as it can be very straightforward.

Capturing audio

Sometimes it is preferable to use audio that comes from the same location that your time-lapse is captured in. It could be the main audio used in the final piece or just a backing track; either way it will help to communicate the feel of the place in the final edit. We do not get audio from shooting a time-lapse alone, so we will need to capture audio on a separate device whilst the camera is shooting the time-lapse visuals. Alternatively, audio can be recorded on the camera itself using the regular video recording function when we are not shooting the actual time-lapse. If you shoot a regular video then you can detach the audio from that and use it as a backing track for the final time-lapse.

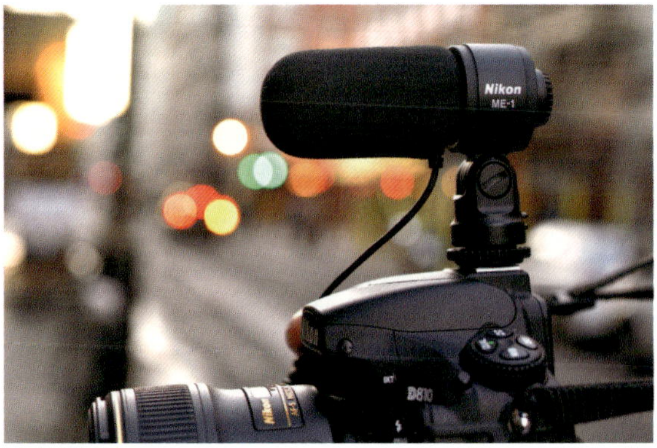

▲ Most advanced cameras have the option for direct audio recording. This shows a small compact DSLR video microphone. These can produce much clearer sound than the built-in microphone and will be much better for audio. On most cameras you cannot capture time-lapse video and record audio at the same time.

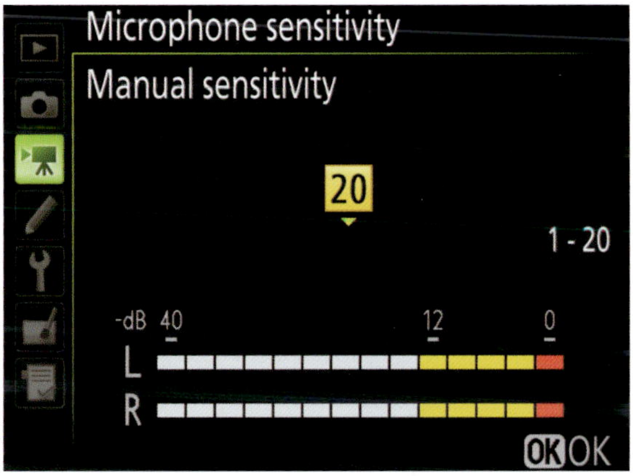

▲ If you record audio for your time-lapse or video on camera, always check the input levels. This will show whether the recording volume is too loud or quiet. If you see any red indicators this means it is too loud and the audio file will be distorted and unusable.

Recording audio on camera

Most cameras will have the facility to record audio. Some cameras have a built-in microphone and/or a facility to plug in an external microphone. Before recording a video clip to capture audio, make sure that you are not covering up the internal microphone because the audio recording will sound muffled or quiet. Another consideration is to make sure that you do not press any buttons on the camera whilst it is capturing audio. If you press buttons on the camera or use the focusing system whilst recording

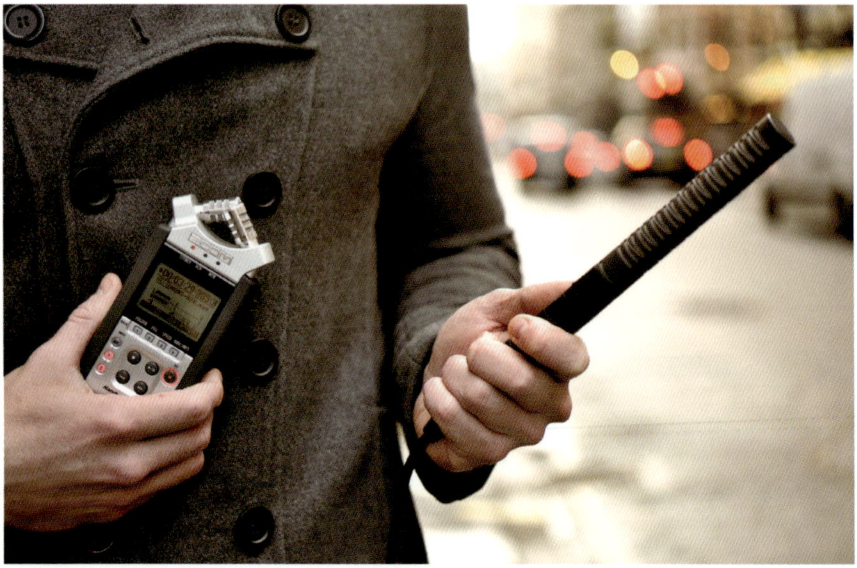

A directional or gun mic being used to pick up ambient city sound to use as backing for a time-lapse video. You can see an external recording device on the left being used. This means that you can capture time-lapse and audio at the same time, because the audio is being recorded separately.

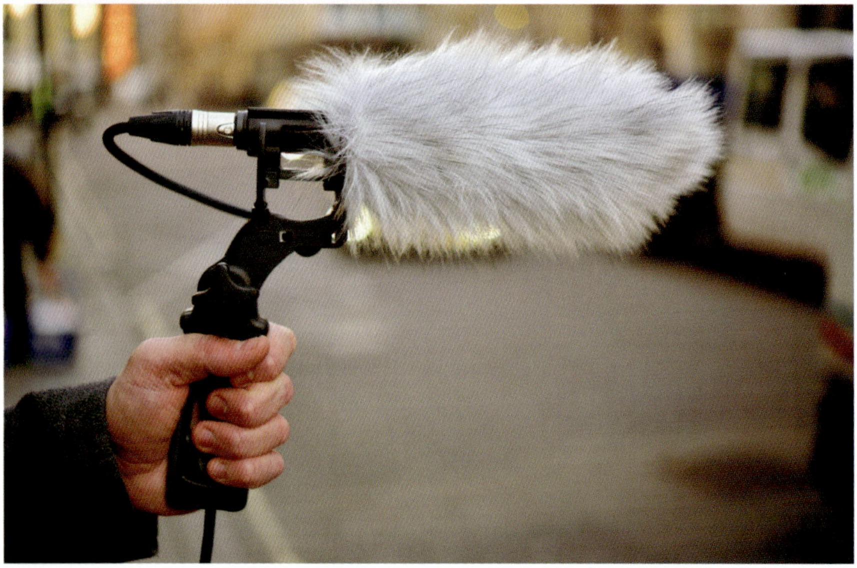

This directional microphone has a very direct and concentrated pickup pattern. It also has a wind shield over it, which will reduce any blowing or hissing noises created by wind blowing against the device.

video, you will hear the clicking noises on the audio track.

Ultimately it can be more tricky to use the built-in microphone than you might think. The audio quality is usually pretty good but a better and clearer audio is easily achieved with an external microphone plugged into the camera or a separate recording device.

Recording audio off camera

For the most part a dedicated audio recording device will be of a higher quality than the camera's built-in microphone and because we will achieve a crisper, cleaner audio signal, it will help to capture the viewer's attention when watching the final video. There are many hand-held devices that are available to us and many are very reasonably priced.

Editing your visuals to audio can be much easier than you think. If you make cuts during changes in the music your video will feel much more confident with its pacing and aesthetics.

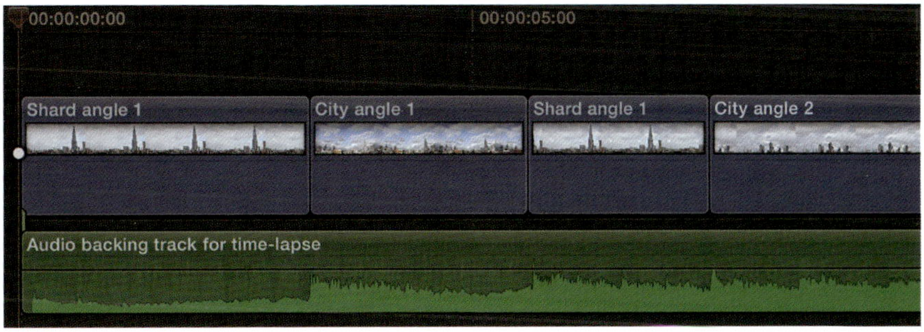

Recording audio off camera often gives us much more flexibility and it means that audio can be captured whilst the camera is shooting a time-lapse video. When using a microphone, the key is to use the correct tool for the job and for most time-lapse videos, a directional microphone will be appropriate.

Directional microphones

Also known as 'gun mics' these are long and thin in shape and, depending on the device, can be plugged into the camera or external recording device. They are very good at isolating a particular subject that is far away from the microphone itself. There are many different directional microphones on the market, which vary in shape. The longer and thinner the microphone is, the further the reach on the pickup pattern. This means we could stand 100 meters away, for example, from a motorway and still record the audio of the traffic by pointing the appropriate microphone at it.

This also means that the microphone will not pick up the clinking of the camera's shutter as it shoots the time-lapse. If you are recording audio separately to the camera, you can be capturing a time-lapse video and recording the audio at the same time. This maximizes the time on location and gives you audio that is relevant to the visuals.

Wind shields

Most commonly when you see a microphone, you will see a wind shield on it. This looks like a piece of foam or synthesized fur that wraps around the microphone. The reason these are on the microphones is so that you do not record any wind noise. If the wind is strong and the microphone does not have a wind shield, blowing or hissing noises will be evident on the recording and will effectively render the audio track useless. The rule of thumb is the more wind there is, the more fur you want.

MUSIC

Making your own music

As you have created the visuals, why not create the music yourself too? If you play a musical instrument then you may already have music you have recorded yourself. This will be a great source of audio for your time-lapse photography. You could compose a piece of music specifically to suit the mood, length and pace of the time-lapse – although of course not everyone has a home studio and a collection of instruments.

Another solution is to create music with software. Most computers come with software that enables you to create music very easily without needing in-depth knowledge. This will give you the creative freedom to customize the music to the time-lapse video. You also might have a friend or family member who makes music, which could be extremely helpful in order to achieve appropriate audio for your videos.

Using well-known music

A piece of music that you have purchased online or on CD will be subject to copyright. This means that this music is protected legally against unauthorized use. Unless you have permission to use this music you are not allowed to feature it in your time-lapse video if you intend to broadcast it in public. If you are simply going to play the licensed music in your own living room, however, this is not an issue.

If you are not sure if a piece of music is bound by copyright, make sure you check before using it. If you put your final video online and you are using protected music, it will be taken offline by the admin team running the website because the music is being used illegally. Another matter to consider if you use a piece of music that is well known is that it could be associated with something else, such as a particular film or television advert, for example. This means that when someone watches your content they will be distracted by associations triggered by the music. Let people enjoy your time-lapse videos in their own right and use music that helps create an emotion or mood that fits your work and is preferably unknown and unlicensed.

Video editing using audio as a guide

Once you have shot your time-lapse and you are ready to put it into the editing software, it will be useful to choose the backing audio prior to editing. The reason for this is that the audio will have such a huge effect on the overall mood and pacing that it will help us make decisions on how the editing is executed.

For example, if our time-lapse is of a busy railway station, the backing music chosen should also be fast and busy. The editing will be influenced by that and can also be quick and fast paced. You can choose the music to complement the visuals and to help with communicating a certain mood or feeling.

Look at the audio track on the editing software; you should see sound waves. This will show you when the music gets louder and quieter or where any obvious changes are. You can then line this up visually when you match the imagery to the audio as you edit. The beat or changes in the music can always be used to make cuts. A strong change in the music is a good point at which to change the camera angle, or go from day to night, for example. Let the music guide the editing and the final product will fit together nicely.

Titles and credits

Creating time-lapse is not always a one-man endeavour – in fact, some of the best time-lapse videos tend to be a team effort and there is nothing like thanking people who have helped you in some way. You may be crediting the artist who composed the audio track that you have chosen to use, but equally you could be thanking your partner who stood in the cold for forty-five minutes holding a spare lens. Saying 'thank you' is always appreciated.

Most video software makes it very easy to put credits at the end. It is best to title your time-lapse at the beginning as well. The video may have a title or a location that you want to communicate. Remember to credit yourself and put your email address for people to contact you. Always make sure people know who produced the piece of work that you have spent hours creating. You never know what might come of it if the right person notices your video.

Choosing software

Choosing the editing software that you use can be a difficult and confusing process, but it really doesn't have to be. Specific software packages will not be discussed here because the technology develops at such a rapid pace. When selecting what software to use, most people go on recommendation from a

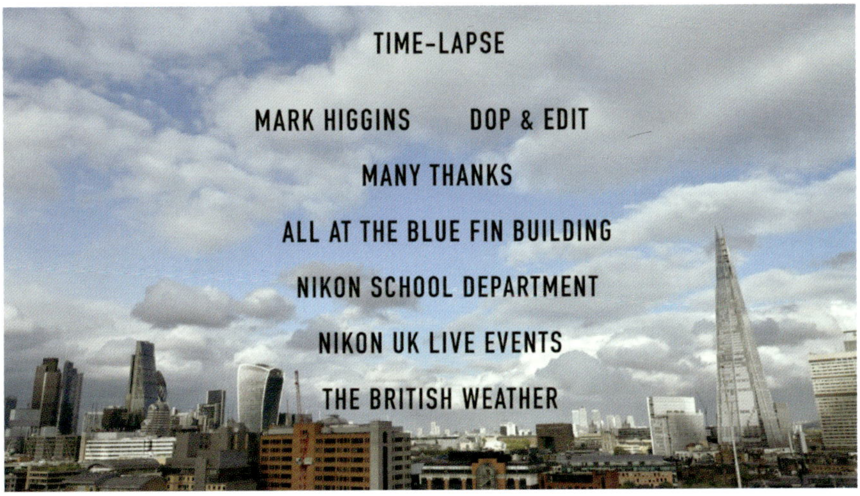

▶ Credits are easy to create even with basic video editing software and can be great promotion for you as an image-maker.

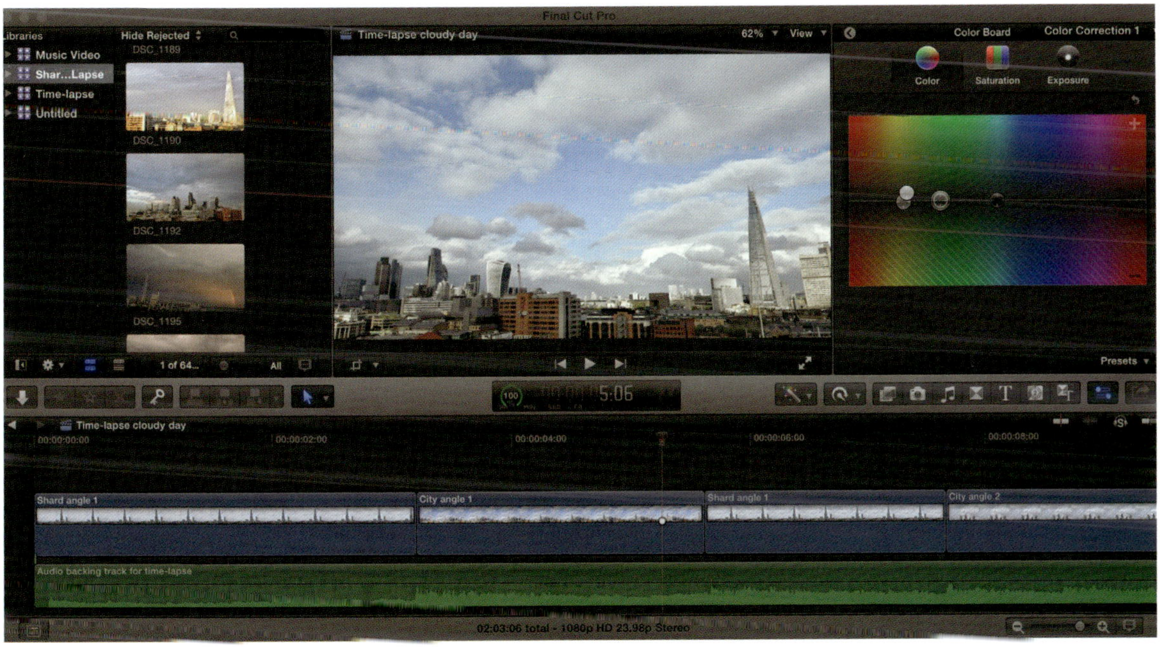

▲ Most video-editing software is fairly similar and will enable you to finalize your work. You can edit all of your time-lapse videos together and add music, titles and credits.

friend or family member or even an online forum or camera club. If you use a program that a friend uses, then they can help you learn, and that is always a huge advantage.

The best thing to do when choosing software for stills or video is to make a list of what you actually need to be able to do. More often than not, the free software that comes with the computer will probably do most, if not all, of it. If you have explored the free software and found that it does not deliver everything you require, then this is the time to move to a more advanced software package.

Chapter 9

Sharing and storing your time-lapse photography

When you are passionate about photography and have created something that you feel proud of, the next step is to present it in some way. You may decide to show your work to family and friends as well as to a wider audience, and there are many ways to exhibit your content. We will explore the different options that are available to us for presenting our stills or video, and the ways in which we can obtain and use feedback. We will look at storing the work that has been created along with different approaches to cataloguing and backing up your digital content so that nothing is lost.

SELECTING WHAT TO SHARE WITH OTHERS

Some say a photographer is only as good as the work that they show to other people. This makes the selection process one of the most important parts of the overall image-making exercise. If, for example, you capture six time-lapse videos in a day, but you only like one of them, show just the one that you like. It sounds simple enough but most of us can be indecisive about what we choose to show. The work that you decide not to display is still very important to your learning process, however. Ask yourself why you did not use that piece of work and what could have been improved.

There may be an emotional attachment to what has been captured and this can make us more precious about our work. We remember the background story and the thought processes that we went through, as well as any experiences we had on the shooting location. When someone else looks at our work they do not share this emotional attachment and therefore experience our still or video imagery in a very different way. If possible, try to select work objectively. If you are able to detach yourself from your work you can be more honest with yourself and choose the strongest work to show people.

Showing your work to others

The camera's back screen

This is one of the most common ways to show others your content, especially when it has just been captured. Most camera screens are very high quality and actually show more colour than most computer screens. The only downside is that the screen is quite small and is difficult to view in direct sunlight. Although limited by size, this way of viewing is a very good indication of how the image or video will look at the end of the process.

Prints

It is very satisfying to see your final images printed on high quality photographic paper. You can print still images taken from your time-lapse videos. The photographic print is more tangible; it is something you can pick up, view on a wall or in a book and therefore the experience of viewing the image is very different to using a digital screen. When you print an image you also see more of the colours

◀ This is an image from a time-lapse shoot in a busy pedestrian tunnel. If you find a location that inspires you, keep going back and build on your experience and knowledge. Camera settings: 1/125s, *f*/4.5, ISO 1250.

that are captured by the camera's sensor. Computer screens are usually quite limited in the amount of colour that is shown. Choose your favourite images and get them printed, if you have not done so already. It is not expensive and is very rewarding. You might even want to print a sequence of images from a time-lapse to represent the movement in a way that is different from playing a video.

Tablets and phones

Using portable electronic devices such as tablets or phones is becoming the most common way we show images or video to others. The main reason for this is that you tend to have this kind of device on you already, even if you don't have your main camera with you. Make a slide show or video to show on your phone or tablet, so when someone asks, you can show them your work quickly and easily.

Laptops

Due to the popularity of phones and tablets, it seems we are using computers less and less to show people our images. However, there are advantages in using a laptop to display your imagery. As a laptop computer gives you additional software tools and processing power, you are more prepared for any eventuality. If you see anything you want to edit or re-edit then you can do so on the spot.

Mobile phones and tablets are being used more for editing images, but their functionality is still somewhat limited. Laptops are very light and are becoming easier to carry around on a daily basis; another big advantage is that you will have a big screen to show your work on. Also, if you are playing a video, the sound quality is better on laptops than on phones or tablets, generally speaking.

Making yourself a showreel

Every so often it is a great idea to make yourself a disc of what you have done in a showreel format, which is simply the best clips put together in one video. This will enable you to watch and review your work and make it easier to obtain feedback. Being able to observe what you have produced on your television at home gives you an idea of how far your skills have progressed, and may help you to come up with ideas for where to go next.

Printing a photo book

The price of getting bespoke high quality photo books printed has decreased dramatically. Getting one printed once every six months or so can be a really productive way to finalize a project or just learn more from your own photography. Seeing your pictures printed in a book is a completely different experience to looking at them on a computer screen and is rewarding and educational.

Showing your content online

The best way to reach a wider audience is to use the internet. It is quite possible to upload a time-lapse video onto a website or social media platform one evening and have hundreds or even thousands of views by the following morning. Most photographers have a website or social media page dedicated to showing their work to others; it is a good idea to have your own website if you are aiming to promote yourself as a professional photographer.

The advantage of building your own website is that you have total control of what happens to your images. When uploading your content to a photography or social media website, you have to agree to their terms and conditions, and you need to be fully aware of what these entail. When you sign up to a profile or account on a website or app, make sure that you read all of the small print so you understand what the legalities of uploading your images are.

Storing and organizing your work

There is always a sense of dread when we talk about storing work and the possibility of losing it. However, storage is getting cheaper and it's also easy to do. Once you have a folder on your computer which holds some great content, you will want to make sure it is safe. If you just keep your work on your laptop there is always the chance of the computer failing in some way. It is very rare these days but it does happen and it may occur when we least want or expect it to.

The approach to take with backing up work is to prepare for the worst-case scenario. Before we back up we need a way of being able to find our work easily at a later date. There is nothing worse than trying to find a particular piece of work and simply not being able to. One popular way is to create folders by years and months so that you can go back chronologically through your work. Another widespread method is to name each folder by event or shoot. Whatever structure you choose, keep it simple and make it easy to follow.

Workflow and hard drives

Once you have put the contents of the card from your camera onto the computer, back it up. When you have backed up the work, format the card in the camera and you are then ready to keep shooting. As far as the computer is concerned, it is best not to keep all of your work on the hard drive because it will start to run slowly as it becomes full. Backing up on an external hard drive is a great way of storing content and also keeping the computer uncluttered. There is always the possibility of electronics failing, which is why backing up is so important. Once you have backed up on one hard drive, make sure it is duplicated on a second and even a third, just for good measure.

It is a good idea to keep one of the hard drives at a different location from the rest, in case you have an accident at home, such as a flood or fire. The next thing to consider how the hard drives should be organized. One example would be to start with three hard drives and label them as A1, A2 and A3. These would hold exactly the same data but you would then have a back-up plan in case one breaks. After those are full you would go on to B1, B2 and B3. This is just one example of a logical and easy-to-follow storage system that would serve you well for years to come.

FEEDBACK

Obtaining and using feedback

It is an unspoken truth that what people say about your work has a huge bearing on your learning progression and confidence. Photographers will react to feedback in different ways. The learning progression often reflects how confident the image-maker feels at that time. If a photographer has lost confidence in their work it can really slow progress down. Conversely, if a positive comment has been made about a piece of work, it can boost the production and quality of their work. The main thing is to be ambitious and always be positive whatever happens.

Feedback at all stages

It is good to recognize that feedback can be obtained at any stage. You might want to seek an opinion when the idea for a project is initially conceived, or you may only want feedback at the end of the process when it is completed. Of course not everyone seeks to gain the opinion of others; you may simply be creating work for your own pleasure and therefore you are your own critic. If you have chosen this route then it will be worth researching your chosen subject area online or in a library to get inspiration in this way.

Who is your feedback from?

Feedback can be obtained from anyone you know i.e. family and friends, but also it can be obtained from someone you do not know online. Whoever the feedback is from, for it to be useful we need to put it into context. Whether the comments are made by a professional photographer or your nan, both parties can provide constructive feedback, but some feedback may be useless or irrelevant.

The most appropriate feedback is from the people that your imagery is aimed at, i.e. the target audience. If you are producing a piece of work for a business, then speak to them and get an idea of what they deem as appropriate; get them to show you examples. If it is not aimed at any specific audience and you are posting your work online, then the viewer demographic could be much more varied.

Most of us will assume that we need feedback from people with a high skill-set within the photography field. However, sometimes honest opinion from someone totally unrelated and with no experience in the subject can be helpful and illuminating. It is easy to spend so much time learning about a subject and then forgetting to take a step back and look at your work from other people's points of view.

Using feedback

Once you have received feedback, it is worth recording and reviewing it every so often to use it effectively, otherwise some valuable information might be forgotten. There could be comments on technical information or creative opinions. Categorize these different aspects of the feedback into 'technical' and 'creative' and use it to progress your work. Technical feedback could be aspects to do with focusing, shutter speed or aperture settings, for example. Creative feedback would be comments that are based more on feelings, composition or subject matter. There could well be a suggestion that opens the door to a huge project for you, or someone may point out a button on the camera that you have never used before.

INSPIRATION AND IDEAS

Sometimes, even with all the enthusiasm in the world, we can occasionally find ourselves lacking inspiration. Inspiration is so important because it fuels our direction when working and also how we feel about the subject in general. You might see a piece of work by a photographer or a film in a cinema that gives you that feeling of awe. When we have these moments it reminds us why we do what we do. If we are lacking inspiration, however, how do we go about finding it?

Inspiration and creativity are not commodities that you can just turn on and off with a switch and this makes it very difficult to find sometimes. It can come from something totally unexpected, such as noticing an image in a newspaper, a commercial on television, or it could be obtained from a visit to an art gallery or even a restaurant. As a time-lapse photographer, you should be able to get inspiration from anywhere with movement so make sure that you are always looking for it and how it can be captured in a time-lapse video. You might be at a train station and notice that the flow of the crowd is quite interesting because it has patterns. You could even find inspiration sitting in a coffee shop looking out the window onto the street. You might not always have your camera on you, but you will have your eyes and this enables you to look for inspiration.

Recording inspiration and ideas

Because inspiration and ideas may come to us at any time we need to be prepared to record them. If we think of a fantastic idea and forget it, we have missed out on what could have potentially been a piece of work that you might have been very proud of. Sometimes the most raw or impulsive thoughts and ideas make way for some amazing content. Other times you may decide that an idea will just not work. Either way, ideas and inspiration cost nothing and are one of our most valuable assets as image-makers. Carry a notepad or have an app for making notes on your phone. First and foremost, enjoy your image-making and good luck.

Index

Other Photography Titles from Crowood

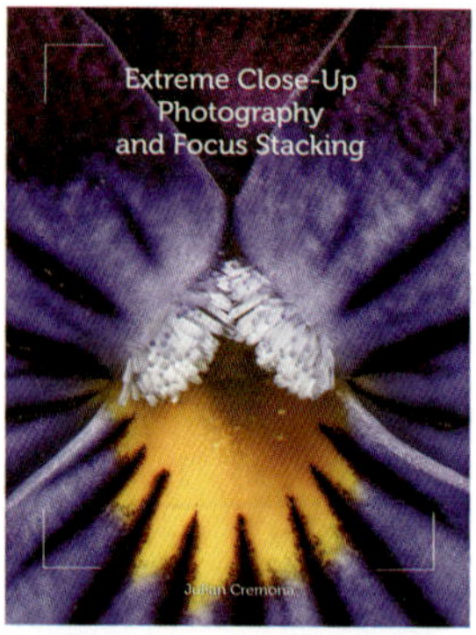

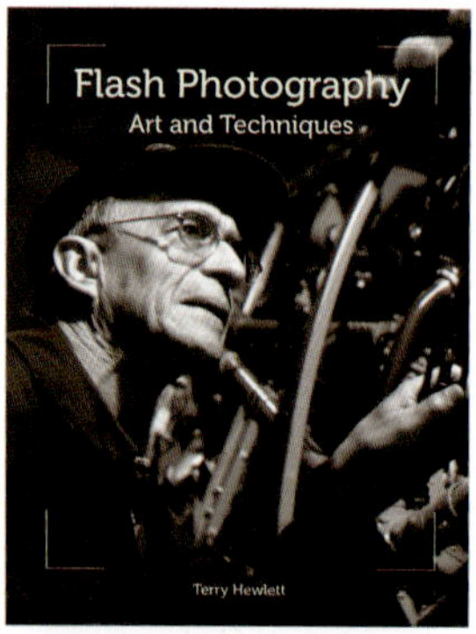

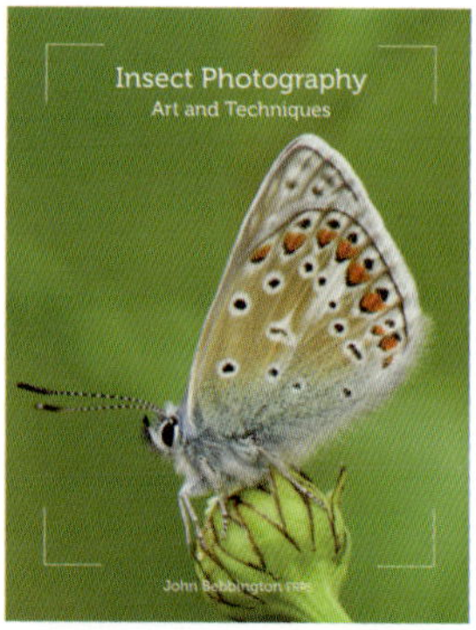

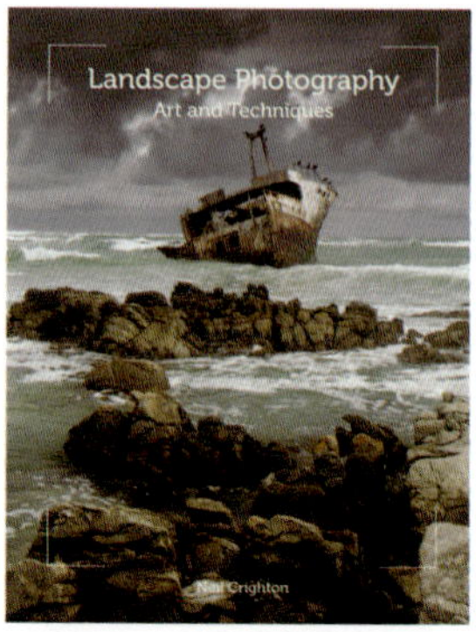

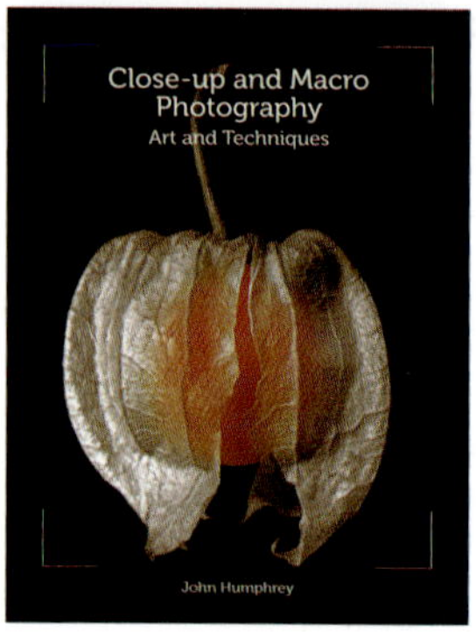

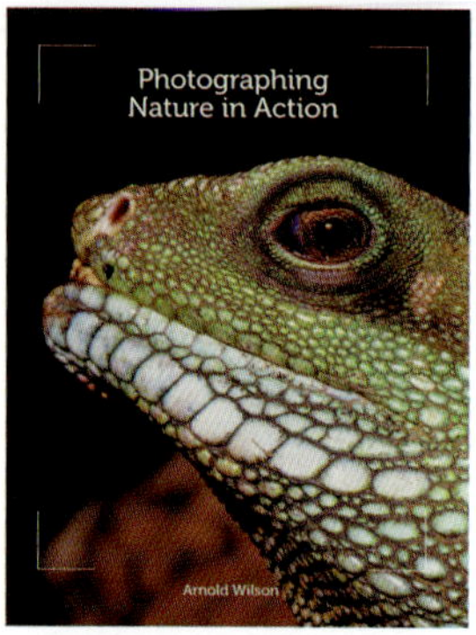

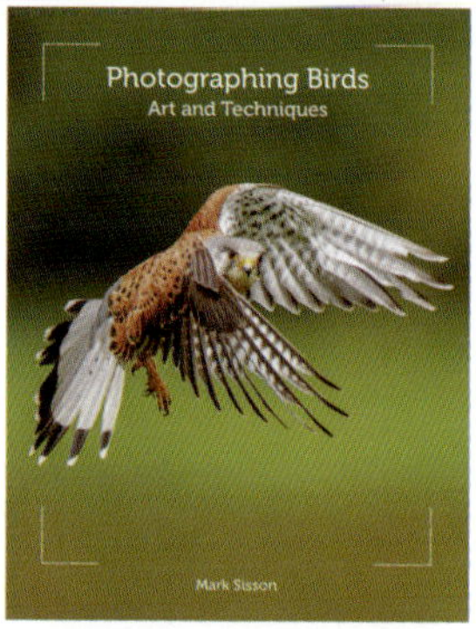

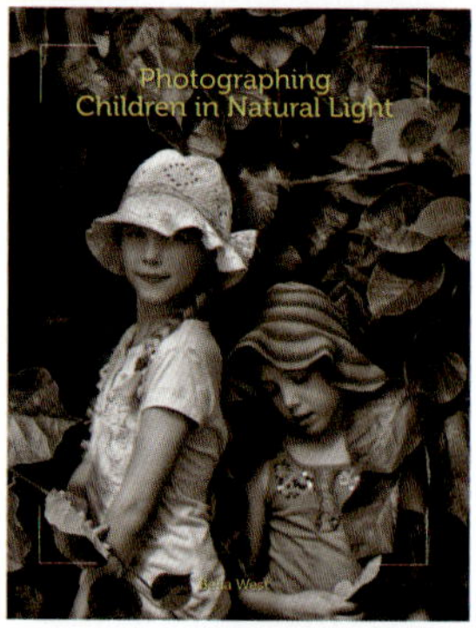

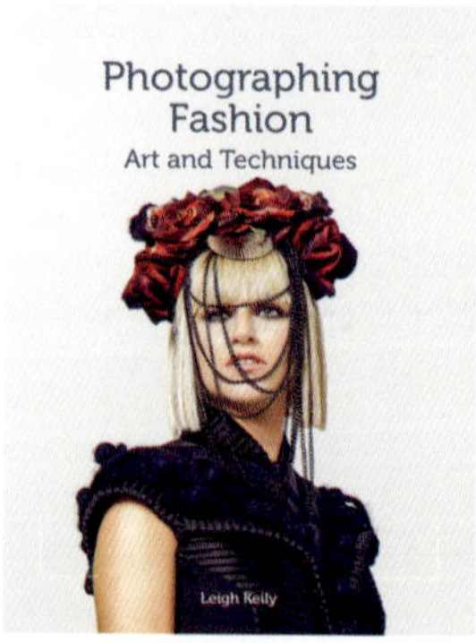

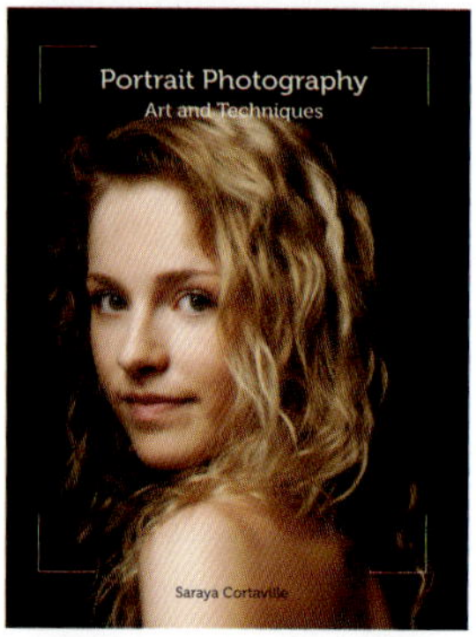

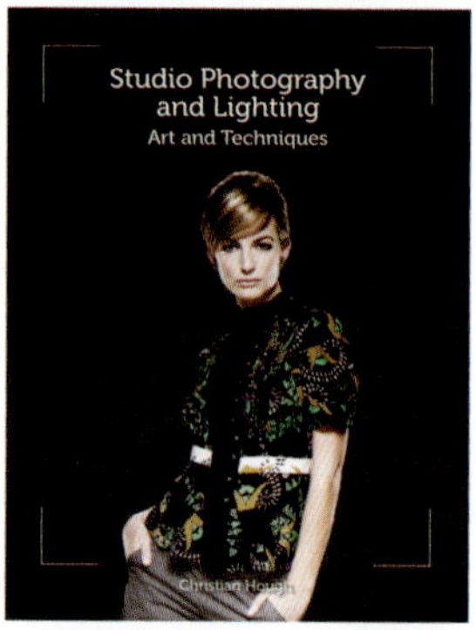

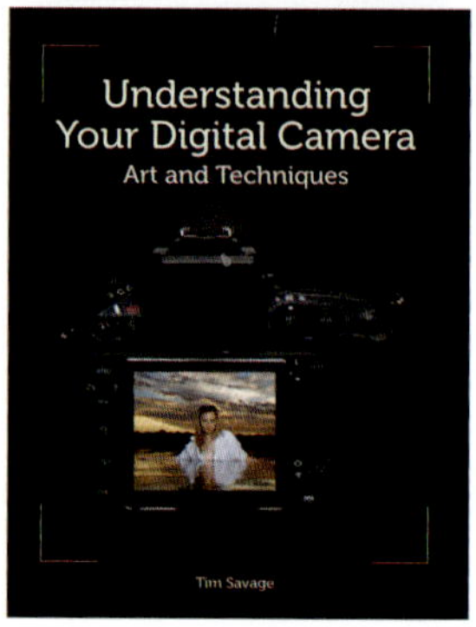

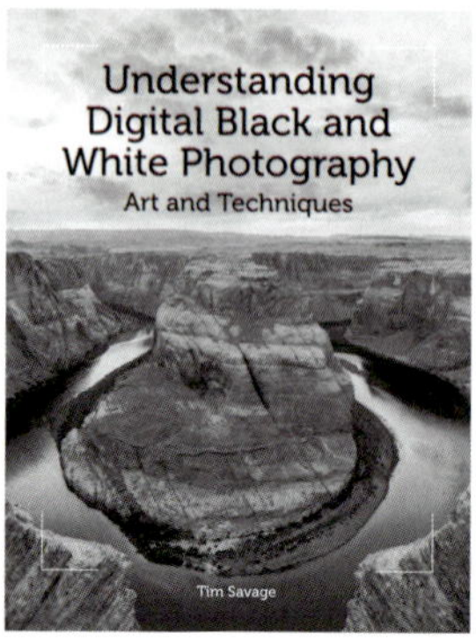

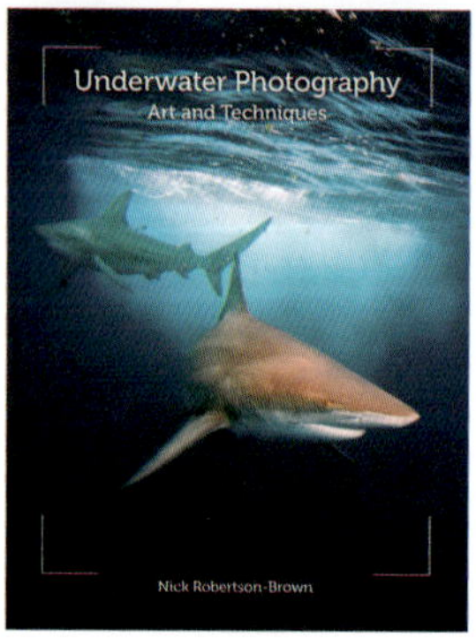

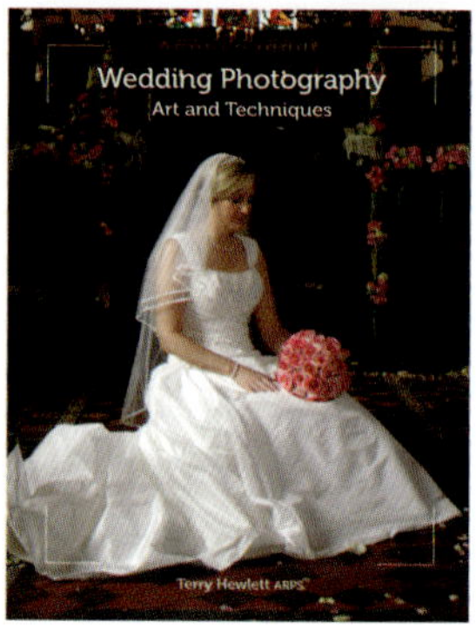